# THE MEDIEVAL GENTRY

# The Medieval Gentry

*Power, Leadership and Choice during the Wars of the Roses*

Malcolm Mercer

continuum

Continuum UK, The Tower Building, 11 York Road, London SE1 7NX
Continuum US, 80 Maiden Lane, Suite 704, New York, NY 10038

*www.continuumbooks.com*

First published 2010

British Library Cataloguing-in-Publication Data
A catalogue record for this book is available from the British Library.

ISBN 978-1441-19064-2

Typeset by Pindar NZ, Auckland, New Zealand
Printed and bound in Great Britain by the MPG Books Group

# Contents

Abbreviations                                                                vii

Acknowledgements                                                              ix

1  Introduction: A Fascination with Choice                                    1

2  Who were the Gentry?                                                        7

3  The Decision-Making Process                                               25

4  Gentry, Warfare and Violence in Late Medieval England                    35

5  The Public Domain: Public Service, Private Lordship and Principles        65

6  The Private Domain: Locality, Neighbourhood and Family                    85

7  The Personal Domain: Contradictory Responses to Conflict                 107

8  Conclusion                                                               125

Notes                                                                       133

Bibliography                                                                149

Index                                                                       163

# Abbreviations

| | |
|---|---|
| *Arrivall* | Bruce, J. (ed.) (1838), *Historie of the Arrivall of King Edward IV in England and the Finall Recouerye of his Kingdomes from Henry VI.* London: Camden Society |
| BL | British Library |
| *Catalogue of Ancient Deeds* | HMSO (1890–1915), *A Descriptive Catalogue of Ancient Deeds in the Public Record Office*, 6 vols. London: HMSO. |
| *CCR* | HMSO (1933–63), *Calendar of Close Rolls, 1422–1509*, 11 vols. London: HMSO |
| *CFR* | HMSO (1931–62), *Calendar of Fine Rolls, 1399–1509*, 11 vols. London: HMSO |
| *Chronicles of London* | Kingsford, C. L. (ed.) (1905), *Chronicles of London*. Oxford: Clarendon Press. |
| *CIPM* | HMSO (1898–1956), *Calendar of Inquisitions Post Mortem, Henry VII*, 3 vols. London: HMSO. |
| *CPR* | HMSO (1897–1916), *Calendar of Patent Rolls, 1399–1509*, 17 vols. London: HMSO. |
| *CSP Milan* | HMSO (1912), *Calendar of State Papers and Manuscripts Existing in the Archives and Collections of Milan*, I, ed. A. B. Hinds. London: HMSO. |
| *English Chronicle* | Davies, J. S. (ed.) (1856), *An English Chronicle in the Reigns of Richard II, Henry IV, Henry V, and Henry VI.* London: Camden Society. |
| *Froissart* | Macaulay, G. C. (ed.) (1910), *The Chronicles of Froissart, Froissart, Jean; translated by John Bourchier, Lord Berners.* New York: Harvard Classics. |
| *Great Chronicle* | Thomas, A. H. and Thornley, I. D. (eds) (1938), *The Great Chronicle of London.* London: Alan Sutton. |
| 'Gregory' | Gairdner, J. (ed.) (1876), 'Gregory's chronicle: 1189–1249', in *The Historical Collections of a Citizen of London.* London: Camden Society. |

| | |
|---|---|
| *Hall* | Ellis, H. (ed.) (1809), *Hall's Chronicle*. London. |
| *Harleian 433* | Horrox, R. and Hammond, P. W. (eds) (1979–83), *British Library Harleian Manuscript 433: Register of Grants for the Reigns of Edward V and Richard III*, 4 vols. Gloucester: Alan Sutton for the Richard III Society. |
| *HOP* | Roskell, J. S., Clark, L. and Rawcliffe, C. (1993), *The History of Parliament: The House of Commons, 1386–1421*, 4 vols. Stroud: Alan Sutton. |
| *Itineraries* | Harvey, J. H. (ed.) (1969), *William Worcestre, Itineraries*. Oxford: Clarendon Press. |
| 'John Benet's chronicle' | Harriss, G. L. and Harriss, M. A. (eds) (1972), 'John Benet's chronicle for the years 1400 to 1462', in *Camden Miscellany Vol. XXIV: Camden Fourth Series Vol. 9*. London: Royal Historical Society, pp. 151–233. |
| *Letters and Papers* | Stevenson, J. (ed.) (1861–4), *Letters and Papers Illustrative of the Wars of the English in France during the Reign of Henry VI*, 2 vols in 3, Rolls Series. London: Longman, Green, Longman and Roberts |
| *NAI* | National Archives of Ireland |
| *Paston Letters* | Gairdner, J. (ed.) (1910), *The Paston Letters 1422–1509*, 3 vols. Edinburgh: John Grant. |
| PPC | TO COME |
| *RP* | Strachey, J. (ed.) (1767–77), *Rotuli Parliamentorum, 1277–1503*, 6 vols. London. |
| *Sheriffs* | HSMO (1898), *List of Sheriffs for England and Wales*, PRO Lists and Indexes, 12. London: HSMO. |
| *Three Fifteenth-Century Chronicles* | Gairdner, J. (ed.) (1880), *Three Fifteenth-Century Chronicles*. London: Camden Society. |
| TNA | The National Archives |
| *Town Chronicles* | Flenley, R. (ed.) (1911), *Six Town Chronicles of England*. Oxford: Clarendon Press. |
| *Warkworth* | Halliwell, J. O. (ed.) (1839), *A Chronicle of the First Thirteen Years of the Reign of King Edward IV, by John Warkworth*. London: Camden Society. |
| *Waurin* | Hardy W. and Hardy, E. L. C. P. (eds) (1864–91), *Recueil des croniques et anchiennes istories de la Grant Bretaigne par Jehan de Waurin*, 5 vols, Rolls Series. London: Longman. |

# Acknowledgements

A great many things in life are the result of chance encounters and conversations. This book is a perfect example of that. After presenting a paper on the composition of the Lancastrian army at the battle of Tewkesbury to the International Congress on Medieval Studies at Western Michigan University in 2002, I found myself speaking, without knowing it, to Tony Morris, then commissioning editor for Hambledon Press who expressed great interest in why some gentry took up arms during the Wars of the Roses. Thus began my journey into the mindset of the fifteenth-century gentry. This book, slightly longer in the making than intended, is the fruit of that investigation. Along the way I have accumulated many debts to friends, colleagues and loved ones. Sean Cunningham, Peter Fleming, David Grummitt, Ralph Griffiths, Michael K. Jones, Hannes Kleineke, Linda Clark and Simon Payling have all been generous in sharing references, ideas and their own research with me. Michael Greenwood, my editor at Continuum Books, has displayed great understanding and patience throughout the writing of this book. However, it is unlikely that it would ever have appeared if it had not been for Professor Jim Bolton who has been steadfast in his encouragement, advice and friendship at all times. It is to him that I owe my greatest debt as friend and mentor. Not only he has read through numerous redrafts of the text and in the process prevented me from making unfortunate typographical and factual errors, he has helped to guide me through some of life's pitfalls. Last, but not least, this book is dedicated to my parents, who have always encouraged me to follow my own path and supported me in my endeavours, and to Isolde, who has never wavered in her love and support as I attempted to balance work, family and writing.

# Introduction: A Fascination with Choice

The Greek philosopher Pythagoras is reputed to have advised people to 'Choose always the way that seems best however rough it may be'.[1] This would seem to imply that there is always one course of action that is better than others and which will ensure a 'good' decision is made. Be that as it may, deciding upon the most appropriate course of action can be difficult at the best of times and poses all sorts of problems for the individual concerned. Evidence drawn from the seventeenth century suggests that decision making during the English Civil War could be particularly unwelcome and unpleasant for those caught up in events. The example of the Norfolk knight Sir Thomas Knyvett undoubtedly mirrored the thoughts and feelings of late medieval gentry. He complained about being put on the spot when rival militia warrants appeared and shattered his tranquil existence; 'I am nowe in a greate straight what to doe', he wrote, after the first warrant had arrived. He continued, 'I was surprised what to doe, whether to take or refuse. Twas no place to dispute, so I tooke it and desired sometime to Advise upon it. I had not received this many howers, but I met with a declaration point Blanck against it . . .' As Knyvett went on to remark, his inclination was to 'staye out of the way of my newe masters till those first musterings be over'. If in doubt the best option appeared to be to hide in the shadows and hope no one noticed. Knyvett's dilemma was by no means unique and his response was just one of a number of potential responses at that moment in time. He could equally have opted to side with parliament or Charles I when the rival warrants appeared. Sir Thomas Knyvett is clearly a salient reminder that many did not know what to do when confronted with a choice and instead sought to buy time and hoped that the issue would go away.[2]

One false move could potentially spell disaster for the unwary. This was exactly the tenor of the advice provided in 1477 by the attorney Godfrey Greene to one member of the late medieval Yorkshire gentry, Sir William Plumpton. Greene wrote to Plumpton advising him that it was a mistake to approach Sir John Pilkington, the duke of Gloucester, or even the king over the matter of the deputy stewardship of Knaresborough. Indeed, he counselled that 'it is thought here by such as loues you at that labour should hurt in that behalue than availe, for it is as long as my lord of Northumberlands patent thereof stands good, as long will he haue no deputie but such as shall please him'. The message was clear:

Plumpton would do more harm than good by going against the wishes of the earl of Northumberland on this matter. That posed a problem for Plumpton. The earl had appointed Sir William Gascoigne in 1471, much to Plumpton's fury, and there had been tensions ever since between the latter two.[3] It should not be surprising that the potential pitfalls of making the wrong choice made many men cautious. In 1487 Sir Edmund Bedingfield had difficulty persuading the Norfolk gentry to assist him executing a commission of array that he had received from the earl of Oxford unless it was authenticated. As Bedingfield said, 'it was thought I ought not to obey no copy of the commission, without I had the same under wax, wherein hath been great argument, which I understood by report a fortnight past, and that caused me to send unto my lord (Oxford) to have the very commission, which he sent me'. The Norfolk gentry wanted to be under no doubt that they would be responding to a royally-sanctioned commission.[4]

The aim of this book is to understand how the leading gentry of fifteenth-century England like Plumpton or Bedingfield arrived at decisions during a turbulent phase of the kingdom's history: the Wars of the Roses. It will seek to identify the principal factors that influenced and shaped their thought processes and behaviour between the traditional starting date of 1455, when Yorkist and Lancastrian clashed at the first battle of St Albans, and the final encounter at the battle of Stoke in 1487. Civil war and the shattering of domestic tranquillity was one of the principal horrors of medieval society. Since the early middle ages political theorists, like John of Salisbury in book 6 of his *Policraticus*, had likened the state to a body with each of the constituent parts contributing to the harmonious existence of the whole. Such analogies persisted throughout the medieval period and were even advanced by Sir John Fortescue, chief justice of king's bench, a key player during the Wars of the Roses. He wrote in the *De Laudibus Legum Angliae* that a body politic, specifically referring to England, was a *corpus mysticum*: the laws were the nerves that united the body, and public spirit was the life-giving blood. Civil war was abhorred because it rent asunder the harmony of the body politic. It could set kinsmen, friends and neighbours against each other and leave a lasting legacy of bitterness and resentment that might affect subsequent generations.[5]

Such was the fascination with the Wars of the Roses that almost from the moment they came to an end commentators have been intrigued by the circumstances that led to the eruption of the conflict.[6] Many chroniclers and scholars have shown awareness in the psychology of choice and have demonstrated a visible interest in the motivation and behaviour of participants, their often contradictory reasons and motives for acting, and how they balance principles and private concerns when making a decision. Tudor historians, including Edward Hall, Polydore Vergil and Thomas More, believed that the past provided a rich source of material from which we could draw political, social and moral lessons. Edward Hall was fascinated by the colourful personalities and motives of the leading figures and was not beyond inventing lengthy speeches in which they justified their actions. Vergil, by contrast, saw the origins of the conflict in the scheming conduct of Richard, duke of York. A similar interest prevailed during the seventeenth century where key individuals like Richard Neville, earl of Warwick, otherwise known as the Kingmaker, drew admiring comments for his chivalric conduct. Richard III, on the other hand, remained a vilified character despite the attempts by Sir George Buck, James I's master of revels, to rehabilitate his name. Yet Buck's attempt demonstrated that some scholars were also capable of taking a more sophisticated view of individual behaviour.

During the eighteenth century a more scholarly approach was also taken to the interpretation of original documents in order to gain insights into motives and behaviour. Thomas Carte drew heavily on government documents stored in the Tower of London where he was keeper of records and applied strict criteria when analysing chronicle sources. He did not accept that Richard III was the reviled character that history seemed to portray; nor did William Hutton who remarked significantly that 'Richard III's character, like every man's, had two sides; he was, at one and the same time, a faithful servant, a brave soldier, an admirable legislator, yet one of the vilest men'. Yet in spite of these observations, other commentators, like Horace Walpole, were still prone to making generalizations. Walpole's general conclusion about the period was that neither side displayed any scruples or principles. To the romantic movement of the early nineteenth century, the Wars of the Roses were decayed and decadent in comparison to the high middle ages, which combined the finest aspects of chivalry and heroism. Sir Walter Scott regarded them as a series of 'civil discords dreadfully prosecuted'. Again, though, some scholars like Sharon Turner produced thoughtful insights into behaviour. Richard III was regarded very much as a man of his times, capable of both great good and great evil. The influential Victorian historian, James Gairdner, spent his entire professional career at the Public Record Office and was able to immerse himself in original source material. In his opinion, one of the principal reasons for the outbreak of civil war was the lack of strong central authority, which in turn led to faction-fighting despite the underlying loyalty that characterized social relationships between the crown, nobility and gentry. The trend among the majority of Victorian scholars was to see the behaviour of magnates and their gentry retainers as fundamentally unprincipled because they regarded the cement that bound lord and retainer together (disparagingly termed 'bastard feudalism' by Charles Plummer in 1885) as a destabilizing force within late medieval society.[7]

It was K. B. McFarlane who first broke with this tradition and suggested that behaviour was not determined by the system of relationships in place but rather the other way around. In a series of influential articles in 1944–5 he advanced the view that there was nothing inherently wrong with bastard feudalism; it depended very much on the personalities of the magnates and gentry concerned. Since McFarlane it has been acknowledged that the impact of lordship could vary considerably. Subsequent studies of gentry from different regions across England have pointed towards their social and political independence in many cases. While the debate on gentry independence or subservience continues, in-depth prosopographical analysis of particular individuals has enabled scholars to look much closer at the range of motives that could potentially shape their behaviour during this crucial period. Goodman's most recent publication on the experiences of the 'soldier' has also sought to tease out some of the elements that influenced behaviour in a new way; but while he has provided some useful detail on the impact of warfare, he continually blurs the differences between nobility, gentry, yeomanry and peasantry in an unsatisfactory manner, grouping them all under a single soubriquet. In so doing, his book fails to highlight the different attitudes and reactions that must surely have existed between these groups within medieval society, certainly within a military context.[8]

Existing studies of the late medieval gentry have generally paid little systematic attention to their involvement in civil warfare other than in standard narratives of the period. While there have been many biographical studies of individual gentry within scholarly articles, they have largely attracted attention through county or regional studies, or through the impact of lordship. This is curious given that the gentry, rather than the nobility, were the natural leaders within their local communities. Indeed, the crown relied upon them to staff local administrative offices and dispense justice, while the nobility relied upon them to act as their mouthpieces at regional and local levels and to supply military manpower. Consequently, the gentry's ability to persuade their kinsmen, friends and tenants to act in a particular way was also crucial, especially their capacity to raise and lead men into battle. This was a critical factor in the eventual success or failure of Lancastrian and Yorkist campaigns. The gentry's behaviour and potential support was of the utmost significance to their political masters. There have been some monographs, like Castor's engaging account of the Paston family, which have shown how thoughts, attitudes and behaviour could shift dramatically in response to political events at a local and national level. But this has been the exception to the rule.[9]

The arrangement of this volume, unlike the majority of investigations into the Wars of the Roses, has been organized on a thematic rather than chronological basis. By exploring the thought processes and concerns of the gentry in an alternative manner we are presented with a fresh opportunity to understand the complexities of the choices that they faced throughout this period of political upheaval and to capture their thoughts, attitudes and behaviour more compre-hensively than before. Their often contradictory responses and differing attitudes to events unfolding around them have yet to be fully explored.

In chapters 2, 3 and 4 we will seek to establish a framework within which we can understand the gentry and how they made decisions. Chapter 2 will consider the vexed question of just who the gentry were and how medieval historians have sought to define them. It will offer a definition of gentry that draws on recent research into the nature of gentry culture that will then be applied throughout the volume. Chapter 3 will build on these ideas and offer a conceptual framework that draws upon current ideas within the social sciences which can be used to understand the decision-making process of the late medieval gentry. Chapter 4 will then explore the gentry's education and military training, their experiences of warfare, and their use of violence within the domestic arena.

Having provided an overview of who constituted the gentry, their decision-making processes and the environments in which they led their lives, the remainder of the book will concentrate on those factors that were likely to influence responses to particular decision problems during the Wars of the Roses. For the purposes of this analysis the dominant decision problem is understood to mean whether an individual would chose to support one side or the other, either militarily or politically. Chapter 5 investigates some of the social, political and cultural forces that affected gentry behaviour in the public domain. It examines the willingness to undertake public service, enter into patron–client relationships with the nobility, the nature of gentry loyalty and the manifestation of deeply held principles. Chapter 6 focuses on the private domain and explores the local environment and issues which could arise within it, including strategic importance, neighbourhood and community relationships, family divisions, the defence and recovery of family status, and destabilizing effects on local elites. Having examined two different types of environment in which the gentry led their lives, Chapter 7 will consider the personal domain and seek to understand those instances where behaviour does not necessarily conform to a particular model and which cannot be easily explained. While there are no incontrovertible explanations of the decisions that were made during the Wars of the Roses, this book argues that we can still understand many of the processes by which those decisions were made, and perhaps come to understand the minds of the late medieval gentry just that little bit better than before.

# 2

# Who were the Gentry?

## INTRODUCTION

Thanks to McFarlane's pioneering work in late medieval studies, it is now accepted that the gentry played a crucial role in the development of English political society during this period. McFarlane asserted that the gentry were not merely political puppets whose strings were pulled by the nobility. He also proposed that a greater understanding of the gentry's sometimes contradictory behaviour would come through more sustained prosopographical analysis. This viewpoint has been endorsed in more recent times by Richmond who has suggested that 'Men were not Pavlovian dogs, jumping at the chance of a fee, a rent charge, a stewardship here, a parkership there. No more were lords puppet masters manipulating their marionette retainers to dominate the provinces or pack parliaments.'[1] Much harder to establish, however, has been what we as historians actually mean by the word gentry and what their defining characteristics were. Contemporaries had no definition for the word gentry, a fact which was reflected linguistically by the interchangeable use of nobility and gentility until the fifteenth century.[2]

Nonetheless, historians have persisted in referring to gentry as if they were a firmly established social or political group; but as the proliferation of studies demonstrates they have experienced considerable difficulty arriving at a consensus about a definition. In the late nineteenth century Stubbs suggested that the gentry of fifteenth-century England simply comprised 'all the landowners between the baronage and the yeomanry.'[3] Simplistic as it might appear, in many respects this definition has much to recommend it because scholars have been increasingly tempted to apply the term out of context. Thomas has even employed the term to describe the thirteenth-century Yorkshire elite, two centuries before the gentry had even become a recognizable social formation. He asserts that the 'Yorkshire gentry, particularly by the end of the Angevin period, resembled their successors in a remarkable number of ways.'[4]

It is generally agreed that by the beginning of the fifteenth century the gentry had coalesced into a recognizable social formation. Before this point, however, a process of transformation was taking place. Coss has argued that the gentry formed 'in an accelerating process from the middle decades of the thirteenth century to the mid-fourteenth century. By the middle decades of the fourteenth century a recognizable gentry was in existence'.[5] The principal change came about when those previously regarded as the lesser nobility became more closely involved in national and local politics during the reign of Edward I. Their participation in warfare was particularly significant as the crown came to rely on their manpower. During the course of the early fourteenth century this process of political involvement gradually widened to incorporate the sub-knightly ranks as well, signalling their absorption into the social elite. Consequently, by the early fifteenth century the nobility were consistently identified with the parliamentary peerage. Below them were the 'gentle classes' who bore the titles of knight, esquire or gentleman. The esquire had also emerged as a clearly defined grade below the knight. Esquires were more than non-knightly members of a family or cadet branches of a knightly line. Moreover, they were more than those who had accepted being distrained for not taking up knighthood.[6] While the term continued to carry with it service and military connotations, the category was sufficiently flexible that it could include those professionals, administrators and merchants who aspired to be gentle. The gradual working out of status gradations, however, took some time to achieve. The final group to achieve a level of definition were gentlemen, who gradually appeared after the Statute of Additions in 1413 stipulated that rank should be recorded on original writs and indictments. It is of no small significance that all of these developments took place as gentry were becoming more politically self-conscious.[7]

It has been observed by some late medieval historians that the profile of the gentry in terms of titular rank produced a broadly based but sharply pointed pyramid. In fact, there was a broad correlation between rank, wealth and office-holding. What generally served to separate the perceptions of elite families at the apex of the pyramid from other members of gentry society were differences in wealth, and the extent of social and political connections beyond their immediate environment. Wealthier knights or esquires within a locality were more likely to be active in regional and county administration, serving as sheriffs, justices of the peace, royal commissioners, and be elected to serve as members of parliament for the shire or a borough; and they often enjoyed business, family and magnate service connections beyond county or regional boundaries. By contrast, the experiences and outlook of a lesser esquire or gentleman, referred to by Fleming as 'parish gentry', who rarely moved beyond the confines of their immediate geographical environment, were probably going to be more localized. For them there is strong evidence to suggest that their lives revolved primarily, although not exclusively, around the manor and parish. They enjoyed strong parochial interests and were active in their local communities. Their testamentary bequests often reflected this identification. Repairs to a road were more likely to appear in a lesser gentleman's will than a wealthy knight's, who would have generally left money for the maintenance of the parish church instead.[8]

## SEARCHING FOR A DEFINITION

The authors of gentry studies have long recognized the problems of arriving at an adequate definition. They have generally sought to overcome any ambiguities by proposing that a definition should be based upon a combination of social, economic and political elements.[9] The first aspect has involved the examination of social distinctions and the exploration of the relationship between the gentry and gentility, that is to say, all those who laid claim to being gentle folk. Evidence from a range of sources, not least texts on household service or evidence used in the prosecution of legal suits, suggests that gentility was regarded as much a mode of behaviour as a characteristic of a particular social grouping. The nobility, knights, esquires and gentlemen could all legitimately make a claim to gentility. The second aspect has involved looking at their relationship to land and landholding. To this has been supplemented income levels and contemporary legislation that regulated office-holding. The correlation between income levels and social gradation, however, is not consistent. Some knights enjoyed incomes in excess of peers. Sir John Fastolf is perhaps the most extreme example. The third aspect has concentrated upon the gentry as the office-holding elite under the crown. Office-holding, though, was a matter of choice and dependent on a variety of factors. There were clearly many who chose not to serve in local government and were perfectly happy to remain free from service obligations.[10]

This all-inclusive approach was adopted by Wright when examining the Derbyshire gentry. Acknowledging the numerous uncertainties, she remarked that 'it is extremely difficult to draw any single line of definition'. Nonetheless, she includes all the families who 'provided a knight or who were distrained, served as a knight of the shire, sheriff, justice of the peace, commissioner of array, escheator or tax collector, together with . . . an income of £5 or over or as a tenant-in-chief'. A combination of defining characteristics is an attractive proposition but ultimately it is still an artificial one. Wright considered this compromise effective because 'the more criteria a family satisfies the better and the less tenuous is our categorising and labelling of them'.[11] Acheson adopted a similar position in his analysis of the Leicestershire gentry. For him, the difficulty in arriving at a definition is not so much 'that our net has been cast insufficiently wide; it may be the case, however, that we have not trawled deeply enough or, perhaps, that the weave of our net has been too open to entrap the smaller fry, the lesser gentry'.[12] In his analysis of Lincolnshire gentry Mackman has also recognized the deficiencies of existing attempts at a satisfactory definition.[13] It is evident, though, that some medievalists are more satisfied with particular criteria than others. Carpenter sees the 'ever closer identification of land and status' as a fundamental feature in the development of lordship, which she sees in turn as coming to define what gentility meant in the fifteenth century.[14]

In recent years, though, some historians have started to move beyond social, economic and political factors for an answer to the question of who constituted the gentry by looking at what else drew them together as a group. Despite asserting centrality of lordship in social relationships, Carpenter has also noted the importance of studying how the gentry saw themselves as a way of discovering their 'attitudes and beliefs'. More recently, Radulescu and Truelove have argued in favour of looking outside the traditional defining characteristics of the gentry. For them, the gentry were 'an amorphous, ever-fluctuating group of individuals'. By exploring and understanding gentry culture, along with the factors that led to the emergence of the gentry, they have proposed that we are better able to understand this diverse group under the single term 'gentry'. This approach draws upon sociological and anthropological studies which have tended to focus upon the cultural practices through which identities are maintained.[15]

This argument has also been echoed by Coss who has suggested that historians' failure to achieve a definition of the gentry is due primarily to an overemphasis on external delineations rather than concentrating on those elements that distinguished the gentry as a 'social formation'. In Coss's opinion, gentry is simply an artificial construct. He presents a persuasive argument for adopting a more flexible approach to how the gentry are defined. He has proposed that they enjoyed a number of overarching attributes rather than being delineated by a rigid set of criteria. He begins by suggesting that they can be regarded as a type of lesser nobility. More often than not local seigneurs, they enjoyed a sense of nobility and gentility with greater landowners that set them apart from those below. Although their status was based on land and landownership, that status was flexible enough to accommodate new entrants into the social grouping, including urban elites and influxes of professional administrators, lawyers, courtiers and royal servants. In addition, they were a territorial elite that bridged the gap between a simple landowning elite and a paid bureaucracy by representing royal authority across the kingdom. The gentry also sought to exercise collective social control over the populace on a territorial basis, which reinforced their individual status and power. Finally, they shared a collective identity and collective interests that required at least one outlet for those views to be articulated; this was first provided through the county court and subsequently through parliament.[16]

What is apparent from the continuing debate on the nature and composition of the gentry is the inability of historians to arrive at a consistent definition. While exposing the problems in the use of an all-encompassing term, the arguments presented by Coss and proponents of gentry culture do not necessarily make our understanding of gentry any better; instead, it could be argued that that they have actually exposed many of the underlying drawbacks without providing a more definite way forward. It may well be that the gulf between those families considered to be gentry is too wide to bridge by one definition alone and that a range of acceptable, subsidiary definitions are needed. With these considerations in mind, this study will follow Stubbs and use the term gentry to refer to all those families between the baronage and the yeomanry. However, the focus of this study is directed primarily at the decision making of those individuals who have generally been referred to by late medievalists as the 'greater gentry'. This is not felt to be a suitable term either, implying a greater degree of wealth, status or influence than some of these might have enjoyed or exerted in their respective environments. Throughout this volume these individuals will therefore be referred to as 'leading gentry' and this term will include long-established families prominent within their local communities, the most active administratively or politically in local, regional or even national governance, or a combination of both. Those gentry who did not display these characteristics will be labelled 'lesser gentry'.

## COHESION, AUTONOMY AND DEPENDENCE

The gulf that existed in the experiences of the gentry is most evident when cohesiveness, autonomy and dependence are examined in greater depth. Gentry network analysis has gone some way towards explaining how they interacted and how they subsequently behaved. Networks were formed in a number of obvious ways: local geography and patterns of landholding; kinship and friendship connections; administrative, legal, political service relationships; and shared cultural pursuits. Recently, scholars have also pointed towards the importance of self-perception in the shaping of identity.[17] Given-Wilson has argued that the cohesiveness of these networks probably varied between different regions. In instances where magnate estates were dominant the gentry might be expected to be more compliant and less assertive in their behaviour.[18]

This position reflects the views of those scholars who assume that entering into a service or affinity[19] relationship with the nobility and the crown was the default position for the gentry. Indeed, Pollard has described service as 'a central feature of all gentlemen's lives'.[20] Service is often taken to mean retaining, yet it is now recognized that service was a much more sophisticated phenomenon than this. It was multifaceted, and ranged from single acts of patronage and services sought by well-wishers from their social superiors, to ties generated by landholding and locality, to the formal connections of service that included the payment of annuities, recruiting feed retainers, and employment as estate officers or as household servants. As Pollard rightly asserts, indentures of retinue and annuities were 'untypical and unrepresentative of the links between man and servant in fifteenth-century society'[21] and were far from widespread. Simple considerations of cost precluded large-scale retaining by all but the wealthiest nobility. In the north east only the Nevilles of Middleham and the Percy earls of Northumberland were able to do this, and in their cases it was down to a combination of political rivalry and their role as wardens of the East and West Marches. What enabled retaining on a larger-scale in this region and not elsewhere was the persistence of *mesne*, or middle, lordship.

Mesne lordship was a vestigial right arising from the original subinfeudation by the first Norman tenants-in-chief during the early medieval period. It provided the holders of honours, liberties and lordships with a variety of rights and privileges delegated by the crown.[22] The honour of Richmond in Yorkshire provided the Nevilles of Middleham with just such an array. While the duties, obligations and fees payable by the subtenants were no longer substantial, the ritual symbolism remained significant and reinforced the sense of belonging to a particular lord. At the same time, however, they also had to take notice of what their retainers said. The earl of Salisbury felt the need to listen to the opinions of his leading retainers before coming out openly in support of Richard, duke of York. When retainers were unwilling to act their lord might have little option but to accept their stance. The earl of Northumberland was unable to oppose the landing of Edward IV in 1471 precisely because his retainers remembered what had happened ten years earlier at the battle of Towton.[23]

Arnold's study of the West Riding has demonstrated that very few gentry held land in chief and were generally mesne tenants of major lordships, primarily of the duchies of Lancaster and York, the comital families of Percy and Talbot, and the baronial family of Clifford. The Percy and Clifford families and the Duchy of Lancaster dominated the north part of the West Riding; by contrast, the Duchy of Lancaster dominated the south part of the Riding. Duchy tenants within this area comprised 60 per cent of the total number of tenants. The remainder were largely tenants of the dukes of York and earls of Shrewsbury respectively. This level of magnate dominance served to increase their local prestige among the gentry within the Riding, especially amongst the leading families. Of these interests within the West Riding, however, it was the Duchy of Lancaster's which held most sway. The stability of magnate power, in Yorkshire and elsewhere in the north east, provided a greater incentive for leading gentry to seek ties of affinity with the greater nobility. According to Pollard such service relationships were the normal state of affairs. Consequently, he shies away from acknowledging an independent quality to gentry behaviour. The nature of landholding society in the north east meant that the Nevilles of Middleham and the Percys were able to enjoy a greater 'degree of commitment and continuity' in service from the gentry.

The question remains, of course, as to whether these men acted in accordance with aristocratic interests. Pollard suggests that the reactions of the gentry to local and national events reflected their ability to effectively balance loyalty with self-interest; they were not indicative of an inherent sense of independence.[24]

Other instances of magnate dominance and the supremacy of vertical ties within landholding society can be seen in the counties of Gloucestershire and Devon. The Berkeleys of Berkeley Castle in Gloucestershire enjoyed a pre-eminence in that shire until the late fourteenth century. The core of their lands was centred on the honour of Berkeley, coterminous with the hundred of Berkeley within the county. However, other lands were also acquired during the fourteenth century through purchase and inheritance. The greatest acquisition was a substantial part of the Lisle inheritance in 1382, as a result of Thomas Berkeley's marriage to Margaret Lisle in 1367, which broadened the family's landed base across southern England. Nevertheless, through the main line of the family and cadet branches, including the Berkeleys of Beverstone, the Lords Berkeley were able to exert substantial influence in the region, manipulate the conduct of local politics, and attract the largest grouping of local gentry into their orbit. However, this dominance was under threat by the late fourteenth century, especially from the Talbot family, rival claimants to the Lisle inheritance. Tensions over the Lisle inheritance exploded into conflict during the mid-fifteenth century.[25]

According to Cherry, Devon was also a county where the influence of the Courtenay earls during the fourteenth century had traditionally dominated political life to an extraordinary extent. Their widespread estates formed a territorial power block that defined the ambitions and actions of the leading gentry. Nonetheless, this dominance had broken down by the early fifteenth century when a series of family mishaps eroded that power. The long minority of Earl Thomas resulted in gentry drifting away and seeking other sources of patronage where appropriate, especially among the more prominent families. Cherry remarks that the Courtenays continued to command the loyalty of the lesser gentry but were unable to compete for the loyalty of those leading gentry who had found alternative sources of patronage. This led to a breakdown in the cohesiveness of local society and to the acrimonious dispute between the earl and Lord Bonville. The death of the earl in 1461 saw his estates being broken up and redistributed to more reliable Yorkist supporters, but a dominant source of authority in the area remained elusive thereafter. The county remained unstable during the 1460s and the continuing survival of Courtenay loyalties appears to be reflected in the number of recruits raised by the Lancastrian army under Queen Margaret in April 1471.[26]

Pollard contrasts the strength of magnate dominance of the gentry in the north with the exercise of lordship in the Midlands counties which was more unstable and fluid. In the Midlands, the uncertainties of local political conditions appeared to make the gentry more circumspect in their behaviour. Nevertheless, Carpenter regards aristocratic ties as the most important influence on the shaping of gentry networks in the Midlands counties. In Warwickshire the gentry aspired to and actively sought out such relationships. Even during periods when unified magnate leadership was weak, the gentry's susceptibility to leadership from above still guided their reactions. The significance of horizontal networks in the conduct of gentry affairs are by no means ignored; indeed their strength and importance is shown to be critical in the conduct of local politics. In Carpenter's opinion, though, it was lordship and the magnate affinity which provided the essential binding force among the county gentry and served to shape their principal reactions. While magnate power and authority in a shire might wax and wane, noble leadership is judged to be the normal state of affairs. Warwickshire is seen as most peaceful during 1413–35 and 1478–83 when local and national leadership was effective. The leadership of Richard Beauchamp, earl of Warwick, during the first of these periods is almost hailed as a golden age for Warwickshire. The Beauchamp earls were able to draw together the gentry, but, when their line died out, local geographical conditions quickly reasserted themselves and the magnate affinity disintegrated into its former constituent networks of gentry.[27]

Carpenter recognizes that vertical ties of lordship did not function well in Warwickshire. Nevertheless, she has suggested that the geographical peculiarities of Warwickshire enabled members of the leading gentry and lesser aristocracy to provide localized 'lordship' during those intervening periods. The leading gentry are seen to be working work towards maintaining peace and preserving their normal way of life under abnormal conditions. Consequently, vertical ties of association are regarded as the dominant model for sociopolitical relationships among the landholding elite. Several key networks survived the death of Beauchamp in 1439. In the Tamworth area a strong network continued to function. At its heart was the existing Ferrers of Chartley affinity. In the north east of the county the situation was different. Here, Edward, Lord Grey of Groby, drew together the existing local networks under his aegis to form a new connection. However, no single magnate was able to pull these groups together. The two most powerful magnates, Humphrey Stafford, duke of Buckingham and Richard Neville, earl of Warwick, were unable to draw the different groups together into a coherent whole. The presence of rival magnates could make local politics more volatile. Unlike Beauchamp, both Neville and Stafford were forced to negotiate and work with the surviving local networks rather than impose their will on the established groups. Neither was sufficiently powerful to be able to do this. Furthermore, such intervention could have a negative impact on local affairs. Warwick's ill-judged support for the Archer family in 1450–1 alienated the Mountfords and other traditional members of the Warwick affinity and undermined his own standing at a local level. As a consequence, William

Mountford gravitated towards Buckingham. Nonetheless, Carpenter still regards the actions of individuals like William Mountford as entirely consistent with external manipulation by the 'dynamics of magnate politics' rather than evidence of independent thought or behaviour.[28]

For advocates of the pre-eminence of aristocratic structures of power, the underlying implication is that the gentry were, by their very natures, predisposed towards patron–client relationships, either noble–gentry or leading gentry–lesser gentry. One particular aspect of gentry studies, which some proponents of vertical ties have criticized, is the concept of the county as a source of group cohesion. Carpenter has sought to downplay or even remove the shire as a unit of importance to the gentry. Others, like Acheson, have acknowledged the significance of the shire on certain levels but have argued that its importance should not be taken too far. The doubts that surround the relevance of the county to the gentry by advocates of vertical ties stem partly from what they perceive to be a misreading of the evidence for those areas where there does not appear to be any obvious indication of these connections.

Proponents of vertical ties have argued, in particular, that the impact of lordship stemming from the monarch – either directly or through the Duchy of Lancaster and Earldom of Chester – has been ignored. According to this reasoning, the gentry were still serving a feudal superior – the crown – as dukes of Lancaster or earls of Chester. In Derbyshire there were the duchy possessions of Tutbury and High Peak, which provided a source of lordship for the local gentry. Castor has argued that the duchy provided the Staffordshire gentry with 'a sustainable distribution of power among the various interests' during the early fifteenth century. It disintegrated, however, when sources of noble lordship reappeared under the Staffords, Ferrers of Chartley and Suttons of Dudley during the reign of Henry VI. Nevertheless, the centrality of vertical ties of association is given primacy.[29] In Nottinghamshire, Carpenter regards the authority being exercised by a noble like Ralph, Lord Cromwell, as simply built upon an old Duchy of Lancaster foundation. In each instance, it is argued that the leading gentry were still actively seeking direct relationships with a feudal superior. Duchy lordship has also been used to dispute the idea of county-based elites. In these areas where duchy estates were prevalent, gentry were attracted by the benefits that this lordship offered rather than the county in which the lordship was located. In such instances, it is asserted that there could not be an elite group of families because the county did not hold significance to the leading gentry.[30]

Even in some southern counties where the nobility were not traditionally dominant, gentry networks have been analysed in this manner. Carpenter's examination of the Stonors of Oxfordshire, for instance, has revealed evidence of a dense network of associated gentry families. The Stonor network was not restricted to a single county but extended into Berkshire, Buckinghamshire and

Oxfordshire. In part it reflected the family's pattern of landholding across these counties. The Stonors' immediate world was shaped by these three, yet they also had interests in Wiltshire, with links to the Hungerford family figuring prominently, and even into Kent where they held some land. The Stonors' immediate range of connections was probably dominated by the local elite, many of whom held major local offices within Oxfordshire. Nevertheless, there is also evidence of a highly localized network of minor gentry and yeomen orbiting the Stonors who were almost continually involved in their affairs within their immediate, local environment. Carpenter suggests that although there was no noble able to provide lordship in Oxfordshire, Berkshire and Buckinghamshire, the crown represented the higher authority and attracted the gentry into its service. In this instance, she asserts that a combination of the crown as a private landowner, a limited magnate presence and the gentry formed the basis of authority in the region. Lordship is still seen as the defining feature of sociopolitical organization.[31]

This state of affairs resembles developments in Kent during the course of the fifteenth century. Evidence here indicates that royal service became increasingly attractive to the leading gentry as the century progressed. Starting from a fluid state at the beginning of the fifteenth century, when some of the leading figures within the shire enjoyed a variety of ties with a handful of magnates, service with the crown was gradually regarded with more favour from the reign of Henry VI. It was not until the reign of Edward IV, though, that the crown sought to exercise lordship within the county actively and draw the leading gentry into its affinity.[32] When it did, an increasing number of families accepted the benefits that a service relationship could bring. The positive benefits now outweighed the negative, but there was by no means a universal desire by the leading gentry to engage actively in public affairs. There were still many gentry who chose not to enter into vertical patron–client relationships. What has perhaps not been fully appreciated in counties like Berkshire, Buckinghamshire and Oxfordshire, is the element of choice again exercised by the leading gentry in deciding to move into royal service.[33]

## GENTRY INDEPENDENCE

Proponents of vertical ties of obligation have gone to considerable lengths to undermine the idea of gentry independence. Yet it is equally possible to interpret their evidence in just such a light. In fact, it could be that they still maintained an independence of interest when it best suited them. The gentry were able to order their affairs without relying on the aristocracy, and in many instances apparently preferred to do so. This is evident from network analyses undertaken for different shires. Carpenter's study of Warwickshire has suggested that leading gentry of the north east dealt mostly with Leicestershire families, while the Trussells, Malorys and Knightleys dealt with families from Leicestershire and Northamptonshire. There was also a strong propensity for north Warwickshire families to own land in Leicestershire, Staffordshire and Derbyshire. Furthermore, this trend was mirrored in the west of the shire where there was significant contact between Warwickshire and Worcestershire families, and in the south where gentry contacts with Gloucestershire were much in evidence. In fact, the Grevilles were more concerned with their Gloucestershire lands than their Warwickshire holdings during much of the fifteenth century.[34] Mackman, too, has found evidence of a network of Lincolnshire families from Lindsey extending into the East Riding of Yorkshire. The marriage alliances of two Yorkshire families, the Constables of Flamborough and the Constables of Halsham, linked them to the Cumberworths, Copuldykes, Hauleys, Skipwiths and Tirwhits. By contrast, the Lindsey gentry did not seek ties in neighbouring Nottinghamshire.[35] In some instances leading gentry even enjoyed significant interests at considerable distances from their native localities, which were often the result of kinship ties, marriage and inheritance. For example, as a means of maintaining their outlying interests, the Stonors of Oxfordshire leased the manor of Horton in Kent to their cousin, Philip Lewis.[36]

Personal links of kinship and friendship, business and financial links, and common service ties to a magnate or the crown could all influence the formation of networks. This feature emerges in leading gentry marriage strategies. While lesser gentry, with restricted social horizons, tended to marry within a county, the leading families could choose to marry into other families of an equivalent social rank from inside or outside a county. The search for an heiress could serve to increase the long-term resources available for future marriage provision and providing for younger children. Equally, it might be used as a way of salvaging family fortunes or for social advancement. As Payling has demonstrated, this trend was more prevalent among those newly established in local society and eager to secure their position in the longer term. Long-standing links to families in other counties stretching back generations might also be exploited to secure an alliance. In other instances tradition dictated the strategy. Three members of the Stanhope family, for example, married into Lancashire families. They all stemmed from the pre-1399 marriage of Sir Richard Stanhope to a daughter of Sir Richard Staveley of Stayley in Cheshire, the steward of the household of Henry, earl of Derby. Ultimately, it seems the choice depended upon personal circumstances.[37]

A desire to maintain control of their own affairs can also be seen in the gentry's use of the arbitration process. Rather than resort to the common law courts, independent arbitrators would be appointed to mediate between respective parties. The essential criterion was to include figures able to command the respect and agreement of either side; it was not essential to have a noble presence on the panel. When arbitration broke down there was little the arbitrator could do. William, Lord Ferrers of Chartley, had attempted to arbitrate between Richard Vernon and John Gresley in 1447, yet the dispute simply rumbled on.[38]

However, patterns of connection on their own do not necessarily account for the reasons that resulted in gentry independence. Arnold has suggested that in Yorkshire geography was an important factor. She does not view the administrative boundaries of the county and riding as socially relevant. However, she does acknowledge that local administration might have encouraged a sense of 'unity and common interest' leading to a gentry body that was 'generally self-reliant'. Yet the gentry there were unable to separate themselves entirely from magnate interests; indeed, they did not seek to do so. Service was viewed by some as an honourable pursuit and not rejected out of hand. The gentry responded to local geopolitical circumstances in an entirely understandable manner. If a lord displayed little interest in a lordship then the gentry displayed an equally indifferent attitude; if the lord maintained an active presence in the locality the gentry were more likely to act in response to overtures. The Talbot earls of Shrewsbury, long-standing lords of Sheffield, showed no interest at all in the West Riding before 1509 and attracted no gentry into their service. On the other hand, the earls of Northumberland and the Lords Clifford were more active in the Riding with predictable results.[39]

Elsewhere, wealth was the determining factor in enabling particular families to achieve a level of pre-eminence within a locality. In Nottinghamshire Payling has suggested that low levels of baronial wealth contrasted with the concentration of non-baronial wealth into the hands of an elite group of families. These families did not look to the resident nobility for leadership. It was, in fact, the other way around, with the baronage depending on them to augment their own influence. That there was cooperation between the two groups is not disputed. Sir Thomas Chaworth and other leading families established close personal relationships with Ralph, Lord Cromwell, and Chaworth actively supported Cromwell in his disputes with Sir Henry Pierpoint and Henry, Lord Grey of Codnor. The growth of Cromwell's power attracted some of the leading gentry into his orbit. There was also intermarriage between the nobility and the leading gentry. Two daughters of John Talbot, earl of Shrewsbury, married into the Chaworth and Vernon families during the 1460s.

Nevertheless, the baronage, with only a peripheral interest in a county like Nottinghamshire, actually looked to the leading families to oversee the administration of their estates. William, Lord Zouche, for example, appointed Robert Strelley as chief steward of his Nottinghamshire and Derbyshire estates. Reliance on a family traditionally associated with an area served a twin purpose: the magnate estates were protected and the local standing of the gentry family enhanced.

The leading gentry were aware that absentee nobility needed their goodwill in order to protect their interests. Vertical ties of service could therefore provide benefits to each party and actually reinforce the sense of interdependence. Wright identifies a similar phenomenon in Derbyshire where the Eyre family of Padley remained prominent in the High Peak area and provided stewards for the Lords Lovell, the earls of Westmorland and the earls of Shrewsbury.[40]

In certain instances the leading gentry might have been inclined towards independence by the potentially disruptive activities of the nobility. The leading gentry of the West Riding, of course, were still subject to tenurial bonds and the demands of their *mesne* lords. The sizeable skirmish at Heworth in 1453 between the Percys and Nevilles drew in gentry tenants from both families in support of their respective lords. Nevertheless, as Arnold also observes, the leading gentry were not willing to support their lords outside of the West Riding during the Wars of the Roses.[41]

An aristocratic presence within a county could severely affect the political geography of a shire. It could serve to disrupt rather than reinforce relationships within landowning society. The leading gentry in particular ran the very real risk of becoming involved in disputes with resident nobility within a county. This appears to have happened in Bedfordshire. Gentry estates were concentrated primarily in the north of the shire; the estates of the dominant noble, Lord Grey of Ruthin, were in the centre and the south. Between 1402 and 1415, Reynold, Lord Grey, actively intimidated the St Amand family's servants and attacked their property at Ampthill. He was also responsible for further disturbances in 1437 that resulted in the appointment of a royal commission of investigation. Edmund, Lord Grey, was also content, it seems, to manipulate local power for his own purposes. He backed Lord Cromwell against the duke of Exeter over the disputed manor of Ampthill during the 1450s, presumably because he was reluctant to see Exeter replace him as the dominant magnate in the area.[42]

While lesser gentry were attracted to service with minor barons such as Grey, for the most part the leading gentry were not. The Greys only appear to have had one knightly client in the county, Sir Thomas Wawton of Eton. Consequently, the kind of behaviour exhibited by Edmund, Lord Grey, was more likely to alienate the leading gentry and undermine political stability. The sheriff of Bedfordshire and Buckinghamshire during the Ampthill dispute was Robert Olney of Weston Underwood in Buckinghamshire, the steward of the Stafford lands in Bedfordshire and Buckinghamshire. As Payling notes, a dispute such as this could place 'intolerable pressure on the serving sheriff'. As Olney later claimed in a petition, he had incurred considerable expenses during his shrievalty and to discharge his responsibilities had been forced to maintain a large number of armed men. He also remarked that his experiences had served to put off others from taking up the shrievalty.[43]

Where lordship was weak or largely absent, the leading gentry were much more likely to conduct their business in accordance with their own immediate needs and requirements irrespective of vertical obligations. Weak lordship can be observed in a number of shires.[44] In Lincolnshire the lack of great magnate estates and the weakness of the vertical ties of lordship meant that these connections did not 'affect life in the county to any great degree'.[45] Mackman identifies networks of gentry connected to the Willoughby and Welles families, but these did not enjoy the same degree of cohesiveness as those identified by Carpenter in Warwickshire. Furthermore, in common with Derbyshire, Nottinghamshire and Leicestershire, the Duchy of Lancaster affinity had witnessed a steady decline in prominence during the early Lancastrian period. By the reign of Henry VI the duchy affinity was 'largely a memory',[46] and while it was preserved in connections between particular families it was not a source of proactive lordship. Indeed, Mackman sees duchy office as something to be avoided like other royal offices. The end result, in his opinion, though, is not an independently minded gentry but a fragmentation of power across the county with nobody able to assume a dominant position of authority.[47]

Weak leadership can be observed in other areas where the Duchy of Lancaster had been a leading landowner. Wright has remarked that duchy offices in Derbyshire 'formed yet another adjunct to the traditional authority of the gentry in the shire'. She has observed that the impact of duchy lordship became increasingly weak as the fifteenth century progressed. Wright has also suggested that the 'apportionment of power' within Derbyshire demonstrated an underlying independence. The gentry were 'a mixture of apolitical and politically independent elements; many had little contact with magnate interests'. They were, in fact, 'individualistic rather than "communal".[48] The Duchy of Lancaster was undoubtedly a source of employment for families, but one for the lesser rather than the leading gentry. During the first few decades of the fifteenth century there had been a 'consistent reappointment of a relatively small number of gentry families' within duchy estates in Derbyshire and Staffordshire. Castor views this as a normal state of affairs in counties where the duchy dominated. In her opinion it made sense for authority to be delegated in this manner and was a 'legitimate reflection of the structure of that society'.[49]

Nevertheless, after the accession of Henry VI the leading families were excluded from the principal offices. The great offices were no longer occupied by Derbyshire gentry, which resulted in the diminution of the crown's influence within the shire. Furthermore, significant portions of duchy estates were granted out. High Peak and Tutbury were granted in dower to Queen Margaret who established her own administrative structure independent of the duchy. Combined together, these trends reinforced the already widening gap between the leading gentry and the duchy. The Montgomerys, who had supplied stewards and constables within Tutbury honour, did not hold office after 1435. Similarly, the Vernons lost their traditional influence in High Peak to Walter Blount, a major landowner in southern Derbyshire, who benefited from close ties to Warwick and Margaret of Anjou. It was not until the early sixteenth century that the Vernons regained their former standing in the region.[50]

The apparent knock-on effect of absentee or weak lordship was to encourage leading gentry to operate independently. This is exactly what the duke of Buckingham's retainers did in Warwickshire according to Carpenter and Castor. Carpenter sees evidence of an attempt by the duke to exercise lordship in Derbyshire and Staffordshire at the expense of Warwickshire; Castor, on the other hand, attributed Buckingham's failure to a fundamental lack of interest in Warwickshire, Derbyshire or Staffordshire.[51] Taking matters into one's own hands in order to achieve a satisfactory conclusion to a dispute suggests that the gentry involved did not display absolute faith in the lordship of the magnate concerned, despite being in an environment where lordship was actively determining social relationships. The Meverell–Basset dispute took place in the Peak District region on the Staffordshire–Derbyshire border where Richard Vernon was the Duchy of Lancaster steward and where the Ferrers of Chartley and duchy connections were supposedly dominant. Yet Vernon chose to join in with the disorder rather than act as peacemaker. Castor describes this as 'maverick' because he was acting outside the accepted limits of behaviour as defined within a vertical hierarchy. Elsewhere she describes the relationship between Buckingham and Richard Vernon as 'hard to fathom'.[52]

In showing themselves willing to act outside an affinity structure in circumstances such as these, the gentry were clearly displaying independence of action. Vernon assessed the situation in the context of his own interests, not those of the duchy or Ferrers connections. Castor points to the failure of Buckingham's lordship and authority in this area of Staffordshire and Derbyshire. She would rather see this as exploiting weak leadership. When Richard Vernon died in 1451 his son, William, was unable to assume the same level of influence in the region. This was inherited by the new duchy steward, and recent recruit to Buckingham's affinity, John Gresley, who was currently involved in a dispute with the Vernons. Not only did it demonstrate poor judgement on Buckingham's part, it also suggested that the local gentry were largely left to manage affairs on their own. It is just as likely that Vernon was aware of the ineffectual leadership of Buckingham, the remote authority of the Duchy of Lancaster and the influence that this afforded him at the local level. It was a tool for the exercise of the pursuit of private interests.[53]

Just as advocates of vertical ties of obligation have attacked the relevance of the county, independence has also been conflated with the notion of a county community. In Kent, Fleming has identified the gentry as the leaders of their community who were able to order their affairs irrespective of the nobility. Their rank entitled them to the deference of the vast majority of Kentish folk who were their social inferiors; their lands also gave them financial independence, and 'The greater gentry's tenure of the more important county offices gave them the means with which to govern the shire – albeit at the king's command'.[54] Bennett and Clayton have both argued that the county of Cheshire represented the major cohesive force within which the gentry ordered their affairs because of its quasi-autonomous status as a county palatine. Royal officials such as the justiciar of Chester, the king's personal representative in the earldom, were heavily reliant on the support of the local gentry who demonstrated a particularly high level of involvement in the county's administration. Clayton and Worthington have both observed that while leading gentry from the north west were often appointed to the principal offices of chamberlain, sheriff and escheator, they were regularly involved in national affairs outside of Cheshire and unable to devote a consistent amount of time to their duties within the palatinate. They were therefore reliant upon local deputies drawn from leading gentry families from the palatinate to maintain administrative oversight.[55] An added element of cohesion in Cheshire was the 'development of military service over a period of more than a century between 1277 and 1403'. Significant numbers of local gentry were recruited by the earl (whether king or prince) who was 'the centre and focus of gentry affiliations aspiring to hold a leading role in the politics of the county'. However, in common with the experiences of the Duchy of Lancaster, the influence of a dominant faction in Cheshire declined after 1399 when the king also became the earl. Notwithstanding the unique traditions and institutions within the shire, broadly based participation by the gentry in local affairs continued and served to shape their attitudes and sense of identity throughout the fifteenth century. In fact, Clayton has asserted that 'during the period 1442–85 the position of dominance enjoyed by the Cheshire gentry could not be challenged by any other class'. In her opinion the leading families of Cheshire very much constituted an oligarchy.[56]

Recently Coss has once again emphasized that the county held significant social and political meaning for the gentry. Indeed, there are instances in which there was a close identification between the gentry and the county, on both practical and symbolic levels. The importance of the county had become apparent during the thirteenth and fourteenth centuries. The emergence of petitioning by elected representatives from the counties, along with active military participation in the king's wars, had increased awareness of national politics and issues among the gentry. These feelings were fed back to all sections of communities through shire organs such as the meetings of the county court. Moreover, the significance of county administrative offices meant that the county represented an identifiable territorial unit for those residing within it. While not wishing to assert the centrality of the county in the lives of the gentry, Acheson regards the political community of the shire as the strongest cohesive force within Leicestershire political society, and with the gentry exercising free will in that structure. It was not forged into a political unit by magnate intervention; political circles within it overlapped and as a matter of course some gentry enjoyed relationships with the nobility and the crown.[57] Elsewhere, scholars have also indicated the importance of the county in determining gentry activity. In Devon, Kleineke has pointed out that it had become common for leading gentry who had landed interests spread across several counties to concentrate their attention within one, and this identification was generally through local office-holding.[58]

## CONCLUSIONS

The preceding analysis has shown that it is perhaps more useful to regard lordship and independence as two mutually coexisting possibilities for gentry at every level of the social spectrum. It is misleading to draw too sharp a distinction between vertical and horizontal ties of association. They can perhaps be imagined as two bisecting axes on a graph that met at different points and thus determined the level of dominance or independence. Indeed, in counties where there was no dominant magnate, the leading families appeared to exercise lordship in their own right with their social inferiors. Neither was inherently more important or dominant than the other. In most counties the management was in Fleming's opinion 'a process of negotiation, not only with the crown, but also with those lords – lay and ecclesiastical – who had interests in the region'. In theory the interests of all landowners coincided as they desired stability in which to conduct their business.[59]

As Coss has argued, 'the interests of the crown, higher nobility and gentry, however much they interlocked, by no means always coincided'.[60] In some counties with a dominant, resident magnate there might have been little opportunity to advance or facilitate personal business other than by entering into such a relationship. Yet this does not mean that all gentry did this or indeed wanted to. Similarly, where magnate landholding was negligible and where the leading gentry appeared to dominate sociopolitical life it did not mean that they were all equally independently minded. There might still have been few opportunities to enter into a service relationship. Some acted as estate officials or accepted fees from more distant lords to manage their local affairs. In some areas, though, the magnate–gentry relationship, a complex reciprocal tie based on mutual respect, was more fluid. The relative dominance of noble or gentry interests within a county might even have shifted in response to external factors, thus altering the relative desirability of options. This, in turn, is likely to have affected the attitude of the gentry, moving periodically from a willingness to enter into service, to acting cautiously and in contradiction to anticipated patron–client conventions.

The gentry were clearly not a homogenous group. Therefore, by extension, we should not assume that they all thought or acted in the same way or regarded the benefits and drawbacks of lordship in the same way. They shared a series of common characteristics – but that is all. They enjoyed different levels and patterns of wealth and landholding, had varying and often contrasting social horizons, and displayed different attitudes towards service and other activities within the public domain. If we can understand how the gentry came into being, the principal characteristics they shared as a particular social formation, especially the sociopolitical environment in which they conducted their lives, and what served to bind or divide them, then we can perhaps better understand those processes that one particular group, the leading gentry, applied to the decision-making process during the Wars of the Roses.

What has not been fully considered by late medieval historians is the extent to which choice was exercised by the leading gentry in different environments and different sets of circumstances. In the next chapter the discussion will therefore move to considering the cognitive process. In particular, it will explore how social scientists have sought to understand the method by which judgements are made and choices reached, and whether these lessons can be applied to our understanding of the leading gentry during the Wars of the Roses.

# 3

# The Decision-Making Process

How did the leading gentry actually make their decisions during the Wars of the Roses? The gentry who chose to support one side through military or political means were not automatons acting blindly without fear or emotion; neither were the gentry who chose to do the opposite cowards. Decisions, whether made in the heat of the moment or after considered reflection, were made at each stage of the conflict. However, is it genuinely possible to ascertain the criteria that fed into their decision-making process? And perhaps most fundamentally of all, given the length of time since these events transpired, can historians hope to understand the actual mental processes that they employed at the time, including the judgements they made on different issues?

Historians often attempt to explain the behaviour of individuals by back-projecting behaviour from a particular event, or reference point. Reference points are subject to manipulation, though. An event alone did not predetermine the choices that would be made and could result in very different responses. Moreover, the assumptions being made about the attitudes that underpinned the behaviour and reactions of the gentry can appear contradictory and remain open to alternative, and equally plausible, explanations. A recent biographical account of the prominent Warwickshire knight, Sir William Catesby of Lapworth, that ascribes certain reasons for his choices, shows the fine line that exists when applying assumptions to the behaviour of gentry. It has been proposed that Catesby's conduct between 1471 and his death in 1478/9 was the result of a chastened attitude after he was impeached for supporting the Readeption regime of Henry VI. Yet a closer look suggests this sits at odds with his earlier behaviour. During the course of his political career he was attached to the earls of Shrewsbury, the royal household and the earls of Warwick. His support for the Lancastrians led him to fight at Towton. A brief spell in exile and attainder was soon put behind him when he secured a pardon. He demonstrated himself to be a man of independent thought and action between 1460 and 1471, following a path that best suited his own interests. His sudden conversion to a chastened man therefore seems out of character.[1]

In this instance it depends on how we choose to interpret 'chastened'. The year 1471 is seen in this explanation as a defining year for the formation of his decision-making process. Catesby had been caught out by the rapidly shifting political and military landscape. The assumption of his attitude according to this model is made on the basis that he was absent from local affairs for almost eight years after 1471. It is also based on the premise that he would still have served in local affairs given the opportunity. It is equally possible, though, that Catesby, without significant patrons to intercede on his behalf, was making a pragmatic, calculated decision in the immediate aftermath of the Yorkist triumphs at Barnet and Tewkesbury. Alternatively, he could have simply decided that it was no longer in his interests to serve in local affairs and like many gentry was opting for a quieter life. Clearly, much hinges on the language that is employed to describe these actions.

The social sciences have much to contribute to the debate on the Wars of the Roses. Their analysis of human behaviour can provide a useful a tool for historians to understand the decision-making processes of the late medieval gentry in a more structured framework. Psychologists define the core ingredients of any decision as a sequence of acts, states and outcomes. Acts are the options available to individuals and from which they must chose, states are the possible ways in which the world might move, and outcomes are the different possibilities or consequences of each act given each possible state. The traditional explanation of people's choices, and one that still remains the dominant model within the social sciences, argues that human behaviour is underpinned by rationality. Each possible outcome is assigned a utility based upon how much the decision-maker valued that outcome. Integral to this model are the twin notions of consistency and coherency. In any given situation it is expected that people will attempt to maximize their utility. When deciding between options, the value of each possible outcome should be weighted by the probability of it happening. Once these have been worked out people would order them preferentially and act in accordance with the highest value chosen. This is sometimes referred to by social scientists as the 'sure-thing principle'.[2] Some psychologists, however, have questioned the validity of this model. The principal drawback of a conceptual framework like this is that no distinction is drawn between known and unknown probability judgements which hold the same value to individuals. Yet experience demonstrates that many people are averse to ambiguous situations; the majority prefer outcomes with known rather than unknown probabilities.[3]

This aversion can be seen in the behaviour of the leaders of urban authorities – for example, when the towns within the Cinque Ports confederation wrote to each other during 1460 and 1461 and despatched riders to gather information from senior local gentry and officials including the lieutenant of Dover Castle.[4] They were afraid of making the wrong move and subsequently being penalized. Responses by leading Kentish gentry are also indicative of risk aversion. Up until the Yorkist invasion of 1460 few had been willing to act in support of Yorkist protests despite any underlying sympathies they might have harboured.

Only a very few committed Yorkists, like Sir William Pecche of Lullingstone in Kent, had been prepared to take a risk earlier in the decade. Pecche had drifted into the Yorkist sphere during the early 1450s and had supported York's protest at Dartford in 1452.[5] Other gentry had remained circumspect. The upsurge of support in Kent reported by chroniclers for the invading Yorkist earls, though, suggested a buoyant, optimistic feeling sufficient to overcome the hesitancy of many leading gentry families resident in the east of the shire. Once confident of the Yorkist cause, leading Kentish gentry were known to have played significant roles at the battles of Northampton, Wakefield and Towton. They had become less risk averse.[6] Not all gentry reacted equally in this way, however. The majority of gentry across the country were not convinced of an outright victory and remained risk averse throughout this period.

Moving forward to the upheavals of 1469–71, we see similar evidence of alterations in the levels of risk aversion. In 1471 there was an upsurge of support among sections of the gentry who saw the fragile regime of Henry VI crumbling and took heart at the return of Edward IV from exile. Victory once more seemed likely and some leading gentry became less averse to risk. The divisions within the Readeption regime and the departure of leading Lancastrians like the duke of Somerset to the West Country to meet Queen Margaret were interpreted by some as signals of the regime's imminent collapse and that the time to act was now. A significant number of Midlands gentry, probably from Leicestershire, Derbyshire and Nottinghamshire, were reported by the chronicler Warkworth to have answered the Yorkist summons during March 1471. Leading Kentish gentry also flocked to the capital in the days leading up to the battle of Barnet in April. By contrast, the Readeption regime struggled to recruit men and the earl of Oxford found himself having to make direct approaches to the East Anglian gentry.[7]

We might suppose that those leading Kentish gentry who remained loyal to the Lancastrian cause in 1460 would be averse to opposing the Yorkist landing and would take no action. Yet Sir Thomas Brown of Tunford did the opposite. He refused to abandon his allegiance to the crown as sheriff of the county when the Yorkist earls invaded. Rather than keep his head down, he retreated to London, and then risked his life and those of his men by fighting his way into the Tower of London despite knowing the possible consequences. With little to lose, his behaviour then became reckless and aggressive. In the process of firing on the Yorkist besiegers he also destroyed the property of Londoners.[8] When the Yorkists captured him he was tried, condemned and executed to appease the City fathers.[9] One might also expect the Lancastrian victories at Wakefield in December 1460 and St Albans in February 1461 to encourage those who had participated to remain under arms as well as helping those previously undecided about joining the cause. Yet there is limited evidence of continuity in Lancastrian forces between Wakefield, St Albans and Towton in March 1461.

This very limited, specific group with a strong element within it was connected to the royal affinity, the Duchy of Lancaster, or magnate affinities like the earl of Northumberland. Thus, we find Symmond Hammes identified as a participant at Wakefield, St Albans and Towton; Sir Henry Bellingham and Sir John Heron of Ford at Wakefield and Towton; and Sir William Tailboys at the second battle of St Albans and then Towton. However, the surviving evidence does not suggest a particularly strong element of overlap in the names of participants.[10]

The majority of leading gentry did not recognize a 'sure thing' and apparently remained content to observe from the sidelines. The extremely low turnout at the battles of Hedgeley Moor and Hexham in 1464 suggests that by this stage even more of the leading gentry, particularly those within that localized region of Yorkshire where both of these engagements took place, considered the probability of a Lancastrian victory to be non-existent. This aversion was low enough to act as a significant deterrent to other gentry. The leading participants at these two battles were long-standing adherents like Sir Richard Tunstall, Sir Thomas Findern, Sir Philip Wentworth and Sir William Tailboys. All had a history of opposition to the Yorkists.[11] The hesitancy of the leading Yorkshire gentry to rise in support of the Lancastrian cause in May 1471 suggests a conflict of interest between loyalty to the Lancastrian dynasty and to their traditional patron, the young earl of Northumberland, who had already shown an unwillingness to oppose Edward IV in April 1471. When it became clear that the Lancastrian cause had collapsed in the wake of their defeat at battle of Tewkesbury, those who had been tempted into active military opposition to the Yorkists applied to the earl to act as their intercessor with Edward IV. The likelihood of a Lancastrian victory, once considered possible or even probable, had diminished to such an extent there was no longer even modest resistance. These gentry had become more risk averse.[12] For some Lancastrian partisans, however, the Yorkist proclamation against them had removed the possibility of a pardon and thus significantly simplified the decision-making process. Death was the only 'sure thing' if they were captured. They needed a Lancastrian victory to ensure their long-term survival. Sir Thomas Fulford and Sir John Delves could be left in no doubt what being 'open and notorious traitors, rebels and enemies'[13] meant. Gentry aversion to risk taking clearly varied in extent and intensity at different moments in time in accordance with the vagaries of political and military fortunes experienced by either side.

A further drawback that some psychologists have identified in a rational model is the suggestion that people's preferences should not be affected by the way options are described or presented for the same situation. Yet once again this clearly happened. A positive presentation of a risky scenario is more acceptable than a negative one. Preference ordering and reversals clearly contradict the traditional model.[14] Evidence of this can be found in the reaction to reports of news during the Wars of the Roses which show people's preferences could hinge very much on what they discovered and how that information was presented to them. The Lancastrian and Yorkist high commands understood the importance of presentation. A positive or negative presentation of the situation could persuade or deter the target audience. The Yorkist articles circulated shortly after the landing on the Kent coast in June 1460 were designed to encourage support in the south east.[15] Similarly, the Yorkist proclamation in the wake of the battle of Barnet in April 1471 was designed to both inform and encourage Yorkist sympathizers, while at the same time deter Lancastrian opponents. The threat of forfeiture for supporting the losing side was a powerful deterrent. Equally, the Lancastrian army of Queen Margaret sent outriders and harbingers during April 1471 to persuade men to join them and counter the Yorkist propaganda that was circulating in the south west. The presence of substantial military forces in the region was much more likely to encourage sympathizers to each cause and influence those inclined to waver.[16]

Psychologists have built upon these objections to rational explanations and developed a more plausible framework of behaviour and decision making. Recognizing that people regularly contravene notions of consistency and coherence, some have argued that they do not necessarily aim to act in a way that maximizes utility. Responses of the gentry during the Wars of the Roses appear to bear this out. Known as Prospect Theory, this has sought to account for behavioural inconsistencies. It recognizes that people still seek to maximize some kind of expectation and aspire to the most favourable outcome. However, the utilities and probabilities that they map in their minds undergo cognitive distortions when they are evaluated, which can substantially alter the relative desirability of any given option. Decision-making is explained as a two-stage process in which the 'frame' is first created.[17] This describes the decision-maker's conception of the acts, outcomes, and contingencies associated with a particular choice. The individual will sift through judgements or attitudes relevant to that decision-frame. In order to make a judgement, the individual looks for signals or 'cues' within one or more environments. These cues determine which judgements are relevant to the decision choice.

Building upon psychological analysis, it is useful within the context of late medieval England to see the leading gentry identifying these cues within geographical, territorial, social, economic, administrative and political 'environments'. These environments resemble the networks proposed by late medieval historians and provided the arenas in which gentry interacted and formed judgements. On the one hand, an environment could be the group of administrative office-holding gentry who periodically came together at the sessions of the peace as justices. Alternatively, on the other, it could simply be a reading circle through which texts were read, borrowed, copied and discussed.

These networks or environments existed at the local, regional and national levels. The importance of a layered approach to studying environments has been recently shown in the work of Holford. He has suggested that within the context of localities a range of frameworks actively shaped cultural identities in late medieval Yorkshire. He has also proposed that there was a national culture of locality based upon the county and wider regional areas, a regional culture advanced by leading families and institutions, and a local culture based upon districts.[18] These were not static concepts; identities were 'plural and fluctuating'. Social and geographical mobility could lead to very different notions of home than a fixed locality. Leading and lesser gentry, with different horizons, were likely therefore to behave in different ways.[19]

This approach also recognizes that by accommodating the impact of emotion and the nature of memory upon the decision frame, the mental processes involved in decision making remain much more fluid than ideas based upon rationality alone. Some theorists have suggested that individuals 'mark' real and imaginary scenarios with positive or negative feelings, which can remain with them throughout their lives. As a consequence, mental representations of decision stimuli can evoke affective experiences which serve to shape perceptions and subsequent judgements and decisions. Accurately identifying and measuring these paradoxical effects, however, is still causing social scientists difficulties and more research is needed.[20] Holford has advanced a similar notion when discussing imagined communities and localities. The words 'country' and 'neighbourhood' carried with them a range of meanings within different contexts and environments.[21] The emotional impact of the exchange of information upon the gentry's actions is shown in Paston, Plumpton and Stonor correspondence. Gentry routinely sought out information and passed it on to their kinsmen, friends, and associates.

Others, though, actively sought to influence behaviour. Clement Paston tried to convince his brother John I of the positive benefits of joining Warwick in London in 1460. Others did not necessarily relay news with that intention of influencing decisions, but the effect could be equally significant. In 1483 Edward Plumpton wrote to his kinsman, Sir Robert Plumpton, informing him that people were troubled by the commandments they had received in Richard III's name and did not know what to do. He provided him with news of the movements of the duke of Buckingham commenting confidently that 'I trust he shalbe right withstanded and all his mallice'. He also reported that the arrival of royal messengers was a daily occurrence. Nevertheless, he stood ready to do Sir Robert's bidding should he ask. Communication between the gentry could therefore inform and shape responses. Sir Robert had received no special favours from Richard III. Indeed, quite recently he had been forced to accept an unfavourable arbitration award over his inheritance by the king. Nevertheless, in October 1483 he erred on the side of caution and the negative news received from his kinsman perhaps reinforced that sense of discretion.[22]

Emotional responses can also be generated by back-projection, where the memory of an event or outcome is distorted in order to justify the present attitude or decision. A famous instance took place in Lancastrian France between Sir John Fastolf and Sir John Talbot. After the battle of Patay in 1429, Talbot accused Fastolf of fleeing the battle rather than coming to his assistance. Fastolf's unchivalric behaviour had resulted in Talbot's capture and detention for four years. Fastolf, of course, saw this as a strategic withdrawal.[23] Similarly, the historical memory presented within legal documents clearly highlights some of the instances where previous events were constructed to suit the needs of the individual. Plaintiff and defendant would each seek to present events in such a way that would present their behaviour in a favourable light. Known as a biasing mechanism, this demonstrates that the way in which people enjoyed or disliked something at the time it happened is less influential than their subsequent recollections of that act.[24]

Experiences are a vital to being able to judge or assess a situation and make what is considered to be an informed decision. Yet these experiences are also subject to cognitive distortion. These are stored in a personal environment and drawn upon by an individual at certain moments in their life along with the emotions felt at the time. Some experiences were of greater significance than others to gentry. A member of the leading gentry, with political and military experience acquired by serving in local government, as a member of parliament, and on campaign in France, Scotland, or Ireland, is likely to have judged the perils of involvement, the likelihood of a summons to service or the possibility of attack, differently to a lesser gentleman whose experiences were largely confined to his immediate locality and who was either unable or unwilling to engage in wider activities. That is not so say, of course, that they could not, or would not, have arrived at the same decision or acted in the same way. However, they are likely to have undergone very different cognitive experiences before reaching that point.

During the Wars of the Roses gentry were faced with an entire range of overlapping and potentially conflicting choices. On the broadest level the decisions revolved around the extent to which they chose to engage with or ignore the conflict between the houses of York and Lancaster. At different stages during the period gentry might be confronted with choices about demonstrating political or military support, answering the summons of the crown or magnate, taking part in open rebellion and insurrection, fighting in battle, communicating with the exiled opposition, targeting enemies in a particular locality or simply declining to take any action whatsoever. Others, however, might have been presented with fewer and even simpler choices. That does not mean that the response of a member of the gentry who did not have any significant connections to the nobility or leading political figures was likely to be substantially different. The consequences of a disastrous decision could also loom much larger in his mind and make him just as risk averse as his social superiors at a crucial moment.

By considering how a member of the gentry might come to a considered judgement about a summons to military service by the crown or a magnate and make a decision, the potential range of responses can be seen. Relevant signals or cues could include the presence within the locality of a Lancastrian or Yorkist army, an unstable local political situation, the attitudes of commissioners of array and royal officials, and sociopolitical relationships. Based on these cues, a judgement about the likelihood of a summons or request for support would be made. The presence of the Yorkist and Lancastrian armies in the West Country in 1471 would have exerted a strong influence on how many judged the political and military situation and ultimately the decision arrived at.[25]

Different cues are evident in the response of the Beverley mercer and gentle-man John Reddisham. According to a petition he sent into chancery during the late 1460s, Reddisham claimed he was sent a commission of array by the earl of Northumberland and Lord Neville directing all the men aged between 16 and 60 years to muster on behalf of Henry VI in 1460. Reddisham obviously pondered how to proceed. Shortly afterwards, John Newport arrived and asked for a copy to send to Sir Thomas Neville, the brother of the earl of Warwick and bishop of Exeter. This he did, only to find himself thrown into prison after the Yorkist defeat at Wakefield in December 1460. The copy that he made seemed to have been delivered into Lancastrian hands by John Newport, and Reddisham found himself accused of treason. Like Henry Vernon, Reddisham was faced by a dilemma about how to proceed. Vernon had hedged his bets and sought to avoid committing himself to either side. Reddisham, uncertain how to proceed, trusted the advice of Newport and sent a copy to the Yorkist rivals. Situations like these must have arisen throughout the conflict and serve to highlight the human dimension of the conflict. Reddisham had to balance conflicting thoughts and feelings. His example contains some of the principal ingredients within the decision-frame that he constructed in order to make a choice: the social norms like the obligation to obey a royal summons to service, the impact of local lord-ship; and personal characteristics such as hesitancy in making up one's mind and doing so in the face of pressure from another. As a result of the relative weight he gave to these factors, he felt compelled to act and accept the risk involved.[26]

It is fair to say that the fifteenth-century gentry responded in differing ways to the same decision proposition and adopted contradictory decision-making strategies during the Wars of the Roses. However, to effectively assess these decision-making strategies it is necessary to keep track of numerous, changing variables, all of which could affect the decision outcome. These often changed over time as a consequence of the decision maker's actions. As individuals experienced more so, too, might their attitudes and opinions shift and, ultimately, the final decisions that they made. During the later 1450s, before the outbreak of hostilities, many were able to apply a compensatory strategy to decision-making. Compensatory strategies allow individuals to sift, combine and process all the information that has been gathered on a subject without the pressure of time.[27] Between 1459 and 1461, and again between 1469 and 1471, gentry are much more likely to have adopted a non-compensatory strategy due to the constraints of time. A greater number were put on the spot during these highly volatile periods and asked to make decisions based on little information much more quickly than they would perhaps have preferred.[28] However, given that these events occurred in the distant past and the challenges presented by the scarce and often disjointed evidence, it is not feasible to make authoritative statements.

Nevertheless, as we saw in the previous chapter exploring gentry culture, particularly their sense of identity, social networks and relationships, and activities in the public and private domains, we are provided with insights into the character and concerns of the gentry as a social formation. Examples of gentry behaviour have been taken as far as possible from a broad cross section of the leading gentry. The actions and reactions of certain individuals have been subject to detailed examination; perhaps by examining these sorts of responses historians can come to understand why the gentry reacted in a particular way during the Wars of the Roses.

Moreover, by combining this with a conceptual framework designed to understand the cognitive process, we have a model that enables us to understand the decision-making processes of particular gentry and to isolate the different types of behaviour that underpinned choices made at the time. It is to these factors that underpinned judgements and the decision-making process that the discussion now moves. As previously discussed, for the purposes of this analysis, the principal decision problem is understood to mean whether an individual chose or declined to support one side or the other, politically or militarily, at a certain moment in time during the Wars of the Roses. There was, of course, a range of subsidiary problems with associated factors, or cues, which impacted to a greater or lesser degree upon the decision-making process. It is unlikely that only one factor was crucial in the process. They are inextricably linked and should not be viewed in complete isolation from the remainder. There is every likelihood that several, often contradictory issues, were running concurrently in the minds of an individual knight, esquire or gentleman at any one moment which could have resulted in contradictory reactions. Some men might have seen the set of factors within a decision frame positively and taken a risk; another group might have seen them negatively and chosen to avoid any involvement. Nevertheless, as the following chapters demonstrate, it is possible to see the relative impact of one factor over another at particular stages of the conflict.

# 4

# Gentry, Warfare and Violence
## in Late Medieval England

## INTRODUCTION

One of the principal influences on the formation of the gentry identified by Coss and others was their participation in the wars of successive kings of England, particularly Edward I and his successors. The very practical need for manpower to captain and lead contingents within royal armies had hastened gentry development and their subsequent importance in the management of the localities on behalf of the crown. In fifteenth-century England there was no standing army. Military resources, not least manpower, were distributed among and across the landowning elite and to a lesser extent urban authorities. When the crown conducted warfare, either at home or abroad, it raised forces in accordance with established conventions; within this context the martial role of the late medieval gentry remained a crucial consideration.[1] The Hundred Years War had become the training ground for much larger numbers of the gentry and introduced many more to the horrors of the battlefield. Moreover, these experiences were not confined to one particular grouping within the collective body of gentry. The traditional portrayal of the elite families being most heavily committed to warfare is at best misleading, at worst wrong. Knights, esquires and gentlemen all participated to varying degrees, and at least some of that participation was probably on the battlefields of the Wars of the Roses.[2]

Yet, were the gentry predisposed to martial pursuits and did this also encourage them to resort to violence as a means of conflict resolution? Did they naturally seek the opportunity to engage in conflict? In this chapter we will explore the relationship between gentry, warfare and violence, and the extent to which this remained an underlying feature of their behaviour during the fifteenth century. In particular, we shall focus on the nature of military education and training, gentry feelings towards the chivalric code, the military equipment of the gentry and attitudes towards its possession, different methods employed to recruit an army and how these related to the conduct of civil warfare, and, finally, the extent to which violence was used to settle disputes within the domestic arena. These considerations have ramifications for how gentry attitudes towards participation in civil warfare are interpreted and when considering the numbers who might actually have been prepared to take up arms at a particular stage during the Wars of the Roses.

## MILITARY EDUCATION AND TRAINING

Keen has suggested that the degree of military experience within a community influenced its collective martial outlook. Denton, on the other hand, has argued that the military community within a shire was normally a distinct element within gentle society. Consequently, 'the size and influence of the pool of gentry with military experience' can serve as an indicator of regional militarization.[3] Education in the martial arts was certainly a common feature of late medieval society across Europe. Orme has shown how education was regarded as an all-inclusive process. Not only did it incorporate formal instruction in reading, writing and arithmetic, but it also included instruction in behaviour and social interaction. While the level of formal tuition received by members of the nobility and gentry varied, there can be no doubt that most received some form of rudimentary tutoring in grammar. Many of the values and cultural mores were inculcated through didactic literature. Education began in the home and the sons of gentry might subsequently find themselves placed in the household of a lord or kinsman where their instruction was taken further. The more able students might study at the universities at Oxford or Cambridge, or acquire grounding in the law at the Inns of Court in London.[4]

The extremes in the level of formal education are evident in two examples. Sir Alexander de la Pole, younger brother of William de la Pole, earl of Suffolk, received a vigorous education and spent time as a scholar at Cambridge. He might even have been intended for a career in the church. By contrast, Sir John Passhley, a middle-ranking member of the Sussex gentry, could still claim in a lawsuit that he had been defrauded because he was unable to read documents placed before him. Presumably, his education had been less comprehensive than Sir Alexander de la Pole's. What tied the likes of Sir Alexander de la Pole and Sir John Passhley together, however, was their military training and military experiences. Like many of their generation Sir Alexander and Sir John went on to fight in France. De la Pole died at the battle of Jargeau in 1429 when the French forces, led by Joan of Arc, successfully attacked and captured the fortress of Jargeau near Orléans. Passhley fought in France over a period of years, perhaps under the experienced eye of his kinsman Richard Woodville, esquire, and survived to tell the tale. Passhley's experiences were entirely in keeping with the times and served to reinforce the notion that the best and most honourable arena in which to acquire experience was on the battlefields of Europe rather than at home.[5]

It is evident that boys were encouraged to play with weapons from an early age and that some boys later developed an interest in warfare. Although from the knightly ranks within gentry society, Passhley was from an established, Sussex family which had sought little influence in the governance of the shire.[6] He had actively engaged in military ventures, perhaps attracted by the opportunities offered in Lancastrian France. Like many of his contemporaries he had probably obtained a rudimentary training as a boy. The age at which most began to receive formal training varied. However, convention dictated that this normally began when they were about 14 years old. Surviving depositions from the court of chivalry cases suggest that this was not an unusual age to be exposed to the perils of combat.[7] The function of teaching boys in arms is likely to have been carried out by knightly masters, fathers and possibly even lords in the case of wards. Who was to take on this role was probably dictated by relative wealth and social standing. There was provision within medieval society to engage the services of a master-at-arms. Such masters were in evidence in urban centres, including London, from the twelfth and thirteenth centuries. The schools of defence that some masters ran, though, were seen as threats to public order and were closed down if the authorities became aware of them. Most masters maintained a shadowy existence, providing their services on a contractual basis, perhaps in a leading gentry or magnate household. In larger households where boys had more companions with whom to practice, the engagement of a master made more sense. Organized matches provided further opportunities to learn the techniques of war. Nevertheless, it is likely that the vast majority of gentry would have had limited access to a master at a school of defence.[8]

Once older, the tournament offered an environment in which the nobility and gentry could choose to hone their fighting techniques. Contemporaries described tournaments as 'Schools of Arms' or 'Schools of Prowess'. During the Hundred Years War tournaments were sometimes staged between knights from opposing armies during periods of truce. The Calais marches were possibly the most popular venue for these *jousts à outrance*. In 1380 Marshal Boucicaut fought Sir Piers Courtenay and later Sir Thomas Clifford there. The latter combat was fought with lances, swords, daggers and axes. An interest in chivalry was often a characteristic of those with strong military backgrounds and experience of warfare. There were different types of tournament. The mêlée tournament consisted of companies of knights fighting against each other and taught them to manoeuvre and charge as a unit. This type of tournament started to fall out of fashion during the fourteenth century, however, and was gradually replaced by the feat of arms which were fought with the traditional weapons of joust and tourney, the lance and broadsword, reflecting the shift in the nature of combat. In battle men-at-arms now fought largely on foot in the 'English' method. The

feat of arms gave a contestant an opportunity to practise his skills on foot with
battleaxe and dagger under controlled conditions, as well as exhibit his superior-
ity in each course.[9]

Although tournaments were highly regulated and stage-managed events, this
did not detract from their practical value as a means of acquiring renown; nor
did it remove the inherent dangers in taking part to the participants involved.
Tournaments did not necessarily always go according to plan. At the Smithfield
contest in 1477 in honour of the marriage of Edward IV's son, the young Richard,
duke of York, to Anne Mowbray, daughter of the duke of Norfolk, Robert Clifford
displaced part of John Cheyne's armour but refrained from attacking that spot
and causing the latter serious injury. For this action he won great praise and a
prize. Nevertheless, some contests did get out of hand. At the same tournament
Anthony Woodville, Earl Rivers, was outraged when, after the contest had supposedly ended, Thomas Hansard took an unchivalrous swipe at him between the
shoulder and the helm, a potentially life-threatening thrust. Seeing red, Rivers
had rained a series of six blows down upon Hansard before officials presumably
separated them. Despite this, the contest had been very much to the crowd's taste
who 'gave lawd to both partys'.[10]

Such was the honour that could be won that men from all over Europe would
travel to participate in such events. During the fourteenth century Bretons,
Flemings and Hainaulters were frequent participants at English tournaments.[11]
Armenians and Cypriots were even at the Smithfield jousts in 1362. Contestants
prized the recognition that their prowess brought them from their contemporaries and within society at large. The Woodvilles and their kinsmen in Kent
displayed a keen practical and theoretical interest in chivalry and martial affairs.[12]
It was Anthony Woodville, Earl Rivers, however, who had acquired a particular
reputation as a jouster and who, when still Lord Scales, had participated in the
famous event at Smithfield against the Bastard of Burgundy in 1467.[13]

A certain kind of man wished to be remembered for his military prowess. Sir
William Oldhall, a leading servant of Richard, duke of York, bequeathed his ban-
ners and pennons to the parish church of St Michael, also known as Whittington
College, in London.[14] The survival, until relatively recently, of the jousting helm
of Sir John Pecche in Lullingstone Church in Kent is testimony to his martial
identity in turn. Pecche enjoyed a successful career within the Calais garrison and
was a noted jouster at the end of the fifteenth century. He participated in jousts
from at least the age of 21 and took part in the 1494 tournament at the Palace of
Westminster with the earls of Suffolk and Essex. Jousting and participation in
other feats of arms remained integral aspects of gentry culture throughout the
fifteenth century. Apart from Pecche's jousting helm, others have survived elsewhere, including one at Melbury Sampford in Dorset, which probably belonged
to either William Browning senior or junior. The two Brownings were active

members of the Dorset governing elite. An interest in jousting placed them at
the heart of the gentry martial tradition.[15]

Inevitably, however, it was the exploits of the most successful warriors that
drew most attention from chroniclers. Sir Christopher Talbot, younger brother of
John Talbot, earl of Shrewsbury, was a jouster of some note. An active participant
in the French wars during the 1430s, Sir Christopher also acquired a reputation
at the lists. In November 1440 it was reported in a letter to John Paston I that a
Spanish knight was about to arrive who would either face Sir Christopher Talbot
or Sir Richard Woodville in another contest.[16] The Hastings Manuscripts provide
details of the exploits of one of the most famous fifteenth-century soldiers, Sir
John Astley. Astley participated in many tournaments during the course of his
career. In 1438 he fought Pierre de Masse in Paris near the Bastile. Four years
later, in January 1442, he fought again at Smithfield. His opponent on this occasion was Philip Boyle of Aragon in what was reputed to be one of the principal
spectacles of the time. Astley joined the Yorkist cause in 1461 although it is
unclear which battles he participated in.[17]

Remaining proficient in the use of arms was a requirement for all levels of
society throughout the late medieval period and was the subject of much parliamentary legislation from the thirteenth century onwards. For the majority of
the gentry and lesser landowners the tournament was not an option. The crown,
however, provided a mechanism for military skills to be preserved. Archery was
specifically regulated and was a skill that the gentry learned as a recreational
pursuit. References to practice sessions at the butts are often to be found among
central government records. However, practise was not without its dangers.
In November 1446 the London skinner Hugh Somervyle was pardoned after
accidentally killing Thomas Edmond, draper. Somervyle had been shooting
crossbows at certain ranges in the company of John, duke of Exeter, and others
in a garden within the precinct of the free chapel of St Katherine by the Tower of
London. Unfortunately, after aiming at a more remote target with his crossbow,
he had struck Edmond with his bolt, which bounced off a tree and wounded him
in the head. Similarly, in May 1453 the yeoman John Hopkynson of Kirmington
in Lincolnshire was pardoned after having accidentally struck John Symson of
Messingham in the head with an arrow and killing him, the arrow having been
carried off-target by the wind.[18]

The gentry also had the opportunity to acquire leadership skills. In times of
war they acted as lesser captains of men, sometimes of their tenants and kinsmen.
They often fought on foot alongside their men in a visible display of solidarity.
When Sir Ralph Percy was captured at Otterburn in 1388 he was bleeding from
numerous wounds and suffering from physical exhaustion.[19] Failure to provide
sensible leadership, however, laid commanders open to criticism. To Froissart
and many of his contemporaries, 'war was not just a matter of hot courage, but

of hot courage married to cool judgement'. It was essential to find the correct balance between the two. Froissart relates the story of the Scottish capture of Berwick by Alexander Ramsay and a force of 40 men. However, a superior English force under the earl of Northumberland then trapped the Scots. When an inferior relief force arrived under the command of Sir Archibald Douglas, Ramsay's cousin, the decision was taken not to risk battle. Ramsay's uncle Sir William Lindsay protested that his nephew should not be abandoned. However, the Scottish garrison was left to its fate. The only survivor was Ramsay, who was spared by Northumberland. This same point was also made, albeit obliquely, by Hall, who commented on the actions of Edmund Beaufort, titular 'duke of Somerset', at the battle of Tewkesbury that 'The duke of Somerset perceiuing that lyke a knight, more courageous than circumspect, came out of his trenche, with his whole battayle, and followed the chace'. Knighthood and chivalry did not mean leaping in without first considering the consequences.[20]

By the fifteenth century, however, Denton asserts that military service among the gentry was to some extent a matter of choice: 'Enthusiasm for any particular campaign depended on its demands and social context'. This parallels Ayton, who has identified periods of 'remilitarization' of the gentry when opportunities for profit and personal advancement increased.[21] France was the principal arena in which the nobility and gentry acquired military experience in the fifteenth century. Within this theatre of operations, however, some individuals obtained a greater level of experience than others. Prestigious campaigns were likely to generate more widespread support than less glamorous noble-led campaigns. It is this prestige which, Denton argues, encouraged the Midlands gentry to serve under Henry V. It appealed to those families who were the natural leaders of regional society and who dominated local office-holding.[22] In very few instances did those gentry who did take up arms commit themselves to a life of service with one particular commander. Indeed, for both gentry and crown the duration of their commitment was vitally important. The gentry were reluctant to leave their lands and domestic affairs for too long. For those who undertook overseas service, studies suggest that most knights enjoyed varied careers, generally combining service in the field with garrison duty.

Keen has proposed that these changing patterns of service after 1420 actually led to the demilitarization of the English gentry. Denton, on the other hand, has argued that this was not the case in the East Midlands where some gentry were able to balance overseas military and domestic responsibilities until the French wars ended in 1453–4. Thereafter, professional soldiers returned home and were able to take up local administrative offices. It was only after 1453 that demilitarization began to set in when this generation slowly began to die out.[23] During the first phase of the Wars of the Roses there were clearly captains well versed in the techniques of war. Sir Thomas Kyriell of Westenhanger in Kent was a seasoned campaigner who had served in France for 30 years. Kyriell gained notoriety as one of the joint-commanders of the English force defeated at Formigny in Normandy in 1450, although this was scarcely his fault. Nevertheless, his experience was highly valued; his defection to the Yorkists in 1460 would have brought much practical experience to their forces. Members of the Scudamore family from Herefordshire likewise served in the French wars and subsequently supported the Lancastrian cause. Sir John Scudamore had fought at Agincourt in Henry V's retinue with four men-at-arms and 12 archers. In 1422 he served with his son at Harfleur and in 1436–7 he was to be found in the retinue of Richard, duke of York. Sir John's brother, Sir William, also served in France. Sir John Scudamore became a leading resistance figure in Wales from 1460–1.[24]

Denton has suggested that very few gentry families performed military service for the first time after 1453. The only East Midlands exceptions he identifies are the Fieldings, Hotofts and Barleys. He suggests that a 'martial family' was characterized by the participation of its head in at least one campaign in more than one generation. He found this to be the case for Derbyshire families including the Blounts, Vernons, Gresleys, Leeks, Longfords and Stathums, while in Leicestershire he identified the Beaumonts, Digbys, Hastings, Trussells and Fieldings. These families continued to serve after 1453. The overwhelming majority of gentry were either those who only served once in one generation before 1453, or those who had simply not served at all. He points to prominent families such as the Willoughbys of Nottinghamshire as a prime example. Active politically, they apparently did not take up arms. Alternative forms of service became more attractive to the gentry as a growing distinction began to emerge between soldier and civilian. The military campaigns of 1475 and 1492 attracted fewer East Midlands families than the 1415 campaign.[25]

Nevertheless, the extent of any 'demilitarization' across England is still uncertain and we should remain cautious in regarding any form of military service as being completely unattractive to the majority of the gentry. There has been no consistent survival of retinue lists for the French wars and certainly not for gentry indenturing for service with foreign magnates. There was still a significant constituency among the gentry who saw honourable military service as part of a career path in royal service. A particularly sought after appointment was a position within the Calais garrison. The nearest that kings of England came to possessing a professional fighting force in the fifteenth century was the Calais garrison. The garrison numbered approximately 1,000 men but, in common with the system of recruitment in this period, it was raised by indentures between the captains and lieutenants of Calais and the crown. The Calais garrison attracted a cosmopolitan group of men. As Grummitt has observed, 'The nature and organisation of war at the end of the Middle Ages served to reinforce the central role of chivalry and notions of virtue and honour . . . Given the performance of

military institutions in Calais, it is no surprise that in the fifteenth century the
Pale fulfilled a role as a chivalric theatre, where men could perform feats of arms,
win honour and engage in the fellowship of arms'.[26] Service at Calais appealed
to gentry with an interest in chivalry and the traditional obligations of gentility
and to those we might reasonably refer to these as 'professional soldiers', such
as Richard Lovelace and Andrew Trollope. Men like these formed the military
backbone of the garrison, serving as men-at-arms and commanding their own
personal retinues. In Somerset's retinue of 1451 Trollope was listed with 24 men
under his command.[27] Although the prospect of regular wages was a problem
that periodically led to mutinies during the first half of the fifteenth century, the
possibility of gaining honour and prestige through military service made positions within the Calais garrison much sought after.

For the ambitious, especially younger sons, it was particularly attractive. The
Paston family were constant suitors of Lord Hastings during the 1470s, seeking
to gain positions in the garrison for themselves and their servants. Places were
usually solicited by the prospective soldier, eager to come to the Pale for his
own reasons or attracted by the prospect of entering the service of a great lord.
In June 1475 Sir John Paston wrote to his brother, Edmund, from Calais, 'I heer
telle that ye be in hope to come hyddre, and to be in such wages as ye schall come
lyve lyke a jentlyman' and advising him of a position in the garrison that had just
become vacant.[28] Some men served in Calais for long periods throughout the
fifteenth century, regardless of political circumstances and changes of dynasty.
Lovelace, for instance, served in Calais for at least 35 years. Another interesting
name with a long service history in Calais that transcended dynastic change was
Hugh Conwey. A Conwey appears as a man-at-arms on foot under Giles Seyntlo
in Somerset's retinue in 1451. By 1461 he had transferred to the Yorkist household, probably via Warwick, and was made beadle of Mark and Oye; in 1464 he
participated in John Neville, Lord Montagu's, campaign to reduce the northern
Lancastrian strongholds, serving in the defence of Newcastle upon Tyne. In
1483, perhaps because of his north Wales origins and links to the Stanleys, he
joined the conspiracy to place Henry Tudor on the throne. Serving in Henry VII's
household, he was made treasurer of Calais in 1504 and died in 1517.[29]

France and Calais were not the only arenas in which men saw service before
and after 1453. The Scottish Marches and Ireland offered other opportunities for
acquiring experience. There were two wardens responsible for the defence of the
Scottish Marches. The warden of the East March was based at the strategically
important Berwick-upon-Tweed, while his colleague on the West March was
based at Carlisle. The wardens were retained by indentures of agreement with the
crown and were expected to recruit men by using the salaries from their office.[30]
The specific terms of the agreements varied during the early fifteenth century,
although the general principal was that the warden of the East March was paid

twice that of his colleague on the West March during periods of war or peace because the East March was the principal route into England. In times of war wardens were expected to double their forces. When John, duke of Bedford, was appointed warden of the East March in 1403 he was expected to maintain a peace-time retinue of 100 men-at-arms and 200 archers. His opposite on the West March was to have half that number. Retaining by wardens by virtue of their office, and as magnates in their own right, became blurred over time. It was common practice for them to recruit members of local families into their service. The Herons of Ford and Chipchase served the Percy earls of Northumberland in their liberties of Tynedale and Redesdale and were integral to the warden's administration. It was Sir John Heron of Ford who reputedly cut down Richard, duke of York, at the battle of Wakefield in 1460 'with great despite and cruel violence'.[31]

Serving on the Marches was a challenging prospect. Roxburgh Castle, set across the border in present-day Scotland, was besieged three times: in 1417, 1436 and 1460, and on the final occasion it was captured by the Scots. Even moving supplies to the castle was fraught with danger for those concerned. Traditionally, the office of constable of Roxburgh Castle fell to the northern nobility and gentry like Sir Robert Ogle who was well versed in the perpetual warfare practised on the borders. As one might expect, a surviving early fifteenth century muster roll for Roxburgh Castle and the West Marches included men from Tyndale and Redesdale. However, service on the borders was not restricted to northerners. The same muster also included other experienced military veterans like the Herefordshire knight Sir John Oldcastle who had seen service in the Welsh rebellion of Owain Glyndwr at the beginning of the fifteenth century.[32]

The other arena in which Englishmen fought, one often forgotten about or ignored by historians, was Ireland. Even before the slide into civil war after 1455, the king's lieutenants periodically recruited Englishmen for service in the Pale and lordship. The counties of Cheshire and Lancashire were fertile recruiting grounds for the king's deputy appointed to take his retinue to Ireland. In only a few instances, therefore, did gentry choose to make a career of serving in Ireland. There was obviously some tradition of service within families from the north west; the 1476 muster of Henry, Lord Grey of Codnor, deputy lieutenant of Ireland, contained members of the Molyneux, Bold and Harrington families from Lancashire as well as from the Venables and Donne families of Cheshire. Sir Robert Bold, in fact, was created lord of the barony of Rathmore and served as steward of the liberty of Meath during the 1470s.[33] Moreover, certain English magnate families had strong links with the lordship as absentee landlords. The earls of Shrewsbury were hereditary lords of Wexford and West Meath. John Talbot, Lord Furnival, was appointed lieutenant of Ireland in 1414. He naturally brought some of his closest followers with him while he was in the lordship. His brother, Sir Thomas, for example, acted as his deputy. Sir Hugh Cokesey and Sir

John Barry also accompanied Talbot to Ireland for periods of service.[34] Perhaps the greatest absentee landlord was Richard, duke of York, who had inherited the great de Burgh earldom of Ulster. York was appointed lieutenant of Ireland from 1447–53 and 1454–9. Various servants of Richard, duke of York, received grants from his son Edward IV for their service in Ireland during York's lieutenancy there. The experience of warfare in Ireland was very different from that in France. The Irish avoided pitched battles, preferring to engage in periodic hit-and-run raids into the Pale. Similarly, the English avoided conducting major campaigns against the Irish. The king's lieutenants and their deputies engaged in similar raids to bring the Irish and 'English rebels' to heel. The description by John Swayne, Bishop of Armagh, of the raid by Lord Grey in 1428 was typical of those of the period. He described Grey's expedition thus: '. . . then my Lord Grey made a good journey on a great Irishman that is called O'Connor and he burned much in their country and took many beasts'. The success of these raids is questionable although the absence of a substantial study of military service in Ireland makes an accurate assessment impossible.[35]

There were also opportunities for potential soldiers outside of the British Isles. John Turnbull was a professional soldier who 'made his living by violence'. He served with Somerset at Calais in 1451–2, in 1454 he was involved in piracy and by the 1470s he was fighting for the dukes of Burgundy. At the battle of Nancy in January 1477 he commanded a company of 96 Englishmen.[36] Service in the forces of European princes clearly offered certain attractions for some men. Lancastrian exiles like Edmund Beaufort, titular duke of Somerset, fought in the wars of the dukes of Burgundy during the 1460s. During the 1470s, Sir Thomas Everingham of Yorkshire also spent time in Burgundy. He was in Burgundian service from approximately 1472 until the death of Duke Charles the Bold at the battle of Nancy. Everingham established a reputation for military valour and went on to become one of Richard, duke of Gloucester's, chief advisers in the war against Scotland in 1482–3.[37] Another option was to go on crusade. Towards the end of the fourteenth century, northern retainers of Henry Bolingbroke, earl of Derby, had accompanied him to fight with the Teutonic Knights against the pagan Lithuanians in northern Europe.[38] Few, options, however, existed during the mid-fifteenth century. Towards the end of the century, though, Sir Edward Woodville, brother of Anthony, served the king of Castile against the Moors in 1486. Spanish chroniclers, clearly impressed, recorded that at the siege of Loja in Granada he dismounted and fought on foot alongside his 300 men-at-arms using their battleaxes in typical English fashion.[39]

Some families even established a tradition of service with the only remaining late medieval crusading order, the Knights of St John, who were based on the island of Rhodes. A document at the British Library refers to the sculptured arms of the families of Kendal, Harcourt, Zouche, Neville, Percy, Ingloys,

Strange, Talbot, Stafford, Courtenay and FitzHugh at Rhodes. Represented here
are families from across the breadth of England. A separate document at the
Bodleian Library also names members of the Danyell, Darell, Weston, Docwra,
Babington, Baskerville, Pemberton, Fairfax and Middleton families serving there
towards the end of the fifteenth century.[40] What attracted families into a crusading order is unclear. A genuine belief in crusading is one possibility; a martial
tradition is another; or even a simple lack of opportunities for advancement
in England. Sir Robert Malory, prior of the Order of St John in England from
1432 until 1439, led an active military career, organizing, among other things,
the Hospitaller contingent that sailed from England to defend Rhodes from the
Sultan of Egypt. Additional members of the Malory clan from Nottinghamshire
and Warwickshire subsequently served on Rhodes. A Sir John Malory served on
Rhodes during the Mameluke siege of 1444. The Weston family from Surrey is
perhaps the clearest example of a late medieval family committed to the order.
Successive generations served during the late fifteenth and early sixteenth centuries. In fact, the Bodleian Library list indicates a strong interest from northern
families, which is suggestive of men seeking opportunities for advancement
outside of England.[41] Englishmen continued to experience the perils of travel
across the Mediterranean throughout the second half of the fifteenth century
and beginning of the sixteenth. Periodically they went on pilgrimage. Sir Henry
Stradling, brother of the Edward Stradling who died at the battle of Towton, followed the example of his father and grandfather and visited Jerusalem in 1476.
He died on Cyprus and was buried at Famagusta that same year. Likewise, Sir
Richard Guildford of Rolvenden in Kent also went on pilgrimage after his fall
from grace at the court of Henry VII in 1505.[42]


## THE ART OF WAR

The study of chronicles like The *Brut* and romances including the Arthurian
legends provides numerous exemplars of military and chivalric conduct. The
extent to which the nobility and gentry owned or had access to books, especially
military texts, is becoming increasingly apparent. The degree to which they
were influenced by the ideas contained within is harder to gauge, however. Any
obvious correlation between book ownership, military instruction as a youth
and subsequent participation in warfare cannot be proven with any certainty.
Nevertheless, it has been recognized that literary tastes had the potential to help
in the formation of opinions and attitudes. The gentry were actively engaging
with the texts that they obtained. The organization of court circles in the later
fifteenth century implied a constant interchange of ideas and books among those
associated with the court. The social, administrative and political activities of

the gentry ensured that ideas were constantly disseminated and transmitted at different levels.

Research has shown that texts were exchanged by people who belonged to the same social or geographical group. The owners of military texts formed a particular reading group. It became the fashion among leading gentry to commission a 'Grete Boke', that is, a chivalric miscellany that could contain a variety of texts including the oath and ceremonies of chivalric orders, Vegetius' *De Re Militari*, Christine de Pisan's *Livre du Corps de Policie* and pseudo-Aristotle's *Secreta Secretorum*. Sir John Astley's anthology of chivalric texts contains the names of Thomas FitzHugh, Brian Tunstall and Thomas Tunstall, suggesting it circulated around court. Sir John Paston certainly had access to Astley's book, which formed the basis for his own 'Grete Boke'. Even where it is uncertain whether owners exchanged books, connections can be proven between them which raises the possibility.[43] Vegetius and Christine de Pisan formed the core of many such anthologies. The relationship between manuscripts and their owners reveal active discourses with the texts, the shaping of personal identities and the development of political attitudes about governance. Other texts such as chronicles also provided exemplars from which the gentry might draw inspiration about chivalric behaviour. *The Brut* chronicle enjoyed widespread popularity during the fifteenth century, and leading families like the Willoughbys and Zouches from Nottinghamshire and Derbyshire – two families particularly active in local and national politics – possessed copies. It is therefore entirely possible that the interest in chivalry, warfare and politics extended much further than historians have appreciated; and that while access to military experiences was declining and some of the leading gentry might not have known as much as they thought they did, it did not mean that there was an active demilitarization and diminution of status.[44]

The chivalric code incorporated several well-known features. At its heart lay the desire to acquire popular renown from one's contemporaries. In medieval literature there were four cardinal chivalrous virtues: prudence, justice, continence and force or magnanimity. The latter meant force of courage, or prowess. In fact, within chivalric texts 'prowess came close to conveying the meaning of a man's life, or even of life itself'.[45] While chivalric literature and romances could provide exemplars for gentry behaviour and conduct, the standard treatise on the art of war was a translation of the *De Re Militari* by the fourth-century Roman writer, Vegetius. Vegetius described a whole series of exercises and techniques for soldiers to learn. Some sections of the book were clearly regarded as more relevant than others and it was these which were adopted, and adapted, by translators of the text. Book 1 discussed selection, discipline and training; book 2 concerned the composition of the legion and as this book seemed of little value to medieval writers, was often abridged or omitted; book 3 looked at tactics and strategy;

and book 4 took up the theme of defence and fortifications. The last 16 chapters, sometimes treated as book 5, concerned naval warfare.

Copies of Vegetius were known to have circulated widely throughout Western Europe. Thomas, duke of Gloucester, owned a copy in French in 1397, a second was given to Humphrey, duke of Gloucester, by Sir Robert Roos, and a third belonged to Sir John Fastolf in about 1450. A prose translation from Latin into English was produced for Thomas, Lord Berkeley, in 1408.[46] A second English translation was made into verse and presented to William, Viscount Beaumont, chamberlain of Henry VI, in the late 1450s and became known as *Knyghthode and Batayle*. Another verse translation was possibly produced for Lord Hastings between 1460 and 1470.[47] The dates of production of some of the Vegetius manuscripts demonstrate that interest in his writing was growing from the mid-1450s onwards. This was a critical period for the English war effort in France and the translators of Vegetius adapted their texts appropriately. The copy made for Lord Berkeley was produced while he was fighting against the Welsh rebels; Berkeley was the commander of the forces that besieged Aberystwyth Castle and elements of the text demonstrate the translator knew of the military conditions there, referring to the guns for shooting stones that were used in Wales and in the north of England as well as describing how a fully armed warrior could be hurt by a stone. The author of *Knyghthode and Batayle* had political issues on his mind as he wrote his text. The author was keen to reawaken a sense of national pride and revive the chivalric ethos among the nation's elite, which was fighting among itself. In dealing with the requirements of a knight, he adds birth and blood as essential, includes tourneying within the training and stresses courage rather than experience as the most important quality. The author wishes to improve the performance of knights so they are able to defend the realm and crush rebellion. He is concerned about the violence, treachery and disorder that has emerged within the kingdom and wants to see the country peaceful and united under a just, strong king.[48]

It has been argued that the presence of *De Re Militari* in most aristocratic libraries indicates that it was simply a status symbol and not necessarily read. Nall, however, has asserted that manuscript evidence suggests that these texts were read by their owners and their ideas digested. The readers' annotations can be dated with confidence to particular periods. Identifying the owners can be problematic of course. Nevertheless, private gentry owners often had their coats of arms depicted in their manuscripts. The Chalons family, leading gentry from Plympton in Devon, owned a copy of Vegetius. That particular copy appeared to have been made for Sir Robert Chalons who died in 1445. His son, John, killed Louis de Bueil in a joust at Tours in 1446. Nicholas Seyntlo, from another prominent West Country family, also owned a copy of the manuscript, as did the Heydons of Norfolk. The Hautes of Kent owned a copy of Christine de Pisan's

*Livre du Corps de Policie*. Which member of the family actually commissioned it remains a mystery. All of these families were from among the elite within local, political society. Yet lesser members of the gentry also took an active interest in these types of text. The obscure William Brandon of Knowle in Warwickshire possessed a copy of *De Re Militari* and *The Brut*.[49]

While Vegetius probably remained the principal manual of practical military training, there were other training manuals circulating in Europe too, although whether they found their way into England is very uncertain and remains unexplored. Two well-known fighting masters, Fiore Dei Liberi from Italy and Hans Talhoffer from Germany, produced their own manuals. The former wrote his book in 1409 while the latter wrote his in 1467. Both men's works were the practical synthesis of years of experience and contained numerous illustrations of techniques. No direct evidence has come to light that Fiore's book was possessed by any of the English nobility or gentry, although it is possible that copies passed through Italy, to France and subsequently into England. The English nobility and leading gentry enjoyed substantial contact with both countries. Englishmen fought in France and Italy during the fourteenth and fifteenth centuries. The illustrations within both manuals demonstrate that in close combat the face, head, and groin were the areas to be attacked and defended. Further evidence that such techniques were actively taught and learnt is found in the wounds of some of the victims of the Towton battlefield that have been excavated. A group of skeletons were found showing clear signs of cranial trauma indicating that the techniques described and illustrated within these manuals were well known.[50]

## METHODS OF RECRUITMENT

It was possible to recruit armies in the late medieval period through formal or informal methods. An obligation to provide for the common defence against external threats had rested upon all Englishmen since the Anglo-Saxon period. The obligation was based upon the notion of unpaid service owed by the men of the shire and boroughs to the king and his officers and it was enshrined in the Statute of Winchester of 1285, which stated that all men between the ages of 16 and 60 were required to be armed and trained according to their status. A wealthy esquire possessing £15 worth of lands and goods worth 40 marks or more was required to come as a mounted man-at-arms, dressed in the coat of mail known as a hauberk, wearing an iron helmet, carrying a sword and a knife and riding a horse. Gentlemen owning lands worth £5 were to come in a doublet, an iron helmet and armed with a sword and a knife. Yeomen, owning less than £2 worth of lands, were to bring cutlasses, spears (halberds), knives and other lesser weapons. The remainder were to bring bows and arrows if they lived outside the forest, bows and bolts if they lived inside. However, the statute's primary intention was not to provide an army but to preserve the peace. This was reflected by the duty of the constables in each hundred or franchise within a county to inspect these arms twice a year. Justices of the peace were required to oversee their work.[51] During the late thirteenth and fourteenth centuries the traditional shire levies were drawn upon by Edward I, Edward II and Edward III for expeditions into Scotland, Wales and France. By the fifteenth century, however, they were only being used to quell internal rebellion or to counter invasion by the king's enemies. The crown issued commissions of array to the leading nobility and gentry within each county. Consequently, levies from northern shires regularly turned out to confront Scottish raids and invasions, while their counterparts in the south were called upon to resist French raids.

During the Wars of the Roses, Lancastrians and Yorkists each sought to harness the arraying process to supplement their own forces. Nevertheless, civil strife and rebellion could work in such a way to reduce the effectiveness of the arraying and the willingness to become involved. Threats of punishment for failing to support the crown were unlikely to have encouraged men to come forward to the array. The success of the process was largely down to the commissioners of array and the cooperation of the local communities.[52] Personal appeals to encourage a positive response produced very mixed results. At Newark Edward IV had to abandon his plans because he was unable to gather sufficient military support from the surrounding region.[53] If the traditional process of arraying failed, then there was the option of approaching individuals directly to undertake that task, effectively bypassing the traditional method of recruitment. Before the battle of Towton in 1461, Sir William Plumpton was asked to come 'with all such people as ye may make defensible arrayed come unto us in all hast possible'.[54] Likewise, in March 1471 the earl of Oxford quoted his royal commission to resist Edward IV in his letters to five Norfolk gentlemen, commanding them to come with 'as many men as ye may goodly make'. In the West Country the Lancastrians attempted to utilize Prince Edward's commission of lieutenancy to raise men in the days immediately preceding the battle of Tewkesbury.[55]

The formal method of recruiting military forces in fifteenth-century England was the indentured retinue. Although used to recruit men for service on the Anglo-Scottish border, Ireland and Calais, its use as a means of recruiting men for service in domestic conflicts was limited. Traditionally the king had relied on his feudal host to supply the manpower for foreign campaigns. During the course of the thirteenth and fourteenth centuries, however, the pressure of warfare in Wales, Scotland and France, combined with the need to raise men on a regular basis, had seen the evolution of the retinue system. The monarch entered into a contract (known as an indenture) with his lieutenants and captains to supply companies of men. Depending on the nature of the campaign and the command structure that was adopted, the king might enter into different contractual arrangements with a number of different captains. He might contract with a single commander to raise the required number of men. The latter would then enter into sub-contracts with other captains. Alternatively, he might enter into individual contracts with different captains. The indenture set out the precise terms of the agreement in what was a straightforward business arrangement. It specified the number of men the captain would provide, length of service, rates of pay and other obligations and entitlements. The captain would then enter into contracts with other knights and esquires that stipulated their terms of service for them and the men-at-arms and archers which they undertook to contribute. Once a retinue was raised and checked at point of departure by royal officials, the captain was supposed to receive an advance of wages and was responsible for their payment and general conduct while on campaign.[56]

It would be misleading to suggest that retinues raised by indenture were not used at all by either side during the Wars of the Roses. Warwick brought over soldiers from the Calais garrison, the only professional fighting force available to the English crown in 1459, only to see them desert the Yorkist cause on the eve of battle. Henry Beaufort, duke of Somerset, brought back with him some men from the garrison after his failed attempt to seize the town in 1460. At least some of these men fought with the Lancastrian forces until the battle of Towton in March 1461. Additional men were drawn from the Calais garrison when the Yorkists invaded England in June 1460. When Warwick turned against Edward IV in 1470 the Calais garrison would not admit him nor provide him with soldiers. The garrison remained loyal to the Yorkist cause. The other principal garrison, although much smaller than Calais, was at Berwick on the Anglo-Scottish border. These men came under the control of the warden of the East March. The Percy earls of Northumberland, who presumably drew upon their numbers during the wars, traditionally filled this office. The extent to which Berwick's resources were employed during the wars, however, remains unclear. During peacetime the warden's retinue for the East March technically numbered 50 men-at-arms and 100 hundred archers and from these he would have provided for the garrison at Berwick and elsewhere. The Percys' tenure in office was ended after the Yorkist victory in 1461 and their Neville rivals took up office. Berwick's forces were then utilized against Lancastrian resistance in the north.[57]

The significant feature here is that the garrison forces were already in existence and were not raised specifically for service in civil war. The conscious use of indentured retinues during the Wars of the Roses was the result of unique circumstances. They were certainly raised by cities and towns during moments of crisis. The notion that towns were completely passive and did not fight in the conflict is incorrect. Reading, Coventry, Leicester, Nottingham and Salisbury all made substantial contributions of men at one time or another. So, too, did the

Cinque Ports, including Lydd, a member of the port of Romney, which sent men to support the Yorkists at the battles of Northampton and St Albans. A force of 36 was sent to St Albans. Finally, townsmen appeared to fight at Towton, possibly under the command of Robert Horne of Appledore.[58]

Once urban authorities had decided where their loyalties or best interests lay, they appointed captains to lead their forces into battle. Towns obviously wished to appoint a competent and experienced individual. William Tybeaudis was selected as captain of Coventry's forces that were sent to support royal forces at the first battle of St Albans in 1455. He was probably an individual with a sound military reputation. William Rokewode, appointed captain of Norwich's forces in 1461, was an East Anglian esquire well practised in warfare. These captains entered into contractual arrangements with the towns' authorities. In turn, they appeared to indent with the men they recruited. Like any contract these could lead to disputes over payment. In one incident there was a dispute over the 11 men from Norwich paid for by Richard Brown to fight with Edward IV at Towton. In a separate episode, the town of Bury appointed William Aleyn, who appears to have been a local man, as their captain in 1461. Some 10 years later he complained that John Smith, an alderman of Bury, had taken advantage of the general confusion caused by the restoration of Henry VI in 1470 to bring a suit of trespass against him in order to recover the wages paid to Aleyn and his company for their service with the Yorkists at Towton.[59]

Apart from the use of contracts to raise men in cities and towns, only two substantial forces of men were raised by indenture during the Wars; both occurred at the beginning of the conflict. They were raised for specific purposes, neither of which was successful. In February 1460, Sir Baldwin Fulford undertook to serve Henry VI at sea with 1,000 men, receiving royal wages for himself and his men for three months. His task was to seek out and destroy the earl of Warwick and other Yorkists after their raid on Sandwich in January 1460. A month later, in March 1460, the duke of Exeter was retained for 3 years with over 3,500 men to protect the seas. However, when Warwick's force appeared in the English Channel, Exeter sought sanctuary in Dartmouth rather than engage Warwick.[60]

Other than these formal methods of recruitment and retaining, the nobility and leading gentry also had the option of employing their own personal followings known as 'affinities'. An affinity contained all those individuals who enjoyed either a service or dependency relationship with a particular individual. These levels of service and dependency varied. At the heart of an affinity was the household. This is where the most intimate form of personal service was performed. Connected to, but not necessarily part of, the household, were the lord's councillors and estate officials who served him at one remove. There were also retainers who enjoyed fees and annuities from his estates in return for performing particular services set out in a formal indenture of retainer. They would become the captains of his men, the bulk of whom were tenants and dependants. The former held land from him that carried service obligations; the latter looked to him for lordship even though they did not necessarily enjoy a service connection. None of these groups were mutually exclusive. It was entirely normal to serve within the household and to hold a position within the estate administration. Similarly, significant tenants might also enjoy a fee or annuity, the terms of which were set out in the indenture.[61]

It is self-evident that the potential size of any force that could be raised was determined by a number of factors. Principal among these were wealth, extent and location of landed estates, and the number of tenants. The number that could be raised was also influenced by circumstance. Attempting to raise men at short notice was likely to result in a low turnout. In such instances they were probably recruited from the immediate household and the closest estates. The male population of a noble household varied considerably and reliable statistics are hard to find. Nevertheless, the household of the wealthy magnate, John Howard, duke of Norfolk, numbered 106 men. That of Lord Grey of Ruthin in the mid-fifteenth century numbered 50 to 60. The household of Lord Talbot at Blakemere numbered about 40. The size of a gentry household could vary considerably as well; a leading knight might have anything from upwards of 20 servants, while a lesser gentleman might only maintain a couple of servants in his household. Luttrell household accounts for the 1420s suggest that Sir Hugh Luttrell had 20 male servants, 4 of them gentlemen. Similarly, the Watertons of Mexborough in Yorkshire had 20 to 25 household servants.[62]

Mustering indentured retainers was a feature of the Wars of the Roses. The number that could be successfully mustered in any one instance is unclear. Evidence from a surviving account for retainers of the earl of Salisbury show that they fall into two groups: the first centred on a group of gentry residing close to the heart of lordship of Middleham; the second, including Sir Thomas Harrington, consisted of 'Salisbury's agents in enemy territory', those retainers who resided some distance away in lands dominated by the hostile Neville Earls of Westmorland. This is not to say they were not powerful men in their own right. Sir Robert Ogle of Ogle and Bothal in Northumberland was a man who fought at the first battle of St Albans in 1455, had served with distinction on the Anglo-Scottish border and later captured Henry Beaufort, duke of Somerset, at the battle of Hexham in 1464.[63]

Indentures of retinue normally stated that the retainer was to bring as many followers as possible upon reasonable notice from their lord. A retainer's willingness to attend his lord was determined by more than the wording of the contractual arrangement. It was largely left to the conscience of the retainer how he acted when forced to make a choice. Bastard feudal contracts were based on mutual advantage. Good lordship offered tangible rewards to an individual, as well as 'intangible' benefits – his patron could exert influence on his behalf. The longer relationships lasted, the stronger the commitment on both sides might become. Nevertheless, the mutual observance of service obligations stipulated in the indenture was taken seriously. This is demonstrated by Sir William Skipwith's claim that Sir John Neville, Sir James Pickering and Thomas Colt forcibly removed him from his stewardship of the manor of Hatfield and constableship of Conisbrough Castle for failing to attend the duke of York at the first battle of St Albans in 1455.[64] Yet if a retainer did not want to fight, for whatever reason, he could not be forced. The unreliability of Henry Vernon during the crisis of 1471 cannot have been unique. Vernon, a Derbyshire retainer of the duke of Clarence, received two summonses from his patron in March 1471. He was requested to join him in the West Country where the latter was recruiting on behalf of the Readeption government. Clarence, continuing to move about the West Country, sent Vernon additional orders at the beginning of April 1471, but to no avail. Vernon sat tight, although he did send Clarence details about Edward IV's movements. Given the level of uncertainty that existed, caution was undoubtedly the best option from Vernon's point of view.[65] Contractual obligations were obviously only part of the story; personal loyalty also entered the equation. Sir Thomas Harrington, the earl of Salisbury's retainer, presumably felt a stronger tie to Salisbury than his indenture of service might initially suggest.[66]

Nevertheless, the numbers of men raised at short notice are generally impossible to determine. After his victories at the battles of Barnet and Tewkesbury between April and May 1471, Edward IV ordered payment of '£100 by way of reward' to Lord Grey of Codnor for the costs which that the latter had incurred in 'attending in his own person upon us in this our great journey as in bringing unto us a great number of men defensibly arrayed at his cost and charge'.[67] Lord Grey presumably recruited from his estates and joined Edward IV on his march southwards. It has been suggested that in response to urgent summonses for military support from Queen Margaret in 1459, Sir Thomas Fitton of Gawsworth in Cheshire raised 67 men who then fought at Bloreheath. Although this has been discredited it remains testimony to the large number of men that Fitton could potentially raise from his neighbourhood.[68] The Scudamores of Bredwardine in Herefordshire also had the benefit of locality on their side at the battle of Mortimer's Cross in February 1461, located about 50 miles to the north of the family's principal residence. Sir John Scudamore brought 30 servants with him. In addition, his son John and his brothers Sir Henry, Sir William and Sir Maurice were there. They would also have brought their dependants. The actual Scudamore presence was therefore likely to have been higher than 30 men.[69]

The recruitment efforts of commanders during the Wars of the Roses were directed principally at leading gentry and their tenants. There was no attempt to utilize external sources of manpower. There is no evidence that English magnates with landed interests in Ireland attempted to exploit these resources. Although some great magnates like Richard, duke of York, held extensive estates in Ulster and even received considerable backing from the Anglo-Irish baronage in 1459–60, particularly from the FitzGeralds, this was not translated into a supply of soldiers.[70] There are just a few brief hints of Anglo-Irish involvement. In 1462 Sir Roland FitzEustace, recently created Lord Portlester, William Griffith and James Dokeray were granted the Irish lands of William Boteler and Richard Bermingham for 'their good service to the king's father and the king in England and Ireland'. They had possibly returned to England with York in 1460 but this remains uncorroborated. Their presence in England could only have been short-lived, however. Portlester returned to Ireland sometime after 19 April 1462 where he was appointed deputy to the king's lieutenant, George, duke of Clarence, with 300 hundred archers, probably recruited in Cheshire.[71] The only Anglo-Irish magnate to actively participate in the Wars of the Roses was James Butler, earl of Ormond and Wiltshire. Ormond had grown up in England and spent little time in Ireland. Irishmen were reported to have served with Ormond at the battle of Mortimer's Cross in February 1461. However, Ormond was attainted and executed after the battle of Towton in March 1461 and there are no reports of Irish involvement thereafter.[72]

Foreign mercenaries from Europe had been employed by English kings, particularly from the Low Countries, during the fourteenth century, often in the capacity as specialists. Gunners and armourers were two key roles that foreigners fulfilled, due partly to a shortage of skilled practitioners in England.[73] However, as more Englishmen acquired military experience during the Hundred Years War this trend had declined. In fact, it reversed as Englishmen sought opportunities abroad as mercenaries. In 1346 Sir Hugh Calveley, Sir Robert Scott and others were even reprimanded by the king for joining the King of Navarre in attacking France.[74] By the mid-fifteenth century the use of mercenaries by the kings of England was virtually non-existant. Nevertheless, Gascons, Normans and other foreigners served with the English during the Hundred Years War, right up to the final loss of Normandy in 1450 and Gascony in 1453. They were not, however, fighting as mercenaries. Some of these men served the Lancastrian government with distinction. Sir Andrew Ogard was a naturalized Dane who made his fortune fighting the French. In the process he accumulated considerable landed wealth in France. It was estimated that his lands were worth £1,000 and that he kept 7,000 ducats in a chest in the house of Robert Whittingham. Ogard served John, duke of Bedford, and Richard, duke of York. During the 1450s, however, he entered the service of Queen Margaret. His death in 1454 removed the need to choose sides in the conflict that erupted the following year at St Albans.[75] Some unfortunate individuals suffered considerable hardship as a result of their loyalty to the crown. John de Mescua, a Navarese knight, had his possessions overrun by the king's enemies in the south of France. De Mescua had served the English with distinction during the early fifteenth century and was apparently one of the few foreigners to receive payments directly authorized from the exchequer at Westminster.[76]

After the collapse of Lancastrian Normandy and Gascony, some French subjects from among the garrisons probably went on to serve the English crown at Calais and perhaps other garrisons like that at Berwick, although the true extent of this is unknown.[77] During the Wars of the Roses there are only scattered references in chronicle accounts to foreigners in the service of Lancastrian and Yorkist armies. Breton mercenaries were reported to have fought with Lancastrian forces at the battle of Mortimer's Cross in February 1461. During the period of Lancastrian resistance in the North between 1461 and 1464, Frenchmen also fought alongside Lancastrians. The support of Pierre de Brézé, seneschal of Normandy for Queen Margaret in the north of England in 1462, is well documented. For a time Alnwick Castle was even surrendered to Lord Hungerford, Sir Robert Whittingham, Sir Thomas Findern and a force of 500 Frenchmen. Two Frenchmen, the Seigneur de Graville and 'Sir Cardot Malorte' were subsequently captured when Queen Margaret, de Brézé, and part of the company fled Northumberland for Scotland at news of the approach of Edward IV and Warwick. They were placed in the custody of Dame Agnes Foster in London.[78] 'Gregory's Chronicle' does refer to Warwick's company of 'goners and borgeners' at the second battle of St Albans in 1461. They were probably recruited from Burgundy. The forces that returned with Queen Margaret in 1471 and fought at Tewkesbury probably included French mercenaries supplied by Louis XII, although no convincing evidence for this has been found to date.[79] Thereafter, the only substantial use of mercenaries was when Henry Tudor invaded in England in 1485. His army contained trained pikemen from a recently disbanded war camp in Normandy. These men had been drilled in the Swiss fashion and their captain was the Savoyard Philibert de Chandée.[80]

Employment with the crown seemed to retain some attraction for foreigners at an individual level. After the failed Gascon uprising of 1453, Gaillard de Durfort, lord of Duras and Blanquefort, had sought employment in English service. Perhaps the most important Gascon to support the English in France, Durefort had served the Lancastrian dynasty with distinction from 1434 as seneschal of the Landes. In 1453 he had been banished forever from France. He was compensated by the exchequer for his losses. When he entered the Calais garrison under the command of Warwick in 1457 his annuity was reassigned there. In 1461 he was elected to the Order of the Garter for overcoming the Lancastrian garrison at Hammes Castle. In 1470, though, he transferred his loyalty to Edward IV and it was largely through his efforts that Warwick and Clarence were prevented from entering the town that April.[81]

It is possible that some foreigners serving within the Calais garrison fought in some of the battles of the Wars of the Roses. One mercenary serving in the garrison was Antonio della Turre of Milan. He had apparently become associated with the earl of Warwick through the papal legate, Coppini, and was a member of the garrison as early as 1460. By 1466 he was a man-at-arms in Warwick's retinue. It also is probable that Sir George Bissipates was at Barnet in April 1471. He appears to have been in England throughout the Readeption of Henry VI. Bissipates was the son of a Byzantine nobleman, who had fled Constantinople as a young man and found service with the King of France before moving to Calais. It could well be the case that Bissipates was the same man as 'George Greeke late of London, knight'. The latter appears in the records of the court of king's bench in the company of Sir Thomas Vere, Henry Wentworth, esquire and others in a dispute with the much disliked Sir William Brandon. Bissipates was perhaps one of those men who had come to England with Sir Geoffrey Gate and was with him when he attacked and released men from the Marshalsea prison in October 1470. What happened to Sir George after the collapse of the Readeption is conjecture. He was pardoned in August 1471, which suggests he was also with Fauconberg's rebels in May. He presumably returned to Calais but subsequently left for France and eventually married into the French aristocracy.[82]

## ARMS AND ARMOUR

The leading gentry were often, although not exclusively, represented wearing armour in funeral monuments and monumental brasses. This was both a reflection of their traditional military obligations and society's expectations of them as a social grouping. There was a strong psychological link between gentility and martial activities, which remained in the popular imagination. In many instances these memorials were commissioned by those families who were simply following the conventions of society. In other instances, however, they wished to celebrate their achievements and were depicted in armour irrespective of the service they had performed. The FitzHerbert memorials in Norbury, Derbyshire, show Sir Nicholas and Ralph FitzHerbert both attired in plate armour, heads resting on crested helm with a clenched gauntlet crest. Sir Nicholas is also wearing the livery collar of the Yorkist suns and roses with the lion pendant of Edward IV. Sir Nicholas, it is clear, wanted to demonstrate his loyal service to the king. What is less clear is whether he specifically saw military service. Yet he undoubtedly possessed the equipment and attire expected of a member of the leading gentry. In other instances, however, we can be certain that the depiction of a knight or esquire in armour reflected direct experience of military activity and warfare. The tombs of Randle Mainwairing, Sir John Hanford and Sir John Savage certainly depict the continuing militarism of the Cheshire gentry throughout the fifteenth century. The tombs of Sir Henry Pierpoint and Robert Barley were also both those of active soldiers from the Midlands. Similarly, the armour in which Sir William Pecche of Lullingstone in Kent was depicted on his monumental brass was likely to have been of the type he wore on the battlefield.[83]

For those leading gentry like Pierpoint and Barley who had accepted the obligations and expectations of their rank within society, what equipment did they have at their disposal in the fifteenth century? During the Wars of the Roses many had access to the most up-to-date arms and armour. At the beginning of the fifteenth century the armour being worn by the nobility and gentry was typical of the style that had emerged during the second half of the fourteenth century. There were a number of common stylistic features: an oval-shaped helmet, known as a 'bascinet', from which was hung a curtain of mail called an 'aventail' to protect neck and face. The body was covered with a short hauberk of mail reaching to the middle of the thighs. Underneath the hauberk was a breastplate; over it was a short surcoat known as a 'jupon'. By the battle of Agincourt in 1415, however, many were dressed in complete plate armour commonly referred to as a 'white harness'. It is probable that a hauberk was still worn underneath armour until about 1420. The bascinet had now become almost round and was now connected with a gorget of plate to protect the throat. The jupon had disappeared and been replaced by a plain-steel 'cuirass', while below the waist the body was protected by a series of overlapping plates known as 'taces'. 'Roundels', or oblong palettes, were placed before the armpits.

Further changes in plate armour occurred during the first half of the fifteenth century. These consisted primarily of secondary defences. Additional plates of steel called 'placates' and 'demi-placates' were fixed to the cuirass. The placates protected the armpits and part of the shoulders, replacing the older palettes and roundels. Demi-placates gave greater strength to the lower portion of the cuirass, and were fixed with their edges upwards. Additional plates were also fixed at the elbows. The left side began to be more fully protected than the right side, which was required to be free in action. Pointed plates, generally two in number, started to be strapped to the lowermost tace which served to protect the thighs. The gauntlets became longer and had more pointed cuffs. They were not always divided into fingers.[84]

Although arms and armour were manufactured in London, the nobility and gentry preferred to wear armour manufactured in Milan, Germany and the Low Countries. Nevertheless, the Armourers' Company flourished in London during the mid-fifteenth century and their armourers regularly supplied the crown with suits of armour. Southwark was an important centre for the production of armour and perhaps also a centre for its importation from Europe. London armourers engaged in both activities. One armourer, Thomas Waryn, provided a new sword for Edward IV in 1461 costing £4, which he probably produced himself.

He also supplied a helmet garnished with jewels to one of Edward IV's principal household servants, the Kentishman Sir William Pecche. Where they could afford it, however, the elite preferred to import their equipment from Europe. In 1473 Sir John Paston did business with the Flemish armourer Martin Rondelle of Bruges, who also supplied the celebrated jouster, the Bastard of Burgundy. The cost of armour produced by the Missaglia and de'Bardi armouries in Italy and elsewhere was not necessarily exorbitant. Transportation costs, however, did increase their price. A new suit of armour could cost anything from £2 10s to £7, although the average price seems to have been £4. The suit of armour given as a gift by Edward IV in 1461 to one of his household esquires cost exactly that. This was a valuable gift to an average esquire whose income was probably in the region of £20 per annum.[85] When the earl of Oxford wanted to purchase armour he instructed Sir John Paston that he was willing to pay up to £7. The household accounts of John Howard, duke of Norfolk, show that he purchased a complete suit of armour costing £7 in 1468 for one of his retainers.[86] The loss of armour could cause considerable worry to some. John Romney, in the service of Ralph, Lord Cromwell, petitioned the crown over the loss of his horse and harness (in this context his armour) at the battle of Northampton in July 1460.[87] If somebody wanted a suit of superior quality then he would have had little trouble finding a supplier. On 7 August 1437, a suit of Milanese armour was supplied for the 'nephew' of the treasurer of England for £7 6s 8d. The treasurer was presumably Ralph, Lord Cromwell, although the identity of the nephew remains a mystery.[88]

Arms and armour were functional pieces of equipment for use in warfare, but they were also highly prized items. Some appeared on the tomb effigies of particular gentry, such as the sword of Sir Robert Harcourt at Stanton Harcourt in Oxfordshire. His sword, of north Italian design, was represented in fine detail. John Digges of Barham in Kent might also have owned a similar weapon. Swords of this design were unusual and were presumably seen by the architects of Harcourt's tomb and Digges's monumental brass.[89] The gilded and bejewelled suit of armour that cost Sir John Paston £20 was probably intended for the tournament at Eltham; it was not intended for the battlefield. The two suits of armour stolen from Sir Laurence Fitton of Gawesworth in Cheshire in 1457–8 were decorated in silver and gilt and were probably also intended for chivalric display as well.[90]

It was clearly anticipated that the arms and armour purchased or inherited from kinsmen and friends would be put to practical use. Sir Giles Daubeney of South Petherton in Somerset seemed to have this in mind when he made his will in 1444. Sir Giles made bequests to his two sons William and Giles. To William he left his suit of armour and two of his best horses. To Giles he left a defensive doublet, haberon, sword, poleaxe and sallet, which were to be wrapped up in his standard and deposited for safekeeping until Giles reached the age of 16 years old. These habiliments of war could even have been used by Giles Daubeney the younger in the service of Henry Tudor at Bosworth in 1485.[91] Sir Thomas Cumberworth of Somerby in Lincolnshire made similar bequests to his kinsmen. His nephew, William Constable, was bequeathed his best suit of armour along with a decorated and gilded dagger. The son of a nephew, Henry Percy, was to receive a suit of armour along with a war axe.[92]

Equipment was carefully looked after by its owners, especially by those who expected to see service in battle. The payment to an armourer of 3s 4d in 1463 by Edward IV's household controller, Sir John Scott of Smeeth in Kent, was probably for minor work and repairs to the armour he had worn in the service of the Yorkists on the battlefield since June 1460.[93] The extent of Scott's personal armoury is impossible to determine. Few detailed inventories survive; nevertheless, it is apparent from those examples that do that certain nobles and members of the gentry possessed significant private stores of equipment in their own right. The inventory taken on the death of Sir John Fastolf, a veteran of the French wars, showed an impressive and unusually extensive collection of arms and armour. In one chamber, described as 'The White Draught Chamber for Lewys and William Worcester', there was a large array of different types of defensive wear and weaponry, the principal items being eight jacks, two stuffed with horn and the remaining with mail; six pairs of cuirasses; three hauberks made in Milan; two pairs of brigandines; thirteen bascinets; ten sallets; a collection of armour for the legs and arms; one spear; three steel crossbows; and a sword. The Fastolf example is unusual, however. Most collections were undoubtedly more modest in size.[94]

Detailed information about the weapons used by men-at-arms in this period is uncommon. Recent research by Grummitt into the Calais garrison during the fifteenth and sixteenth centuries, however, has provided valuable new insights into the wide variety of weapons in use there and that were, by implication, available to commanders and their forces during the Wars of the Roses. The weapons used in hand-to-hand combat by the man-at-arms and the ordinary foot soldier are all represented within the records of the garrison. The principal types of weapons were bills, axes, swords and daggers, although there were varieties within each basic category. The records from Calais suggest that the most favoured weapon was probably the bill. The inventories reveal large numbers of bills stockpiled in Calais, which reflect the importance of the garrison as an arsenal as well as their intended use by the garrison. In 1481 in the Calais armoury contained 84 'white' bills and 119 'black' bills. Another important weapon was the 'battleaxe', probably the two-handed poleaxe, the favoured weapon of the armoured man-at-arms on foot in the fifteenth century. This was particularly effective at both slashing and thrusting. In the same inventory there were 60 'gylt' axes and 172 'ungylt' ones.

The numbers suggest that in the late fifteenth century the heavy poleaxe was the polearm of choice for well-equipped English soldiers, replacing the lighter bill. References to 'long spears', possibly pikes, which begin to appear in the 1440s and 1450s, indicate that English armies were influenced by European developments. The growing importance of longer polearms within English armies may have been a reaction to the success of Swiss pikemen against the armies of Charles the Bold at the battle of Nancy in 1477.[95]

The equipment of lesser gentry and yeomanry was much less elaborate than the armoured men-at-arms. The Bridport Muster Roll of 1457 presents a perfect indicator of how they would have been expected to be arrayed. The equipment of the average gentleman was a jack, sallet, sword, buckler, bow and sheaf of arrows. This is not dissimilar to that found in the possession of the minor Norfolk gentleman John Dawes in an inventory of his goods taken in 1475 when he was outlawed. It is exactly that which one would expect for his status within society as defined by the Statute of Winchester. The inventory recorded that he owned a pair of brigandines, two sallets, a sword, a dagger, bow and a poleaxe which all together were valued at 12s 6d.[96] Dawes's possession of a bow lends weight to the continuing importance of archers in English armies throughout the fifteenth century. The bow also features prominently in Calais accounts.[97] Longbows were probably procured on a private basis, although during periods of intense military activity they were presumably supplied centrally. In 1460-1, 380 bows were received by the victualler, of which 147 were apparently sold to the soldiers with the remainder placed in the stores.[98] The Calais accounts make it clear that the soldiers of the Calais garrison employed a wide range of other weaponry including crossbows, a weapon not traditionally associated with the English. By 1436 the crossbow was firmly established in the hands of English soldiers and was ideal for use within the restricted confines of a castle during a siege where its slower rate of fire was less of a disadvantage.[99]

## THE GENTRY'S RESORT TO VIOLENCE

The gentry's attitude towards violence has been the subject of considerable debate among late medievalists. In recent years it has become fashionable to regard arbitration as the main method of conflict resolution. Wright has suggested that the Derbyshire gentry seldom waited for the judicial system for a solution and preferred to settle matters themselves by peaceful means. Arbitration was a way of resolving existing disputes, making amends for previous conduct and avoiding further outbreaks of violence. For these reasons it was a popular and regular means of resolution. The success of arbitration has also led some medievalists to conclude that levels of violence in local society were relatively low. After examining the evidence of East Anglia, Philippa Maddern has concluded that gentry violence was a rare occurrence. Limited acts of violence were accepted if they fell within the perceived natural order. When violence did erupt it usually took the form of vandalism or seizure of property rather than violent assault or murder. It was only when those limits were breached and threatened to disrupt local society that violence was regarded as a threat. Carpenter's findings in Warwickshire have largely corroborated Maddern's arguments. While acknowledging that medieval landowners were prepared to resort to violence, it was seen as a last resort. Payling has also suggested that 'disputes which degenerated into lurid acts of violence, like those between Pierpoint and Foljambe and Pierpoint and Plumpton, were exceptional'. The Pierpoint–Foljambe dispute in Derbyshire during the 1430s had seen each party trying to influence the legal process through legal and illegal means. In Nottinghamshire, he has argued that arbitration was successfully employed to settle many disputes, not least that which erupted between members of the Willoughbys of Wollaton over the division of the family inheritance. The final settlement document produced in 1449 sought to cover every possible cause for dissension and is possibly one of the best surviving examples of its kind.[100]

While arbitration undoubtedly had a place maintaining stability within local society, it was not necessarily the preferred option. Structural problems within local society could make the peaceful resolution of conflict at the local level difficult to achieve. The exercise of lordship was no guarantee of a favourable outcome either. Magnates with particular interests in a locality might be deemed a suitable choice to act as arbiters, although this depended on the weight behind the decision desired by each party. The dispute between John Gresley and the Abbey of Burton in Derbyshire during the 1450s resulted in the active intervention of the duke of Buckingham. Yet he proved unable to impose any settlement and the dispute rumbled on for years. Nor was resorting to the judicial system necessarily any more likely to ensure justice could be obtained. A major drawback of the public law courts was that the delegation of responsibility for the local administration of justice to the leading gentry, through the offices of justice of the peace and sheriff, could lead to abuses of that power and the corruption of the legal process. The very men who performed public service to the crown also had the ability to bring substantial numbers of men into the field to defeat or intimidate their opponents in the pursuit of resolving their own private disputes.[101]

Moreover, magnates could actually exacerbate a dispute. When an individual secured assistance from a noble patron the scales could be weighted unfairly in favour of one party and lawlessness was often the end result. Leading gentry families preferred to avoid conflict but appeared willing to redress the balance if particular circumstances warranted it. When Henry, Lord Grey of Codnor, actively supported Sir Henry Pierpoint during the 1430s, other gentry, notably Richard

Vernon and John Cockayne, favoured Thomas Foljambe. Payling also points to the continuing destabilizing effect of Codnor's actions in Nottinghamshire during this period. In 1439–40 he actively intervened on behalf of John Brokestowe in the latter's dispute with John Preston. Grey was subsequently accused of 'grete main-tenaunce and lordship' by Preston. A series of accusations were brought before a commission of oyer and terminer at Nottingham in November 1440.[102]

While a resort to arbitration suggested a desire to avoid the use of violence, it did not preclude its use. Therefore, the question still remains whether the gentry were predisposed to violence and, furthermore, whether they would resort to its use when it was felt necessary. From a chivalric viewpoint the picture appears relatively clear. Many contemporaries admired violence here. Warfare was a recognized arena in which renown and individual reputation could be achieved. Furthermore, loyal service on behalf of king, prince or lord was one of the principal methods of realizing that desire. Military prowess brought a knight 'worship', that is to say, an increased reputation among his contemporaries. Since the greatest opportunity for exercising prowess was war, a delight in martial pursuits lay at the heart of chivalric ideology. Sir Thomas Malory reflected contemporary sentiments when he expressed an admiration 'for men who can beat other men in armour, on horseback, with lance and sword'.[103] At the same time prowess was also a deeply ambiguous force that could easily spiral out of control if unchecked.

It has been argued that the early centralization of power and authority in England had resulted in a greater degree of control over the employment of vio-lence as a means of settling private disputes. Furthermore, it has been suggested that this policy against 'war within the realm – that is, open warlike violence or even carrying offensive arms' met with a greater degree of acceptance than elsewhere in Europe.[104] It is Kaeuper's thesis that the gentry did display a natural predisposition to violence. Chivalric literature acknowledged the impulse to settle any issue, especially any perceived slight to honour, by resorting to arms. There was a further recognition that when the law did not serve their purposes sufficiently, individuals' natural impulse was to resort to 'warlike violence'. The situation became that much more complicated when the king or the law was no longer judged to merit obedience. In abnormal circumstances violence might then be regarded as licit. Sir Thomas Malory was clearly prepared to resort to violence to achieve his own personal ends and was accused of committing a number of violent crimes including robbery, extortion and rape in his native Warwickshire in 1450. The impulse to settle a conflict by force was certainly felt by many nobles and gentry in the conduct of their daily lives and Malory was not alone in this behaviour. The records of the common law courts are littered with similar allegations, which has led Kaeuper to observe, 'knightly violence so prevalent in chivalric literature was ... practised in everyday life, with serious consequences for public order'.[105]

It is perhaps unsurprising that those gentry who experienced unsatisfactory outcomes through the public legal system might opt to use extra-legal methods to obtain a more acceptable result. These might well be through the informal methods of arbitration. But where arbitration failed, the resort to arms was a natural, almost inevitable, consequence. However, it was not used automatically or without forethought. The leading gentry used violence when it suited their particular purposes at every stage of the Wars of the Roses, whether they were political 'ins' or 'outs'. The Vernons of Derbyshire, who found themselves on the political margins of the Yorkist polity after 1461, certainly employed violence in their quarrels with the Strelleys, FitzHerberts and Grey of Codnor to obtain successful outcomes. They were not discouraged simply because the wheel of fortune had turned against them.[106]

## CONCLUSIONS

The gentry's relationship with warfare and violence was clearly a complex one. While the obligation to be practised in arms and to possess the necessary equipment according to their degree was enshrined in statute law, it is by no means certain how adept they actually were. Any sustained training in arms was weighted in favour of the leading gentry and those who opted for a long-term military career. It was also the leading gentry who were more likely to engage in military service or who enjoyed increased access to chivalric texts, romances and chronicles. Yet even they were not consistent in the degree of service they performed or the level of interest they demonstrated in chivalric ideals. Of those who served in France, the actual number exposed to battle were probably fewer still. Many more probably undertook a tour of duty in a garrison and were content to leave it at that. The pool of leading gentry who experienced bloody conflict was therefore unlikely to have been that significant, although this should not be seen as an active process of demilitarization. By the mid-fifteenth century there was still a cross section of gentry with practical experience of warfare; nevertheless, there were unlikely to have been any with direct exposure of the perils of civil war. The last major battle on English soil had been the battle of Shrewsbury back in 1404. Being asked to support Lancastrian or Yorkist parties provided the current generation of gentry with a new moral dilemma. Unless an individual adopted a narrow, partisan view of the conflict – and there were some who did – there was unlikely to be any discernable renown gained by the slaughter of one's friends, kinsmen, neighbours or social acquaintances.

Some leading gentry seem to have been more inclined towards violence than others, but this was a behavioural rather than cultural phenomenon based on chivalric concepts. Violence was not an automatic response in gentry behaviour.

It was not always the preferred option in settling disputes. As Mackman has suggested in Lincolnshire, the response in the county to the conduct and crimes of William Tailboys would appear to suggest that such behaviour was the exception to the rule. Thus, it is perhaps more appropriate to analyse gentry attitudes to violence within the context of the sociopolitical environment in which they conducted their business.[107] As psychologists have already suggested in their analysis of behaviour, it is much more likely that the gentry opted to settle disputes by arbitration or through the use of violence in accordance with the particular circumstances of the situation. Their environments determined what the relevant cues, or factors, were that needed to be taken into consideration. A disposition towards either option was determined by these considerations.[108]

A shift in structural conditions was more likely to have an effect on the propensity towards violence in a locality. If a community was divided between itself or local sociopolitical conditions changed, then other methods for achieving an acceptable outcome to a dispute might be chosen. In Derbyshire, Wright has observed that noble interference in the shire during the 1450s caused existing feuds and disputes to intensify by which means some gentry were briefly drawn into national politics. Although she does not indicate the extent of crime after 1461, she does assert that 'routine and larger-scale disturbances engineered by gentry continued, apparently undiminished, throughout the fifteenth century . . . In the years following the Readeption, the region south and west of Derby continued to generate a high level of gentry-related crime and violence'.[109] Similarly, in Devon, Kleineke has argued that the lawless conduct of Sir John Dinham was due largely to a shift in structural conditions. With the waning of Courtenay power at the beginning of the fifteenth century there was a power vacuum which presented Dinham with an opportunity – one that he seized. Once the Dinhams had cemented their status and power in the second half of the century, there was less need to assert themselves through illegal activities.[110]

These observations clearly have implications for how we explain gentry attitudes towards the Wars of the Roses. Ultimately it would seem that responses to events generated by the conflict were more likely to have been influenced by factors other than underlying chivalric values, previous military experiences or any predisposition to violent behaviour. In the next chapter we will therefore move on to examining decision-making by the leading gentry in the public domain, which has been seen as one of the environments where they were traditionally active.

# 5

# The Public Domain: Public Service, Private Lordship and Principles

## INTRODUCTION

By the fifteenth century the leading gentry had become the delegated servants of the crown in the localities, exercising royal authority on its behalf within the shires. Where local and regional conditions were also favourable to magnate interests gentry might enter into a service relationship with them, too. Together, the aristocracy and leading gentry were integral to the governance of the realm. They provided counsel to their sovereign and applied his will across the land. The crown, aristocracy and gentry were all familiar with the notion of the 'common weal' and the good governance of the realm for the benefit of all. The king was expected to rule in the interests of his subjects, employing the four cardinal virtues of prudence, justice, temperance and fortitude, and to maintain the peace and safety of the realm. He was regarded as the means by which communal ideas and values were realized. However, the concept of the commonweal was antithetical to traditional chivalric values, which laid an emphasis on the individual and his actions, including prowess, honour and martial virtue – the traditional values of the aristocratic and knightly elites. Taken to their extreme, they could be used to justify violent action in defence of personal interests. While the king was competent, these contradictions and tensions remained under the surface. Nevertheless, the question of how to respond and to behave arose when the ability of the ruler came into question.[1]

In this chapter we will explore those relationships that the leading gentry entered into within the public domain in order to ascertain how these shaped their decision making. Loyalty and dependability underpinned service relationships to the crown and magnates. In some instances it may have been blind loyalty to the exclusion of all else; in others, it could have equated to a temporary political accommodation. It may also have meant loyalty to an individual or loyalty to a principle. Either way, those who entered into a service relationship tacitly accepted a range of widely held assumptions about duties, obligations and rewards, along with notions of what constituted acceptable and unacceptable behaviour. Watts has argued that the attitudes of the leading gentry at least were going through a process of evolution as a consequence of the debates of the mid-fifteenth century. These changes can perhaps be summed up by Sir John Fortescue's statement that the 'beginning of all service is to know the will of the lord you serve'.[2]

Yet as we have seen, there was no imperative among the gentry to undertake service. While loyalty and obedience were coming to be seen as essential bastions of the common interest and gentry attitudes towards public, administrative service or service within a magnate affinity were likely to have been shaped by relevant cues within their environments. Therefore, are the ideological shifts identified by Watts indicative of practical changes in behaviour during the Wars of the Roses or were gentry attitudes towards service and loyalty more malleable? And, crucially, how did the gentry respond to the practical demands of royal and aristocratic service during periods of political instability?

## THE GENTRY AS PUBLIC SERVANTS

How far were the gentry public-spirited, serving the crown from a sense of duty and obligation? In fact, is this concept even relevant to leading gentry motivation and behaviour? The answer is of course unlikely to be black or white. Although by the fifteenth century Fleming regards local administrative service as 'the most compelling and characteristic obligation of the gentry' in Kent, it is unlikely that the leading gentry there, or elsewhere, fell exclusively into one category or the other.[3] As we have already noted, during the course of the thirteenth and fourteenth centuries the leading gentry had emerged as the traditional servants of the crown in the localities, undertaking the rigours of local administration on its behalf. A distinct hierarchy of office-holding had also emerged over the course of time. By the fifteenth century the leading gentry were well established in the roles of sheriff, justice of the peace, escheator and royal commissioner. As sheriffs and justices of the peace they exercised significant authority on behalf of the monarchy. Moreover, as the authority of the justice of the peace had increased at the expense of the sheriff, a place on the commission of the peace was a very visible honour and demonstration of standing within the community.[4]

Participation in local administration created sets of judgements that influenced the behaviour of those families who served within that environment. There were undoubtedly some who undertook the office purely from a strong sense of public duty and as part of the *cursus honorem* for a person of that rank within society. Their status determined their actions. Tradition, too, might play its part in encouraging men to come forward to serve. Clayton has suggested that the Cheshire gentry were especially aware of their liberties and reacted strongly in their defence. They participated in local government because they wanted to and they were not forced to attend the county court either, but did so willingly.[5] While service within the formal structure of county administration could be interpreted as revealing a public-spirited attitude, it also implied a greater degree of acceptance and trust upon the part of the crown and its ministers, who acted as sponsors, that the nominated individuals would perform their responsibilities loyally and diligently. Moreover, the crown was prepared to reward those who served it faithfully. Occasional financial rewards were one method of recompense, although in the longer run there was also the prospect of more lucrative grants of royal offices or even a place within the royal household.

It is unlikely that the majority of gentry acted out of a sense of public duty alone. Local administrative office attracted no fixed salary. Evidence from petitions suggest that to recover the costs that they incurred during the course of their tenure some leading gentry resorted to dubious means. The example of Sir Hugh Willoughby, who was accused of extorting over £29 from several men in Rutland and Kesteven during his term as sheriff of Lincolnshire in 1439, is by no means an isolated case. The cost of local office could be onerous and leave incumbents and their families with considerable debt. The records of central government are littered with petitions requesting assistance with outstanding debts incurred through office. These sit side by side with government prosecutions attempting to recover those sums. Favoured individuals were sometimes able to secure financial assistance but that could not be taken for granted. The tally of reward granted to Ralph Willoughby, sheriff of Norfolk and Suffolk, in 1483–4 was presumably for undertaking office on behalf of Richard III in a county where the king had little support after the usurpation. Willoughby, connected to Richard when still duke of Gloucester, was from the Nottinghamshire family resident at Wollaton but had married into the East Anglian gentry. In the tense period after Richard's accession support for the crown from men like Willoughby was invaluable.[6]

Moreover, among leading gentry there is ample evidence to suggest public service was not perceived as an honour throughout their adult lives. Those who asked to be excused from these obligations show this.[7] While their excuses might be genuine, however, some gentry were more successful than others at avoidance. The aged Sir Robert Moton of Peckleton in Leicestershire petitioned to be excused service as sheriff in about 1451, but despite his advanced years the request was flatly refused. His only concession was to be allowed to account by deputy. In the West Riding there were also indications of avoidance. Sir William Rither secured an exemption in 1438, Henry Vavasour in 1442 and Sir William Fairfax in 1478. Like Moton, Rither's experiences show that if the crown was determined enough an individual could be browbeaten into service. Just five months after his exemption was granted he was appointed sheriff.[8]

Payling has argued that the identity of service families changed over time along with their level of commitment to public service. In Nottinghamshire the new generation of appointees to local office apparently felt little or no engagement to the Lancastrian regime by the late 1450s. Despite the presence of the court in the Midlands, the confidence of some leading gentry in the royal administration and in the king himself had clearly declined. Their decision frames had shifted as the judgements that had previously indicated that royal service was worthwhile now indicated that it was not. Three leading Nottinghamshire gentry, Robert Strelley, John Stanhope and William Babington, readily supported Yorkist interests in 1460. Payling suggests that local office-holding had not benefited them, which created a lack of any feeling of commitment to the crown or its interests. This is an entirely plausible position, as men traditionally involved in these activities assessed the costs and benefits of public service during an increasingly unstable period.[9]

In fact, studies of Nottinghamshire, Derbyshire, Leicestershire and Kent have demonstrated that the actual numbers of gentry who regularly undertook public service was restricted primarily to a small percentage of families. Payling has shown in Nottinghamshire that between 1399 and 1461, 27 Nottinghamshire men were appointed to the joint-shrievalty of Nottinghamshire and Derbyshire, serving a combined total of 41 terms. Of these 27, 17 (serving 23 terms in total) came from the 13 families who constituted the county elite in Nottinghamshire. Fleming has highlighted similar circumstances in Kent. Between 1422 and 1509 just 14 families provided half of those appointed to the shrievalty. While justices of the peace were drawn from a broader cross-section of the gentry community, the emphasis was still on the upper reaches of society.[10] Interestingly, Arnold's evidence suggests declining numbers of gentry with the relevant skills in the West Riding. A diminishing number of families in the Riding exercised the shrievalty during the reign of Henry VI and reflected a wider trend within Yorkshire as a whole between 1437 and 1509. No family had a tradition of service and there were no particular or noteworthy connections between these families. The local administrative environment, perhaps because of Duchy of Lancaster influence, was such that it apparently created different attitudes and responses among the leading gentry.[11]

The profiles of many sheriffs suggest that the crown preferred individuals with previous experience in local administration. There was also a desire that the appointee could command the respect of other gentry. Consequently, military experience could also be regarded as an asset. The Leicestershire and Warwickshire sheriff Sir Thomas Everyngham had served in the French wars of the first half of the fifteenth century before opting to support the Yorkist cause after 1461.[12] Sir Thomas Kyriell, who regularly served in Kentish administration after 1450, had also seen substantial service in France from the mid-1420s to 1450.[13] The crown was certainly in a position to exert its influence over appointments, and after 1461 the increasing influence of the royal affinity in local administration reinforced a sense of service to the crown and to the commonweal of the realm. Sir William Trussell was established as knight of the body in the royal household for about three years before he was pricked as sheriff of Leicestershire and Warwickshire in 1475.[14]

In addition, the small pool of men with the necessary skills for local office no doubt accounts for the reappointment of all but the most notorious offenders, along with the crown's acquiescence in this process. Yet it also accounts for the willingness of royal authorities to intervene when reliability was not forthcoming. A political crisis showed royal intervention at its most obvious. The political turmoil in 1460–1, 1469–71 and 1483 saw increased intervention on the part of the crown to achieve a balance between local, vested interests and acknowledged supporters. In 1460–1 the sheriff of Cheshire, Sir William Booth, was able to remain in post. It would seem that his long career in public administration was seen as a valuable asset. By contrast, the choice of Sir Robert Fullhurst as sheriff of Cheshire during the restoration of Henry VI in 1470–1 indicates that the Lancastrian regime desired its own trusted men in these positions. The criteria upon which men were selected had shifted, albeit subtly. Fullhurst was one of the principal gentlemen within the county. He had served as an esquire of the body to Henry's son, Prince Edward, and also had substantial experience of the Cheshire administration. He had weathered the political storms of 1460–1 and as an alternative to the Stanley family was a very attractive proposition.[15]

Appointments to commissions of array, oyer and terminer, and other ad hoc commissions, often indicate better than any fixed annual appointment those whom the regime was prepared to trust as well as those leading gentry who were prepared to be identified with it. The commissions issued at the royal court in Coventry in 1459 and 1460 illustrate quite forcefully the diminishing pool of gentry who were acceptable to the Lancastrian regime. The leading gentry on the commission of oyer and terminer appointed on 22 June 1460 covering the strategically sensitive counties of Kent, Surrey, Sussex, Middlesex, Hertfordshire and Essex were Sir Gervase Clifton, Sir John Cheyne and Sir John Heron. The inclusion of Heron is particularly interesting. As a Northumbrian, his southern links were negligible and his appointment was perhaps owed to his Lancastrian and Percy connections.[16] Similarly, the leading gentry appointed to the commissions of array issued by Edward IV in late April 1471 were carefully selected. Gentry excluded by the Readeption regime were much in evidence in Kent, reflecting the former dominance of the Yorkist affinity in the shire. Yet some counties clearly posed problems. In Warwickshire the only member of the gentry on the commission was the sheriff, Sir Simon Mountford. Similarly, the Hastings family dominated the commissions for Leicestershire and Northamptonshire.[17]

Local political instability served to dissuade potential office-holders from seeking appointments even more. The handful of families that consistently served in Warwickshire has been used by Carpenter to suggest that long-term survival of a family was often achieved by maintaining a low political profile. The majority of potential candidates among the leading gentry were presumably aware of the pitfalls of being identified with the current regime. Their decision frames included judgements about how they might be asked to undertake duties that could bring them into conflict with their friends, neighbours and kinsmen. Under such conditions many leading gentry did not rush to take up office or put their names forward as candidates. Those who were willing to undertake office stand out from other gentry who preferred to keep their heads down.[18]

When Henry VI was restored in 1470, the Readeption regime – an uneasy coalition consisting of the earl of Warwick, moderate Yorkists and partisan Lancastrians – struggled in certain areas to find men willing to serve within local administration. In some areas making appointments was a relatively straight-forward process. In Kent the regime was able to draw upon a nexus of Neville associates grouped around John Guildford and Henry Aucher, with Aucher appointed sheriff. Appointments to the bench of justices of the peace proved more difficult, though, and they had to resort to bringing the aged war veteran Sir Richard Frogenhale out of retirement to sit with men of known experience such as John Guildford and George Brown. Frogenhale's background suggests that it was his former Lancastrian loyalties that mattered since his only previous administrative service had been as escheator of Kent and Middlesex in 1445. His adult life had been spent largely in military service in France; his first-time appointment to the bench could have been an attempt to bolster the authority of a much-reduced body.[19] In Essex and Hertfordshire, the sheriff was Sir Henry Lewis, who combined Beaufort connections, local office and the governorship of the royal household.[20]

More substantial difficulties emerged elsewhere though. The Midlands counties proved very problematic. The lower social status of some candidates appointed would appear to indicate more serious problems among the elite of that shire. It showed that the usual pool of families were not coming forward to serve or were not regarded as reliable. The Lincolnshire sheriff in 1470–1 was the relatively untested John Ascough.[21] Leicestershire was another problematic county. The appointment of John Bellers to the commission of the peace was unexpected given his exclusion from office under the Yorkist regime but appears to have resulted from former ties with the Beauforts. Even those whom the struggling regime felt safe in appointing were offered some financial inducements.[22] The strategic importance of the county was reinforced by the granting of tallies in 1470 to William Fielding, the sheriff of Leicestershire and Warwickshire. He was allowed the sum of 120 marks assigned on the issues of his bailiwick. While his standing with the restored regime might have been high, it was still acknowledged by those in power that his continued support could not be taken for granted in the long run should the inevitable challenge from the deposed Edward IV come. In the event, Fielding did not disappoint when called upon by the rapidly disintegrating Readeption government. He was among those knighted on the field of the battle of Tewkesbury. His will, made shortly before the eve of battle, also hints at a man who knew that his survival could not be taken for granted.[23]

## LORDSHIP

Given the ambiguity of gentry attitudes towards public service, it is worth considering what patron–client relationships meant on a practical level to gentry, and why some entered into them and others did not. How did they regard the duties and responsibilities that accompanied service, or the impact of a magnate affinity on the affairs of local society? The relationship between patron and client clearly encompassed service on a number of different levels. Moreover, they were of varying length and were not necessarily permanent. The most commonly accepted approach to explaining the patron–client relationship has been to look at the degree of proximity to their lord enjoyed by servants. This has often been described as a series of concentric circles. Membership of an affinity could mean personal service within the lord's household, as an estate official with occasional contact, or as an annuitant or retainer in receipt of a fee for specific services rendered. Historians are generally comfortable with the idea of levels of service based on concentric circles. At the heart of the circle was the household, which remained the centre of the magnate's activities. Thereafter the degree and extent of contact became weaker. Yet, none of these levels of service was mutually exclusive and there could be overlaps between all of them.

It was these men who were drawn upon at moments of crisis to provide the necessary manpower to pursue a quarrel or form the core of a military force. However, indentured retainers were just one form of retainer and only one category within a noble affinity. Given that the bond between patron and client could vary in strength, it was only natural that the members of an affinity could also show a range of reactions and, indeed, a varying degree of commitment.[24] Geography alone meant that service within the household or estate was more likely to lead to stronger ties of loyalty than for an individual in receipt of a fee or annuity resident on an outlying estate whose service was only called upon in extraordinary circumstances. The payment of an extraordinary fee to maintain oversight of the interests of a lord in an area where he traditionally held little authority was an implicit acceptance of the independence of the member of the gentry concerned. Gentry chose to enter into such a relationship and could equally choose to leave it if it was not deemed to be in their interests. The complexity of these relationships can be seen reflected in the activities of members of noble affinities during the course of the Wars of the Roses. Moreover, the degree of commitment felt by members, and the extent to which they identified their interests with those of their patrons, can be seen in their subsequent behaviour, while the judgements that they formed on the beneficial nature of service could exert a fundamental impact upon the strength and effectiveness of an affinity.[25]

Chivalric writers were emphatic about the faithful service owed by the knight to his lord. Equally, lordship carried with it an obligation for magnates to maintain peace within their own affinities. Within an area like the north east where the Percys and Nevilles of Middleham dominated landed society this responsibility was particularly pronounced. It would be a mistake to assume that magnate interventions within local society were necessarily malign. The aristocracy could, and did, exercise a positive intermediary role in dispute settlement. Many of the principal figures during the fifteenth century exercised this element of good lordship and sought to mediate in local disputes. By the second half of the fifteenth century, however, it was increasingly accepted that loyalties were often directed to the pursuit of one's own private interests. Watts suggests that this kind of unprincipled behaviour had become quite normal in the opinion of Sir John Fortescue who was writing throughout this troubled period.[26]

It would have been quite natural for gentry to seek good lordship to further their personal concerns. The taking of multiple fees or livery from more than one lord over time suggests that certain gentry were not strongly attached to any particular individual; rather they were more attached to the idea of securing a favourable outcome for the issues that concerned them most. Some lords were wise to this and recognized the destabilizing impact. Carpenter suggests that Warwick deliberately avoided assisting a troublemaker like Richard Archer in Warwickshire during the 1450s for this reason. Instead he sought to build bridges with the old, established families. Archer therefore attempted instead to enlist the support of one of Warwick's enemies, Henry Percy, Lord Poynings.[27]

Despite the reciprocity implicit in the service relationship, the gentry made particular choices based on their own circumstances according to the structure of their own decision frames. There were, of course, those who eschewed service of any kind, preferring to manage their affairs independently and avoid conflict or litigation where possible. It is for this reason that many remain at best shadowy figures within their localities, rarely making an appearance in documentary sources. Others, however, opted to stay outside of magnate affinities for more discernable reasons and are more visible as a consequence. At one end of the gentry social spectrum some remained aloof largely because of their own status as 'county magnates'. Kleineke defines them as those 'whose political position was based essentially on landed wealth, spread like a magnate's across several counties, but whose limited horizons prevented participation in national politics'. This summed up the attitude of the Dinhams until the elevation of Sir John

Dinham to the peerage in 1467. A wealthy family with landed interests spread across five counties, the focus of their attention remained Devon. Nevertheless, until that point the family had existed outside the Courtenay affinity within the shire, remained aloof from the proceedings of the county court and declined to accept royal office other than royal commissions.[28]

Antipathy to active noble intervention in local affairs was another cause for avoiding a service relationship. As we have seen, only a small percentage of the leading gentry of Derbyshire, Nottinghamshire and Leicestershire entered into service with the Duchy of Lancaster or non-resident nobles. Moreover, these were normally lesser rather than leading gentry. While the more senior families did not turn their backs on the possibility of service within an affinity, Acheson regards this service as professional rather than political and not necessarily indicative of political affiliation. Exactly how impartial officials were depended in part on the relative balance of gentry and magnate estates within a shire. Where magnates enjoyed significant landed interests then the degree of independence or sense of public duty felt by the gentry was possibly constrained by an acknowledgement of the wishes of a patron or acknowledgement of his interests. Magnates obviously exerted influence to secure the appointment of members of their affinities. In Leicestershire the appointments of Sir Leonard and William Hastings were closely linked to the career of Richard, duke of York, from the mid-1450s onwards. In contrast to the Duchy of Lancaster, the Duchy of York was not a major landholder in Leicestershire. They were more likely to have been attracted to the service of York on a personal level. It is entirely plausible that they also recognized the potential for advancing their careers by serving as sheriffs, which increased their willingness to participate in local administration. William Hastings was a young and inexperienced sheriff at just 24 years old when he was pricked in 1455. By remaining loyal to the House of York the Hastings family subsequently acquired substantial influence within the Yorkist polity.[29]

When magnate interference became too overt in a locality, though, the result was often parliamentary complaints about the conduct of the magnate's affinity, including those serving in local administration. What was condemned was the deliberate abuse of authority on behalf of a noble patron, or the protection by a noble of a client's interests. Of most concern to the gentry were maintenance, the illegal giving and taking of livery, and the illegal retaining of followers or being so retained. Of the three, maintenance was the issue that most exercised the minds of knights of the shire and burgesses. The practice frequently involved tampering with juries of indictment and of trial, or with the justices. Despite legislation from the reign of Edward I onwards to counter illegal activities of magnate affinities, maintenance remained common and the illegal behaviour of officials was routinely condemned.[30]

## DEEPLY HELD PRINCIPLES

Watts has remarked that the Wars of the Roses began with a series of statements of constitutional principle and 'the disorderly events of the fourteen fifties, fourteen sixties, and fourteen eighties were accompanied by a rich debate over the rights and duties of rulers and subjects'.[31] However, the historiography of the period has blurred the debate over the impact of principles on behaviour. Principled behaviour became associated with 'constitutional' behaviour, and while there has been a gradual movement away from this Victorian viewpoint, championed among others by William Stubbs, current scholarship still tends to regard political principles and personal concerns as mutually exclusive.[32] It is very clear that the use of principled language could be used to mask what we would call unprincipled behaviour. The good of the community, the 'common weal', was a principle which all levels of society were familiar with and ultimately aspired to. That kings, magnates and commons used it to justify their actions does not mean that the principle itself did not positively encourage an individual to act in its defence. Yet the principle could also be divisive. Lancastrian and Yorkist alike hijacked the 'common weal' during the course of the conflict. The end result was that principled conduct by one side was viewed as unprincipled and destructive by the other; this can only have served to reinforce a reluctance to adopt a clear political position or provide military service.[33]

The legacy of Henry V and his conquests in France resulted in strong emotional reactions in some of those who had served there and a series of unique judgements to be made by particular leading gentry. It demonstrated how sustained belief in an idea, activity or policy could result in equally strong positive or negative responses by the leading gentry. The wars of Henry V had become a national enterprise, and although not universally popular, had continued to attract men who strongly believed in the defence of the Lancastrian claims in France. As Grummitt has remarked, 'For a national military effort on the scale of the one made in the early summer of 1436 the crown relied on the goodwill of its greatest subjects, the nobility and other lay and ecclesiastical landowners, and those in turn relied on their own tenants, servants and friends to fulfil their military obligations'.[34] However, the failure of Henry VI's government to emulate, or even hold onto, Henry V's conquered lands led to hostility both in Lancastrian France and in England. It aroused great passions in a way that the erosion of the English Pale in Ireland did not.

Personal losses suffered as a consequence of the military collapse in the Duchy of Normandy were inextricably linked to concepts of honour and chivalry among some veterans of the wars. The fiasco in Normandy aroused great passions. When Sir François de Surienne, an Aragonese knight in English service, was blamed for the disastrous attack in 1449 on Fougères in Brittany, thereby precipitating the final overrun of Normandy by the forces of Charles VII, he angrily resigned from the Order of the Garter. De Surienne returned his garter because he felt that his trust had been betrayed. He had been in the service of the crown for at least ten years and perhaps, if his own petition is to be believed, since 1424. After seizing the fortress at Fougères, however, he was left to his fate and a relieving force led by Sir Robert Vere never arrived to save him. De Surienne surrendered and was allowed to leave with his men. Yet he was subsequently labelled a truce-breaking mercenary and this was too much to bear. He left royal service and returned to Aragon.[35]

The loss of Normandy in 1450 and the failure to recover Gascony in 1453 were still fresh in the memory of many when Yorkist and Lancastrian forces came to blows at the first battle of St Albans in 1455. In the minds of some who followed York it was regarded as a betrayal of the legacy of Henry V and the position maintained by Humphrey, duke of Gloucester. The duke had been steadfast in his opposition to any concessions to the French and vehement that the Treaty of Troyes, which acknowledged Henry V's claims to sovereignty in France, should be upheld.[36] Notable veterans of the wars, including Sir John Fastolf, advanced continuing support for this position.[37] Bitterness over the events of 1449–50 in particular lingered in the minds of some leading gentry associated with the duke of York, which was compounded by the behaviour of some of Somerset's retainers. This served to alienate a significant element of the Anglo-Norman establishment. York was particularly angry at the way in which the garrison at Rouen had been forced to surrender, and the confrontational attitude of Sir Osbert Mountford during the course of the negotiations with the French. Similar acrimonious feelings were undoubtedly present among some English veterans five years later who felt a deep sense of injustice at the way in which they were treated in 1449 and 1450.[38]

In fact, it is quite possible that the veterans on York's council put pressure on him to take action over these issues. One of York's own servants, Sir Henry Redford of Castlethorpe in Lincolnshire, was obviously swayed by some of his experiences in France. Redford had been a highly respected soldier in France and had served as York's lieutenant of the palace at Rouen before being appointed *bailli* there. He was still *bailli* when the garrison at Rouen was forced to surrender to the French in 1449. He had been held hostage thereafter and was still a prisoner in July 1451 'having noo goods wherewith to contente his finaunce'.[39] Briefly returning to England, he was appointed mayor of Bordeaux in 1452 at a time when the English grip on Gascony was weakening. By 1455, Redford was probably a man nursing several grievances against those who had brought about his personal problems. He had fought hard in the service of the crown but had suffered personal losses which seemed to stem from Somerset's mismanagement of Norman affairs. It is probable that the grant to Redford of the stewardship of

the lordship of Kirketon in Lincolnshire on 24 May 1455 was a reward for supporting York at the first battle of St Albans.[40]

The personal hostility of men like Redford to what happened in 1449–50 was
raised to the level of principle. Their honour had been taken from them and
they had suffered considerably as a result. Lack of much wider evidence among
the leading gentry would suggest, however, that a significant proportion of this
group did not espouse this view. Lancastrian forces included many veterans of
the French wars as well, some of who had also incurred substantial losses in 1450.
While the memories of the recent disasters in France played on the minds of men
who had suffered considerable personal and financial losses, this did not prevent
many others remaining loyal to the crown despite the personal sacrifices they
had made and the losses that they had also incurred. In fact, three veterans of the
wars were defending the town barrier at St Albans in 1455 on behalf of the king
while negotiations were being conducted between the dukes of Buckingham and
Norfolk. Sir Richard Harrington, Sir John Hanford and Sir Bertin Entwistle, the
latter erroneously described by Holinshed as a native of Normandy, had all served
in France.[41] The career of Harrington is known about in some depth. He had been
stationed at Evreux in 1433 with a retinue of 35 men-at-arms and 105 archers.
By 1435 he was a knight-banneret under Bedford. About this time he became
captain of Caen and by 1443 was *bailli* as well. Harrington was a trusted military
commander; nevertheless, after the fall of Normandy he moved into the service
of the royal household. That he was considered trustworthy within royal circles
at this time is shown by his appointment to the commission of inquiry into the
alleged embezzlement of soldiers' wages from the garrison in Caen.[42] Harrington
certainly did not harbour any significant personal grudges that affected his loyalty
to Henry VI.

By contrast, Hanford and Entwistle hardly appear in the records of English
central government, suggesting that they had sought a military career in France,
perhaps because of limited prospects in England. Similar examples have been
found in a study of military society in Cheshire during the fourteenth century.[43]
Entwistle and Hanford were contemporaries and served under Bedford during
the 1430s. Hanford had been a knight in the household of the duke of Bedford
and served under him as captain of the garrison guarding the bridge at Rouen.
He was clearly also a beneficiary of land grants in Normandy and, as Massey has
shown, he took an active role in maintaining and protecting his rights to them.
Little else is known about him, particularly after his return with English forces
in 1450. In 1451 he briefly appeared as a commissioner to take the musters of the
Kentish esquire Gervase Clifton and the troops sent by the London authorities
for action across the Channel. By 1452, however, he was serving as lieutenant of
the constable of England, Edmund, duke of Somerset. His appointment was no
doubt the result of connections he had forged with Somerset during his service

in Normandy.[44] Similarly, Entwistle, a native of Lancashire, had purchased the lordship of Bricqbec in the district of Valognes near Cherbourg from William de la Pole, duke of Suffolk, where he had then based himself. He had subsequently served as bailiff of the Cotentin. Cherbourg had been the last town to surrender to the French in 1450, so the memory of his personal loss would have been very fresh in his mind. Yet, unlike Redford, he did not put his own personal loss before the interests of the crown.[45]

## GENTRY LOYALTY

Magnates and gentry alike prized loyalty as an ideal. The loyalty of the leading gentry augmented the dignity, status and authority of the nobility within local and national arenas; equally, it could enhance the prestige and influence of the gentry and enable them to play a significant role as leaders of their own communities. In practice, loyalty, as the Wars of the Roses demonstrated, was a malleable concept that could be, and was, moulded according to circumstances. Each party to the relationship was realistic enough to know that there were few instances where absolute loyalty could be guaranteed. Loyalty was not normally equated with unswerving and partisan behaviour. During moments of political crisis and tension, though, it assumed a greater degree of significance to each side. In these circumstances tacit acceptance of the new regime was demanded from the public. Outspoken opposition or even mild dissension became a risky proposition as the notary John Clerke discovered shortly after Edward IV's victory at Towton. He was presented before the local wardmote at Farringdon in London in 1461 for remarking that he would prefer to go duck hunting rather than watch the coronation procession of Edward IV. Similarly, John Brunever, apprentice to Richard Manston, vintner, was arrested after his master had reported him for seditious words spoken against the restored regime of Henry VI in 1470–1.[46]

Within the sphere of royal and magnate affinities and those gentry serving within them, loyalty assumed an enhanced significance as well. Both parties sought good lordship and loyal service equally. Traditions of service existed between some gentry and leading magnates. Richard, duke of York, Edward IV, Richard, duke of Gloucester, and Richard, earl of Warwick, were all capable of inspiring men to follow and serve them loyally. The Conyers family of Hornby in Richmondshire were long-standing servants of the Nevilles of Middleham. It was Sir John Conyers who became most closely identified with the Nevilles, primarily the earl of Warwick. He fought for the Yorkists at Blore Heath and Ludford Bridge and was attainted in 1459. He became Warwick's steward of Middleham and as long as Warwick served Edward IV, so did Conyers. When the split came in 1469, however, Conyers followed his patron's lead. That loyalty transcended his oath of allegiance to the king. It is highly probable that he was 'Robin of Redesdale' who led a northern uprising against Edward IV in 1469. Conyer's son, John, died at the battle of Edgecote shortly afterwards. Sir John was also active in fomenting rebellion in Yorkshire again in 1470. In the wake of the collapse of the Readeption he transferred his loyalty to the new lord of Middleham, Richard, duke of Gloucester, who seemingly represented the heir to the Neville inheritance. He carried with him members of the Conyers clan into Gloucester's service and loyally served the duke throughout the 1470s and later entered Richard III's household. Sustained loyalty and the ability to generate those feelings did not go unnoticed or unrewarded: Sir John Conyers became a knight of the body and was raised to the Order of the Garter. The 'wight' Sir William Conyers was recorded in the 'Ballard of Bosworth Field' as one of the Ricardian casualties at the battle in 1485.[47]

An equally obvious display of disloyalty could have significant repercussions for an individual. Some saw not honouring service commitments as a betrayal of a sacred bond and this occasionally lead to recriminations on and off the battlefield. Take the example of Richard, duke of York's, servant Sir William Skipwith. Skipwith's conduct had obviously been found wanting by some of his colleagues. In 1459 Thomas Colt and Sir James Pickering were both accused by Skipwith of having put him out of the stewardship of York's manor of Hatfield and the constableship of the castle of Conisbrough in Yorkshire for refusing to follow the duke against Henry VI at the first battle of St Albans. Colt and Pickering were two of the duke's councillors and members of his retinue. Skipwith had also been a retainer of the duke but had chosen not to serve when called upon. By 1459 Skipwith had determined that his interests were best served by identifying with the Lancastrian court, which had prompted him to petition the crown for the restoration of the offices. Skipwith had balanced his own interests against those of York and decided that continuing loyalty to the crown was the better course of action at that time.[48]

A deep-rooted tradition of service among some gentry had also existed towards the House of Lancaster. As dukes of Lancaster in their own right, Henry IV and Henry V had enjoyed the ability to inspire their men. Unfortunately, Henry VI did not and certain families that had served the duchy gradually drifted away.[49] Yet loyalty to the House of Lancaster was still highly prized. Such was the strength of feeling that, for some serving at the heart of a noble affinity, the lack of commitment by other colleagues was seen as a betrayal of a sacred commitment. Service relationships were taken seriously by many gentry and interpreted by some as meaning that military service should be undertaken in defence of the interests of their lord, even to the extent that personal safety should be disregarded. In the tense opening months of the first phase of the Wars of the Roses some men who had once been close colleagues on a daily basis now found themselves on opposing sides of the political and military divide. In the strategic manoeuvring that occurred before the battle of Northampton in July 1460, when forces were being gathered together by both sides, one group of gentry associated with the royal household, led by Sir Edmund Hampden, Sir John Chalers, Edward Longford, Thomas Tresham, John Pury and Everard Digby, attacked the Yorkist sympathizer Sir Robert Harcourt at his home in Stanton Harcourt in Oxfordshire. They allegedly held him prisoner for seven weeks. Harcourt was to claim in a subsequent lawsuit that this had prevented him from joining his Yorkist colleagues at the battle.[50]

It is conceivable, of course, that Harcourt felt himself to be the victim of malicious gossip from those who had been at the battle and needed to justify his absence because of the loss of honour he had experienced. Whatever the exact circumstances, Harcourt felt it necessary to provide a reason. Yet there has been little consideration of the feelings that prompted Hampden and his associates to act in the way they did. Presumably, in their minds Harcourt had betrayed Henry VI in favour of the Yorkists. Harcourt had an excellent Lancastrian pedigree and, like many of his generation, his early career in Lancastrian service had been spent in France. In 1445 he had been among those sent to France to receive the new queen and escort her to England, after which a special attachment seems to have been formed between them. In 1453 his baby son even received a gift of a tiny Lancastrian livery collar. Harcourt had apparently enjoyed a close relationship with many at the heart of the Lancastrian court and his failure to support Henry VI and Queen Margaret probably contributed to Hampden and his colleagues' sense of anger at the betrayal. Chalers, in particular, had been a long-standing associate of his and Sir Robert's kinsman, John Harcourt, and had even married one of Chalers' daughters. Harcourt's actions could quite possibly have appeared as a betrayal on three levels: of loyalty to the crown, kinsmen and friends.[51]

There were clearly some members of the gentry who, in supporting the Lancastrian or Yorkist parties, demonstrated deep-rooted loyalties to their cause and who were clearly prepared to risk death, forfeiture or exile in the service of their lord. These judgements apparently dominated their decision frames. To some this was how loyalty could and should be interpreted. The career of Sir William Oldhall exemplified a man who placed personal loyalty to his lord and patron, York, above his own personal well-being. Oldhall had enjoyed a successful military career in Lancastrian Normandy and had purchased York's manor of Hunsdon in Hertfordshire from the wealth he had accumulated. Oldhall was closely associated with his master's policies from 1450 onwards. In the backlash against the Lancastrian regime he was even elected speaker of the commons in parliament in 1450. Oldhall was identified as one of York's most prominent counsellors and was deeply implicated in the aborted uprising of 1452.

He was subsequently targeted by Somerset and the Lancastrian regime. Forced to find sanctuary at St Martin-the-Grand, Oldhall did not re-emerge until the first battle of St Albans in 1455. He was attainted and his impressive new house at Hunsdon granted to Somerset. Oldhall was with York at Ludford Bridge in 1459 and subsequently condemned along with the duke's closest retainers and supporters. However, he died in 1460 before the kingdom descended into open conflict.[52]

There were also a number of Lancastrian exiles who remained loyal to the dynasty up until the outcome of the battle of Tewkesbury in 1471 ended the direct Lancastrian line. Perhaps one of the most outstanding examples of loyalty was Sir Richard Tunstall, who had served at the heart of the Lancastrian royal affinity for at least three decades. From the moment the first blows had been dealt by both sides in 1455, he maintained a consistent loyalty to the Lancastrian cause. After 1461 his commitment did not waver. Tunstall had followed Henry VI, Queen Margaret and Prince Edward north into Scotland after the battle of Towton. Together with the Queen, Robert Whittingham and John Hampden, he had besieged Carlisle with an Anglo-Scottish army in June 1461. He was reported to have been captured and executed at Carlisle in June 1462. In fact, he surrendered Naworth Castle and made good his escape before seizing Bamborough Castle in October 1462.[53]

One month later, in November, he was at Dunstanborough Castle with Sir Philip Wentworth, another Lancastrian rebel. Wentworth had also accompanied the Lancastrian forces northwards; he remained at large, precisely where is unknown, until he ended up at Dunstanborough. Most of the defenders in the castles received safe-conducts to leave the realm. Wentworth and Tunstall managed to escape. Perhaps like Tunstall he returned to Scotland and rejoined Henry VI and Queen Margaret. In the event, he was with Lancastrian forces at Hexham in 1464. Few Lancastrians managed to escape the battle with their lives. Wentworth was captured and taken to Middleham where he was executed along with Oliver Wentworth, who was possibly his brother.[54] Sir Richard Tunstall was perhaps the only man of any consequence to escape the slaughter and he was forced to spend the next couple of years moving from one hiding place to another with the sad, pathetic figure of Henry VI in tow. The Lancastrian cause had now reached its lowest ebb. Even after Henry was captured in 1465, Tunstall remained in opposition and sought refuge in Wales at Harlech Castle until its capture by the Yorkists in 1468. He was then a prisoner in the Tower of London until his release during Henry's brief restoration in 1470–1 when he was appointed master of the mint. There is no evidence to suggest that he fought at either Barnet or Tewkesbury in 1471 and, indeed, after Edward IV's victory, he made his peace with the Yorkist regime and entered royal service.[55]

Some Yorkist supporters were equally capable of displaying a single-minded loyalty and were prepared to go into exile with their monarch when forced to choose. Reports vary over the exact number of men that accompanied Edward into exile in Holland in 1470. Some say 700 to 800, while others claimed it was 1,500. Attention has generally focused on the leading supporters of Edward IV, including his brother, Richard, duke of Gloucester, Lord Hastings, Lord Rivers and Lord Saye and Sele. The speed with which Edward's position had collapsed in 1470 meant, however, that many loyal supporters remained in England. Among the group of gentry exiles who appeared to accompany the king was Sir Maurice Berkeley of Beverstone in Gloucestershire, brother of William, Lord Berkeley, who remained conspicuously loyal to Edward IV at a moment of crisis. Berkeley had served as an esquire of the body during the later 1460s and was closely involved in the manoeuvres that were taking place in 1469. Edward IV used him to warn Clarence of the movements of Robin of Redesdale, little knowing the close connections that his wayward brother enjoyed with the Nevilles. By remaining with Edward, Berkeley faced an uncertain future. It was a political gamble, perhaps prompted by emotional ties to the House of York, that ultimately paid off, but he would not have known this as he sailed across the North Sea to the Netherlands. Berkeley's appointment as sheriff of Hampshire in April 1471 perhaps reflected the king's desire to have a reliable supporter on the south coast who enjoyed connections within the county in advance of Queen Margaret's anticipated landing in that region. Among the men that Berkeley raised in support of the Yorkists was another Hampshire gentleman, William Sandes, who was knighted after the battle of Tewkesbury. Berkeley subsequently benefited from his loyalty and progressed into the inner reaches of the royal household, serving as a knight of the body.[56]

Two further exiles with Edward were Sir Robert Chamberlain and Sir Gilbert Debenham, who were sent to assess the reception that Edward IV could expect if he attempted to land in East Anglia in March 1471. Both men were part of Edward's inner household. Like his father and namesake, Sir Gilbert Debenham the younger of Little Wenham in Suffolk had a reputation for violence and thuggery, although perhaps to a lesser extent. The Debenhams were traditionally associated with the Mowbray dukes of Norfolk. However, Gilbert Debenham had also moved into Yorkist service by the mid-1460s and had prospered under this new source of patronage. It is perhaps unsurprising that Debenham's magnate and royal connections rapidly brought him into conflict with the retinue of the earls of Oxford. Indeed, it was Sir Thomas Vere, brother of the thirteenth earl, who mustered the local levies against a Yorkist landing in March 1471.[57]

Deep-rooted loyalty manifested itself once again in 1483 when a significant section of Edward IV's royal affinity turned against the usurper, Richard of Gloucester. The rebels retained a strong sense of loyalty to Edward IV and his heir, Edward V. While willing to acquiesce the overthrow of the Woodville grouping

around the king, there was a point beyond which many were not prepared to go. That tradition of service, for instance, was maintained by William Berkeley who rebelled against Richard III in 1483. Berkeley and his kinsman Robert Poyntz had participated in the moves designed to remove the influence of Sir Edward Woodville from the navy and the Isle of Wight during the protectorate. As soon as Richard abandoned the role of protector and took the throne for himself, though, he alienated the Yorkist affinity including the likes of Berkeley. Leading members of Edward IV's household then formed the nexus around which the rebellion formed. Sir John Cheyne of Falstone-Cheyne in Wiltshire, for example, had served as Edward IV's master of the horse during the 1470s. He had married the widow of William, Lord Stourton, and found himself linked to the Berkeleys of Beverstone, also loyal servants of Edward IV.[58]

Richard III was clearly capable of inspiring the loyalty in some of his Yorkshire retainers that his opponent Henry Tudor was unable to. Dominic Mancini remarked of Richard, while still duke of Gloucester, that he 'kept himself within his own lands and set out to acquire the loyalty of his people through favours and justice. The good reputation of his private life and public activities powerfully attracted the esteem of strangers. Such was his renown in warfare, that whenever a difficult and dangerous policy had to be undertaken, it would be entrusted to his discretion and his generalship. By these arts Richard acquired the favours of the people . . .' The significant numbers of northern gentry who served with Richard of Gloucester in Scotland in 1482 subsequently served with him at Bosworth in 1485, despite the very short notice allowed for them to arm and muster. Most did not have to think twice about answering his summons. This strength of feeling for Richard was subsequently recognized by Margaret Beaufort, the mother of Henry VII, who praised Sir Ralph Bigod to some of her servants when he refused to allow them to impugn the name of his former master. He was held up as an example of loyalty that transcended personal and political enmities.[59]

## CONCLUSIONS

This chapter has demonstrated that the public domain and the lives of the leading gentry intersected in a number of ways that could affect their decision making. The opportunities existed for them to serve in public administration and in magnate affinities if they wished to. Yet the nature and extent of these opportunities varied geographically according to the relative dominance of magnate and gentry power. Furthermore, while their willingness shifted in accordance with local political structures, it is evident that many leading gentry chose not to serve within the king's administration or as a member of the nobility; and even those that did enter into a service relationship did not demonstrate a continual willingness to serve throughout their lives. It would appear that those who did serve were a minority within gentry society as a whole.

Service, whether in public administration or with a magnate, was not constantly undertaken by the leading gentry. The majority of gentry, not least the leading gentry, probably regarded public service as a double-edged sword. Many leading gentry whose wealth and status within a locality in many instances enabled them to retain their social importance, remained unwilling to put themselves forward for office. Those that performed these duties did so for a variety of reasons according to their own decision-making frames and personal circumstances. While some may have served from a sense of duty or have seen the practical advantages of a spell in office, there were some very distinct disadvantages that no doubt acted as a disincentive to other men. Many leading and lesser gentry regarded service within a magnate affinity with equal circumspection. Partisan loyalty was more likely to be exhibited by those leading gentry intimately connected to a principal magnate or to the crown. For men such as these, along with those who shunned any form of service but whose lineage and prestige enabled them to remain important men in their localities, there were presumably other factors that shaped the decision-making process.

# 6

# *The Private Domain: Locality, Neighbourhood and Family*

## INTRODUCTION

If service connections, patronage relationships or deeply held principles were not the dominant elements in the decision-making process of all the leading gentry, it is necessary to identify alternative influences that helped shape and determine their framing processes. There is a powerful argument for focusing our attention upon the regional and local environments in which the leading and lesser gentry conducted their business and personal affairs, referred to here as the private domain, because these would have impacted upon more than a just a small proportion of gentry society. In this chapter we will examine the two most significant influences upon the stability of these environments. The first influence was the possibility of an alteration in the strategic importance of localities at particular stages of the conflict. External political or military factors could exert a temporary or permanent influence upon the resident gentry and could place them under pressure to make uncomfortable choices. The second influence was changes to the social dynamics within local and regional gentry society. The stability of neighbourly relations, the extent and intensity of family disputes, questions of landed inheritance and preservation of status, and the arrival of newcomers into local society were each potentially disruptive to the local environment and could exert a powerful, divisive effect upon local society.

## THE STRATEGIC IMPORTANCE OF REGIONS AND LOCALITIES

Gentry decision frames were normally created through a gradual process of selection in which relevant judgements were balanced against each other in order to arrive at an informed choice. When unanticipated events occurred, though, the decision frames were likely to have become distorted and the judgements that were brought to the decision choice were based on less reliable information. This is evident in instances where the strategic importance of an area altered, giving rise to gentry involvement at unexpected moments. While certain parts of England were more closely involved in the Wars of the Roses than others, no region remained completely unaffected or immune from the conflict. In the immediate context of local circumstances some of those leading gentry who would otherwise have opted to remain on the sidelines were drawn into events. Royal intervention in Kent during the later 1450s apparently exerted a strong negative effect on local sensibilities. The crown was very aware of the underlying support that existed for the reform programme of the earl of Warwick and the duke of York. A steady stream of traffic continued to move between those elements sympathetic to the Yorkists in the region and the earls at Calais in 1459–60. Sandwich, with its large well-equipped port, rather than Dover, remained the centre of royal operations during in the final years of the decade, but relations between royal forces and the town remained tense. The large build up of forces in the town must have added to the local sense of unease and the hostility towards Lancastrian forces under the command of Lord Rivers. It is perhaps also unsurprising that the leading gentry in the region responded enthusiastically to the Yorkist invasion in 1461.[1]

Urgent demands for manpower to either thwart or support an invasion might have also presented the leading gentry of particular areas with a quandary. The introduction of one or more new cues, particularly within their immediate environment, disrupted their traditional decision frames. Changes in the strategic importance of a region could clearly have had a direct impact on the short-term decision-making processes of some leading gentry, especially some of those who had been involved in previous disputes and confrontations. In certain instances their decision frames possibly enabled them to adopt a more flexible cognitive approach. Having encountered similar situations before, they were able to employ a non-compensatory strategy to make what they considered the most appropriate choice. The battle of Mortimer's Cross in February 1461 included a significant proportion of gentry from Herefordshire and the Welsh Marches fighting on behalf of the Yorkists and Lancastrians. William Worcester remarked upon these men in his *Itineraries* and also went to some pains to find out and record their military backgrounds.

Herefordshire had been the scene of considerable upheaval during the mid-1450s. The activities of Sir Walter Devereux and Sir William Herbert in support of their patron, Richard, duke of York, had created significant unrest in the Welsh Marches. Ranged against Devereux, Herbert and others at Mortimer's Cross was at least one leading gentleman, Sir Thomas FitzHarry, who had come into conflict with them during the preceding decade.[2] Similarly, the battle of Blore Heath in 1459 appears to have been the only significant engagement in which substantial numbers of Cheshire gentry were involved. Despite the inconsistencies in the contemporary evidence it seems clear that a significant proportion of the leading gentry of the palatinate fought and died for the Lancastrians under the command of James, Lord Audley.[3] In the aftermath of the battle, however, the leading gentry remained on the sidelines and waited upon events. Some, including Margaret, the widow of Sir William Troutbeck, were coming to terms with the financial implications of losing their husbands. Not only did Margaret have to contend with distraint of knighthood, she had had to pay £100 for the wardship of her son, and had lost her husband's horses, armour and other military equipment at the battle.[4]

Nevertheless, to cope with unexpected developments many leading gentry continued to employ compensatory strategies, basing decisions upon the gradual accumulation of information. Clayton's analysis of the palatinate records of Chester suggests that in the tense transition from a Lancastrian to Yorkist government between June 1460 and March 1461 the leading gentry were increasingly unwilling to conduct any significant business in the county court. The leading gentry and their families were apparently standing back and observing the impact and ramifications of the Yorkist takeover. After the Yorkist victory at Northampton a warrant was sent to the sheriff, Sir John Mainwairing, ordering him to release the earl of Salisbury's sons, Thomas and John Neville, from custody. Following the accession of Edward IV in March 1461 the administration of the palatinate began to function once again without any significant repercussions. In fact, as Clayton shows, the majority of gentlemen taking part in the business of the county court and exchequer were largely the same as before. Like other areas of the country, Cheshire was affected by periodic unrest during the early years of Edward IV's reign, but there is little evidence of wider gentry participation.[5]

This is not to say that leading members of the Cheshire gentry did not become involved in events elsewhere in an individual capacity. In some instances this was perhaps the result of their broader, sociopolitical horizons. It was probably sometime between 1460 and 1461, at about the time of the battle of Northampton in June 1460, that Sir Ralph Brereton of Malpas was involved with Sir Gervase Clifton in an attack on the Leicestershire property of John Bourchier, Lord Berners at Groby. What prompted the attack is unknown; yet the involvement of Cheshire gentry outside of their native county is clearly a distinct possibility. Such instances, though, seem to have been rare.[6] Similarly, the troubled period between 1469 and 1471 made little impact upon gentry decision making within the shire. An attack upon Sir William Stanley by local yeomen and tradesmen from Nantwich in November 1470 suggests some degree of resentment against a family closely identified with Yorkist interests, but that was not sufficient to prompt gentry to leave the county for the West Country. The support that Queen Margaret had hoped for from Lancashire and Cheshire before the battle of Tewkesbury was certainly not forthcoming. It is entirely possible that Sir John Delves, Readeption sheriff of Staffordshire, who had landed interests in Staffordshire and Cheshire, sought to recruit within the palatinate, but he was largely unsuccessful for there were no recorded gentry from the shire at the battle.[7]

Mackman has shown that like Cheshire, Lincolnshire's experiences of the Wars of the Roses were also limited and sporadic. Yet they did affect the county, especially in 1470. For a brief period the county assumed an increased strategic significance. The Lincolnshire rebellion that year was a direct result of the post-1461 Yorkist political settlement and the shift in the balance of power within the county. It also reflected the breakdown of law and order seen elsewhere in the country as individuals seized the opportunity to settle private scores. A likely scenario advanced by Mackman is that the troubled state of the country in general in 1469 was aggravated in Lincolnshire by its involvement in the Yorkshire rebellions, which in turn prevented local administration from functioning properly. In these circumstances, Lord Welles took the opportunity to pursue a grudge with Sir Thomas Burgh. But his attack on Burgh's house at Gainsborough backfired. Burgh was able to use his position as master of the horse, one of Edward IV's most intimate body servants, to persuade the king to intervene directly in the county. Welles now found himself summoned to London. Warwick and Clarence apparently made approaches to Welles, but he lost his nerve and subsequently took up the offer of a royal pardon. Welles's son Robert, however, continued with the plans discussed with Warwick and Clarence and the rebellion went ahead in 1470. Sir Thomas de la Launde followed his nephew Sir Robert Welles into rebellion and was captured after the battle of Losecote Field. He was subsequently executed at Grantham.[8]

## NEIGHBOURHOOD AND COMMUNITY RELATIONSHIPS

For many leading gentry what really mattered to them was a stable, local environment in which to lead their lives. It has been suggested that in many instances their own social horizons were as narrow as the lesser gentry. Consequently, it remained an important consideration within their cognitive framing process.[9] Evidence suggests that in some instances certain families went to considerable lengths to demonstrate their association with a particular place. New families, those in crisis or those who were simply ambitious adopted a number of different techniques to reinforce this personal identification. One of the most common was visual display, such as a tradition of the commemorative laying-down of effigies in churches. The Willoughbys of Willoughby-on-the-Wold in Nottinghamshire established this practice during the late thirteenth and fourteenth centuries. They were a new family in the locality and this was a method of asserting 'gentry cultural identity amongst the parish community'. In fact, by the fifteenth century with the family firmly anchored in local society the church had become a crowded family mausoleum. The Cliftons of Clifton in Nottinghamshire also engaged in commemorative display but went one step further and established a college there. Both were designed to bolster and strengthen their identity in the region.[10]

A deep-rooted sense of belonging might have exerted an influence on gentry willingness to act in support of Lancastrian or Yorkist interests, although on its own it did not determine whether this would be a positive or negative response. It was the judgements forming the decision frame that determined whether they acted to protect their local interest or avoided involvement to avoid losing their position in society. Generally speaking, though, the aristocracy, leading gentry and other landowners wanted peace and stability in order to conduct their lives. It is likely that good neighbourly relations were maintained during the Wars of the Roses, subject to the normal caveat of personal disputes that often involved the ownership of land. Relationships within a locality were usually given expression through the concepts of country and neighbour. Holford has noted that these reflected a system of attitudes and values rather than defining particular geographical regions. They served to guide the conduct of social relationships. The interaction of neighbourhood, country and friendship had the potential to cement local society together. The values enshrined within such concepts were employed, for example, by the Pastons during the 1460s. In 1465, John Paston I advised Margaret and others to use an appeal based on neighbourhood to combat the attacks by the duke of Suffolk on their properties. Of particular significance to neighbourhood was the idea of friendship. As John Paston's actions demonstrate, such appeals could include those for armed or military support but it can only be speculated the extent to which this was used during the Wars of the Roses.[11]

While the wars undoubtedly exacerbated existing disputes in some instances, and certainly generated new disputes based on Lancastrian or Yorkist preferences, there were also leading gentry on opposite sides of the political divide who continued to coexist within a locality without apparent difficulty and still remained on friendly terms. Their decision frames were structured on the basis of local environmental cues in such a way that they were seemingly able to arrive at decisions independently of patrons or other external circumstances. One example of peaceful, neighbourly relations transcending political differences was the relationship between William Fielding and Sir Thomas Malory. Malory and Fielding were neighbours in both Leicestershire and Warwickshire and had been involved in each other's affairs on a number of occasions including the marriage settlement of Fielding's son, John. Malory had become increasingly identified with the earl of Warwick by the late 1460s; Fielding, meanwhile, had maintained a low profile during the 1460s, although his previous Lancastrian associations were widely known. The Readeption enabled the two to coexist in political harmony as the interests of their political masters now coincided.[12]

In certain circumstances the decision frames of leading gentry were shaped in such a way that they were able to reconcile a desire for stability with their position as traditional leaders within their communities. Where an external threat arose they were prepared to provide military leadership to their communities. The aftermath of the loss of Normandy exerted a particularly strong influence on the inhabitants of east Kent in 1450 and during the decade up to 1460. It had increased the sense of vulnerability felt by the leading gentry and the inhabitants of Cinque Ports to attack from French pirates. In the same way that the gentry of northern England accepted their responsibility to defend against Scottish incursions, leading local levies against attack was an obligation accepted by the leading gentry of east Kent. A handful of contemporary chronicles record rumours of a French descent on Kent in the early summer of 1457. Sir Thomas Kyriell, lieutenant of Dover Castle, was appointed to keep a watch. Then, on 28 August a French fleet from Honfleur, commanded by Pierre de Brézé, seneschal of Normandy, landed at Sandwich. Part of the town was burnt and John Drury, the town's mayor, was killed. A local force from the Cinque Ports was raised and led by Kyriell, Gervase Clifton, Robert Horne and Richard Culpeper. They managed to drive the French back to their ships and kill about 120 men in the ensuing fight.[13] This raid became something of a cause célèbre in England in the late 1450s, and for the residents of east Kent was regarded as evidence of the failure of the Lancastrian regime to provide for the defence of the realm.

The gentry may have also adopt a leadership role in communal protest, although subsequently justifying this type of action could have posed significant difficulties. In some instances gentry participation in communal protest was probably reactive rather than proactive. This was the case in Kent where Bohna has demonstrated that the constables, themselves lesser landholders, provided the communal military leadership during Cade's rebellion of 1450. While there was undoubtedly some leading gentry involvement, they probably felt a compulsion to act rather than a sense of communal responsibility to do so.[14] Nonetheless, the defence of local interests against unjust demands and exactions from an outside agency was still an accepted response by the gentry. The gentry's role as the leaders of communal protest emerges in the 1469 Yorkshire rebellion by Robin of Holderness. The cause of the protest was the ancient tax levied by the hospital of St Leonard at York, albeit stirred up by members of the earl of Warwick's affinity. The hospital had the right to exact a quantity of corn called a 'thrave' from every ploughland in Yorkshire, Lancashire, Westmorland and Cumberland. In 1468, Sir Hugh Hastings had gathered together a following in the East Riding to prevent the servants of the hospital from gathering their entitlement. The leader of the 1469 protest, Robert of Holderness, is normally identified as Robert Hillyard, Hastings's brother-in-law. Even the rebellion by Robin of Redesdale was grounded in popular discontent at unfair taxes. Redesdale is traditionally identified as a member of the Conyers family who were leading gentry within Richmondshire.[15]

Communal responsibilities taking precedence over royal demands are apparently evident in the reactions of the Kentish gentry in 1460. As Yorkist forces moved towards London from Sandwich, the three local esquires who were also royal servants were faced with a stark choice: resist or capitulate. As the rebel earls approached the city walls of Canterbury, John Fogge, John Scott and Robert Horne offered no resistance. Instead they opened up the city gates and joined the invading army. Contemporary chronicles are silent on underlying motives. Surviving correspondence for the Cinque Ports, however, demonstrates that the residents of east Kent were aware of the steps being taken to resist any landing on the south coast. Direct confrontation with a much larger force was an unwelcome proposition and also ran counter to local feelings and sentiments.[16]

In the case of Fogge, Scott and Horne, existing Lancastrian connections were not allowed to stand in the way of a decision choice weighted in favour of local conditions. All three could point to family service in defence of the crown's interests. Fogge's father, Sir Thomas, had been the only Kentish retainer of John of Gaunt and a soldier of some renown in his day. Moreover, Fogge was also the former son-in-law of Sir Thomas Kyriell. They were undoubtedly in close communication throughout this period about the state of local conditions. John Fogge had emerged as a trusted royal servant during the early 1450s. Along with Scott and Horne, he even had been commissioned to disperse Cade's Kentish rebels. Fogge had even incurred some degree of local unpopularity in September 1452 when he had been identified in a small-scale uprising as an oppressive royal servant.[17] The Scotts had also been loyal Lancastrian servants. Scott's father, William, had served the Lancastrian regime as sheriff and escheator of Kent and participated on various local commissions. He had enjoyed connections to leading figures at court including the king's deceased uncle Humphrey, duke of Gloucester. John Scott was also the stepson of the prominent Lancastrian servant Gervase Clifton.[18] Robert Horne's connections with the regime are uncertain. The Hornes were long-standing residents of Appledore in east Kent, with close ties to the port of Romney. By the time Robert began participating in the county administration in the early 1450s, the family had produced sheriffs and justices of the peace, and was closely connected to prominent local families including the Guildfords and Darells. Robert seems to have pursued a military career and served in France under a number of captains including Sir Richard Frogenhale and Sir Thomas Hoo, leading figures within the Norman administration. As a military man Horne was presumably also well known to Sir Thomas Kyriell and probably had regular communication when the latter was serving as lieutenant of Dover Castle in the late 1450s.[19]

The judgements that Fogge, Scott and Horne arrived at emphasized the importance of the local community and maintaining their pre-eminence within it. Similar considerations probably entered the decision frames of other leading Kentish gentry as the Yorkist forces moved up from Canterbury along the old Roman road towards London. Those whose homes lay closest to the route of march either kept their heads down or joined the swelling ranks of their fellow Kentishmen. Depending on their decision frames either strategy could be adopted to protect their local standing. A mixture of pragmatism, kinship connections, and perhaps a desire to distance himself from the Lancastrian affiliations of his Woodville kinsmen, presumably prompted William Haute to join his son-in-law, Fogge. Haute was an old man by this time but had served in France during the Agincourt campaign of 1415.[20] The groundswell of support in the county might mask the identity of some men who felt pressured to join through local circumstances rather than any genuine sense of enthusiasm. By the time the Yorkist earls reached London they reputedly had an army containing 40,000 men from Kent, Surrey and Sussex. Despite the exaggerated numbers, it indicates the strength of popular feeling at a local level, which the gentry tapped into. The large list of rewards of annuities and crown offices made to the leading Kentish gentry in the wake of the battle of Towton in 1461 provides some indication of the likely participants at the battles of Northampton, Wakefield, St Albans and Towton, and the role that they played as military leaders within their communities.[21]

## FAMILY DIVISIONS

The relationships between different family members were not consistently harmonious. Kinsmen were, however, aware of the potentially divisive effects of disputes. Evidence suggests that where families and kinsmen were divided in their political allegiances, the outcome of a battle could have fundamental consequences for their fortunes and for the division of the family lands. This quite naturally acted as a deterrent for many, yet not all. The decision frames and the behavioural strategies adopted by opposing kinsmen suggest that these factors did not necessarily assume a dominant position in the cognitive process. It was equally possible for father and son to support opposing sides in the conflict and, in theory, to have lined up against each other on the battlefield. This might have been the case with Sir Thomas Green, senior and junior. The Greens were a substantial Northamptonshire family. Sir Thomas the Elder had enjoyed a distinguished career in royal service, fighting in France under Henry V, and subsequently holding local office in his native shire. Green's loyalties appeared to waver in favour of the Yorkist cause. His election as sheriff in 1454 certainly hints at his acceptability to the protectorate, while his removal from the commission of the peace in 1459 would imply mistrust from the increasingly partisan regime of Queen Margaret.[22] His son, by contrast, actively supported the Lancastrian cause. Connections to the Beaufort family had apparently eased his way into the royal household as an esquire. He subsequently served in local administration as escheator of Northamptonshire and Rutland in 1455–6 and then as sheriff of Northamptonshire from 1456–7. He was obviously regarded as an active Lancastrian supporter, for in May 1461 his estates were seized on the orders of Edward IV.[23]

Perhaps the most extreme example of a divided family, however, is the Mountford family of Coleshill in Warwickshire. Their wealth and concentration of Warwickshire property made them the greatest knightly family in the shire. The family had already divided before the Wars of the Roses erupted. Nevertheless, the rivalry between Edmund and Simon, son and grandson respectively of Sir William Mountford by two marriages, rose and fell in accordance with the successes and failures of the Lancastrians and Yorkists. The family had been faithful supporters of the Lancastrian dynasty even before the accession of Henry IV in 1399. During the course of the 1450s the tension between Simon and Edmund assumed a much greater intensity. Edmund was the son of Sir William's second marriage, while Simon was the son of Sir Baldwin, son of Sir William by his first marriage. Edmund had extended the tradition of family service to the House of Lancaster and eventually became a carver, one of the King's most intimate body servants. Edmund rubbed shoulders with some of the leading political figures within government at that time. By contrast, Simon was much less well connected. Nevertheless, in common with his father he had gravitated towards service with Richard Neville, earl of Warwick, at a time when he was increasingly at loggerheads with the court. In 1454 an arbitration award had sought to assign the Mountford inheritance to each son in a peaceful manner. Coleshill was awarded to Edmund's feoffee, the duke of Buckingham; the manor of Ilmington to Baldwin and, ultimately, Simon. Not surprisingly, the agreement broke down and between 1456 and 1458 Simon found himself imprisoned in Gloucester Castle for failing to surrender his claims to Coleshill and Ilmington.

The accession of Edward IV after the battle of Towton in 1461 had far-reaching consequences for Simon and Edmund as well as the possession and division of the Mountford inheritance. Edmund was attainted while Simon sought by means of a parliamentary petition to lay claim to the Mountford lands, asserting that Baldwin and Simon had only surrendered their claims to Edmund under duress. During the course of the 1460s Simon also entered the service of Lord Hastings, firmly nailing his colours to the fortunes of the Yorkist mast. The restoration of Henry VI caused considerable concern to Baldwin and Simon in

1470, who feared the return of Edmund from exile. In the event, their claims were unfounded. Although Edmund returned to England he did not have time to make good any claims. By 1474 Edmund had instead reconciled himself to Edward IV and entered the service of the duke of Buckingham. He was not allowed to take possession of any Warwickshire property, though. Instead he was allowed to take possession of his father's Berkshire lands. Simon, meanwhile, retained the Warwickshire lands and his influence in the shire grew steadily at the expense of Clarence, who was, in theory, the dominant magnate in the region. It was Simon Mountford who linked the senior gentry across the shire and who, in the opinion of Carpenter, 'provided the cohesion amongst the local gentry for which the nobility had formerly in large measure been responsible'. Tewkesbury had effectively signalled the triumph of the senior branch of the Mountford family.[24]


## DEFENDING AND RECOVERING FAMILY STATUS

The decision frames of many leading gentry are likely to have incorporated judgements regarding the very real risk of forfeiture, disinheritance and loss of local influence if they took to the battlefield and finished on the losing side, or the consequences arising from the death of a family member in battle. It was possible, of course, that a death could act as a disincentive for other members of the family to take any further part in war. While there is no evidence to prove that the Northumbrian knight Sir William Euer was deterred from further support for the Lancastrian cause after the death of his son Ralph at the battle of Towton, the consideration must have crossed his mind, if only briefly, and then been balanced against his connections to the Neville earls of Westmorland.[25]

The desire for revenge was the more normal emotion felt after the violent death of a kinsman. Contemporary chroniclers suggested that the duke of Somerset, the earl of Northumberland and Lord Clifford took up the Lancastrian cause with such vigour after 1459 because of the deaths of their fathers at the first battle of St Albans in 1455.[26] A desire for revenge and to uphold family honour probably prompted Sir Henry Pierpoint to fight for Edward IV at Towton in 1461. His decision was perhaps the result of a personal vendetta against the Plumpton family who had killed his father in an affray on Papplewick Moor in Yorkshire just a few years earlier. The root cause of that conflict was disputed possession of lands in Nottinghamshire at Holme Pierrepont. Previous attempts at arbitration had failed. In the event, Pierpoint's choice turned out to be fortuitous. He remained committed to Edward IV thereafter, particularly during the upheavals of 1469–71. He was subsequently rewarded with an assignment from the exchequer for the payment of his previous debts as sheriff and for attending the king at Barnet and Tewkesbury. Whether Pierpoint had looked at the possible benefits to be gained through sustained loyalty to the Yorkists is open to question. Yet a decision based partially on personal loss suffered in a private dispute had resulted in positive gains being made in the long run.[27]

For those who suffered attainder the subsequent results could vary. Their decision frames required them to identify the relevant cues and make judgements based upon the likely success of recovering their position. Some found themselves pitted against those who had benefitted from their forfeiture and thus unwilling to surrender those gains. After 1461 Sir Nicholas Latimer of Duntish in Dorset had to struggle to work his way back into royal favour and recover his lands. Latimer, linked to the Beauforts, had fought at the battles of Wakefield and Towton. He was subsequently attainted and some of his lands were granted to Sir John Howard and Edmund Grey, earl of Kent. Latimer remained in arms in the north with Queen Margaret and the Lancastrian resistance until 1463 when he swore allegiance to Edward IV along with Somerset and Sir Henry Lewis. He received his pardon at the end of 1463. Latimer claimed in his petition that the earls of Warwick and Worcester had promised him all of his lands. This did not happen – although restored to the king's laws his property remained in the hands of his opponents. Nevertheless, Latimer set about negotiating the return of his property. He was pragmatic enough to realize that this was necessary. Protracted talks were arranged and conducted with Howard over a two-year period. It is entirely plausible that Howard then interceded on Latimer's behalf and secured him a grant of his former lands in 1466 and sponsored the reversal of his attainder in 1468. It would appear that Howard had balanced the likelihood of holding onto his gains in the long run against how much he could benefit through an accommodation with Latimer.[28]

Some victims in the conflict seem to have been more unfortunate than others. In part this was undoubtedly due to the extent to which they were identified with the Lancastrian or Yorkist regimes. Yet in some instances there also appears to have been a personal dimension. The treatment that Sir Thomas Tresham received during the 1460s at the hands of his former opponents seemed to have a direct bearing on his subsequent decision making in 1470–1.[29] Tresham had entered royal service by the late 1440s. During the 1450s he was increasingly associated with the court. He was even cited as one of those responsible for the first battle of St Albans in 1455, although he was not one of the eventual scapegoats. Nevertheless, during the increasingly unstable years of the decade he was still able to rise in royal service and by 1459–60 had become controller of the household. In 1459 he was also elected speaker of the commons in parliament and presided over the act of attainder which convicted York and his allies. He also profited personally from the redistribution of patronage. It is perhaps unsurprising that Tresham was attainted in 1461.[30] His own lands and the dower lands of his wife were taken into Yorkist hands and redistributed to their own supporters. His

Northamptonshire lands went primarily to John Donne, an usher of the chamber, although the Hastings family also profited. Ralph Hastings, esquire of the body, obtained a number of parcels of land in Buckinghamshire and Northamptonshire. Tresham's prominent Yorkist stepfather Sir William Pecche displayed a singular lack of interest in assisting his reconciliation to the Yorkist regime. Pecche was one of Edward IV's carvers, and as one of the King's closest body servants, ideally positioned to help his stepson. Yet there is no evidence to suggest he did.[31]

A general pardon in 1464 enabled Tresham to begin the process of re-purchasing his former property but it was a slow and expensive business. His petition to parliament in 1467 for restoration emphasized his new-found loyalty to Edward IV in contrast to other Lancastrians. If it is to be believed, he spent over 2,000 marks in the attempt, something which he would only have been able to do with the assistance of loans from others. Although it received royal assent Tresham still became embroiled in Lancastrian intrigue and was imprisoned in November 1468. Nevertheless, to add to his difficulties the escheator of Norfolk entered his lands and took away numerous goods and chattels. Word went around political society in East Anglia and even further afield that Tresham's 'livelihood . . . is given away by the King'. In particular, Tresham's deeds and documents were seized. For some reason he was not liked by the regime and it looks as if he was, in fact, being victimized by unnamed individuals. Although subsequently released, once again Tresham's personal circumstances were extremely uncertain. He began proceedings to recover his property and while he made some progress, political events overtook the legal process. Possibly serving as speaker of the commons in parliament in 1470–1, he was probably instrumental in overturning the Lancastrian attainders. Tresham inevitably came to the conclusion that supporting the restored regime of Henry VI and fighting for Queen Margaret at Tewkesbury in May 1471 were the best ways of completing the recovery of his former prosperity and maintaining his position within local society. He paid for that decision with his life.[32]

Defending family and protecting estates and inheritances from predatory attacks were always going to be relevant judgements within the decision frames of those contemplating taking up arms or struggling with the consequences of finding themselves on the losing side. The relative anguish experienced by some individuals was perhaps determined by the strength of an association with a particular place. Whatever their emotional attachments to one or more places, gentry at all levels of the social spectrum would have been concerned about the potential damage to the current and future prospects of their immediate family if they ended up on the losing side. There would have been a need to balance one likelihood against another. Their aversion to taking risks influenced their preference ordering of the available responses and the eventual choice that was made.[33]

The practical effect of death, attainder and forfeiture for leading gentry caught on the losing side varied considerably. Many were very much aware of what could happen to them if they chose to take sides. Nor would this fact have been lost on their friends, family and neighbours. Evidence of the impact of these considerations can also be found in surviving wills of the period, which display an underlying anxiety about events. Sir William Tyrell of Beeches in Rawreth in Essex, who fought for the Lancastrians at Barnet, perhaps under the earl of Oxford, drew up a will shortly before the battle seeking to make appropriate provision for his family. It is no surprise that in the wake of deaths in battle some widows remarried men who were likely to help protect the family patrimony. William Fielding's widow subsequently married the royal justice, Richard Neel. At least one reason for this must have been the legal expertise he could bring to the inevitable legal challenges to the family's landholdings.[34]

Sir Thomas Harrington's reaction in 1459 bears all the hallmarks of somebody aware of what was about to happen. Harrington, a retainer of Richard Neville, earl of Salisbury, and member of his comital council, could see the threat of war looming and decided to entrust his lands to a group of trustees, all of whom were men of opposing political loyalties. Harrington had been among those summoned by the earl in November 1458. He was 'sente for to come to Myddleham to Erle of Sarisburie – and there ate that time it was concludid by the said erle and al hys hole counsel that hee and all suche other men of worshipp as (then met) sholde take ful parties with ye ful noble prince the duke of Yorke'. Harrington was clearly hedging his bets should anything happen to him on the battlefield.[35]

The death of the head of the family or principal heir could result in a number of unwelcome consequences. The widow could become prey to unscrupulous suitors, the children disinherited. Considerations like these could become matters of crucial importance at any moment in time. They had the power to stop an individual participating when first called upon or possibly the moment a cause seemed lost. The reference point in the decision frame would now shift and the relative weighting given to choices alter. The increased risk aversion is evident in the actions of the long-standing Lancastrian servant and war veteran Sir John Scudamore of Bredwardine in Herefordshire during the early stages of the Wars of the Roses. Shortly after his defeat at the battle of Mortimer's Cross in February 1461, Henry VI's half-brother and die-hard supporter Jasper Tudor earl of Pembroke, had retreated to his Pembrokeshire estates in south Wales where he sought to rally remaining support. Letters were sent to key servants at the strongholds of Pembroke, Denbigh and Harlech, urging them to resist the Yorkist forces commanded by Lords Herbert and Ferrers of Chartley. Despite Tudor's pleas, Scudamore delivered up Pembroke Castle after token resistance on 30 September 1461.[36]

Like many of his contemporaries who were faced with a similar situation, Scudamore's decision to surrender Pembroke Castle appears to have rested to a large extent on the desire to protect his family's safety. His decision frame undoubtedly incorporated those judgements that had formed in the wake of the recent Lancastrian defeats and which now exposed his family's vulnerability. He had received a written pledge from Herbert and Ferrers stating that his life would be spared and his estates would not be seized. They both promised to speak to the king on his behalf. In his mind Scudamore had imagined the potential outcomes and impact upon his family. These had subsequently affected his decision. In the event, the promises of Herbert and Ferrers had proven empty. A bill of attainder was brought into parliament. This failed to pass, but towards the end of this parliament his estates were seized by royal ordinance instead. Scudamore was allowed to retain his life and his goods but he was effectively consigned to a political and financial limbo. Scudamore's lands in Herefordshire and the Welsh Marches were eventually granted to Lord Herbert's brother, Sir Richard Herbert. This sense of simmering resentment remained with Scudamore for the remainder of the 1460s. It is perhaps unsurprising that he was one of a small group of gentry appointed to the commission of the peace in Herefordshire during the Readeption of Henry VI. There is no evidence that he fought at the battle of Tewkesbury, but in common with other former Yorkist opponents he made his peace with Edward IV. It was only in the parliament of 1472–3 that Scudamore felt able to petition for their return. Even then he did not secure the immediate return of his property. In 1475 his lands were granted to John Herle and Margaret, late wife of Sir Richard Herbert.[37]

Issues surrounding a family's inheritance could, and did, create a disgruntled constituency of gentry families and could lead to dispossessed opponents or their children to assume arms at a later date when these private concerns showed no signs of being satisfactorily resolved. A number of instances between 1461 and 1471 naturally involved former Lancastrians and their heirs. The experiences of some of the leading gentry who had fought with the Lancastrian army after their decisive defeat at Towton in March 1461 serve to highlight just how fickle fate could be. Much depended on how they were regarded by the new Yorkist regime and the nature of their own contacts within the new governing elite. These were the relevant cues which helped them to form judgements and ultimately shaped their choices. Somebody who subsequently displayed sufficient public remorse at his actions was more likely to benefit from a favourable response to a petition than somebody who appeared to simply go through the motions.

The effects of the 'sins of the father being visited upon the son' are particularly visible in the experiences and actions of George Brown. Brown had found himself pushed to the political sidelines during the 1460s, primarily as a consequence of the actions of his Lancastrian father, Sir Thomas, who had been executed for his role in the defence of the Tower of London in 1460. Sir Thomas was already unpopular within Yorkist circles and had clashed in the past with the duke of

York. By prolonging the siege of the Tower of London and supposedly firing upon the city's inhabitants, he effectively sealed his own fate while handing the Yorkists a propaganda coup in the capital. An attempted breakout failed and Thomas, Lord Scales, was killed in the process. When Sir John Wenlock succeeded in entering the Tower, Brown was captured and brought to trial. Along with some of his men, former servants of the duke of Exeter, he was condemned at the Guildhall and executed at Tyburn.[38]

Memories of what happened to his father must have exerted a considerable impact upon Brown, resurfacing when he sought reconciliation with Edward IV. In his 1472 parliamentary petition he remembered the 'grete malice of dyvers his [i.e. Sir Thomas's] ennemyes and evell willers'. Indeed, in the wake of his death, Sir Thomas's enemies quickly swooped in to seize his property and possessions. Prominent among these was the Yorkist, Thomas Vaughan.[39] At first Vaughan had appeared to act as protector of Sir Thomas's widow, Eleanor, and her children. Together they offered £1,000 for the goods and chattels of Sir Thomas. Shortly afterwards they were granted his lands for another £1,000 with the intention that the lands would be divided between Brown's sons. Inevitably, Vaughan married Eleanor, but the sons found themselves excluded from their inheritance and left in limbo. Vaughan and Eleanor were granted their estates to hold jointly for term of their lives.[40] Vaughan was able to hold onto the lands even after Eleanor's death, which occurred sometime between 1466 and 1472. There are indications that relations between stepfather and one of his stepsons, George, were not good and that Brown took matters into his own hands in order to secure their recovery. It was not until the 1472 parliament that George Brown was able to successfully petition for all the judgements against his father to be reversed.[41]

Keeping lands within a family, albeit with a stepfather in control, was clearly not a guarantee of long-term peace and prompted some men to resume arms at a later date. In fact, George Brown's troubled relationship with his stepfather and his inability to secure his landed inheritance appeared to be the catalyst in ensuring that he first came out in support of Warwick and Clarence against Edward IV in 1469–70, and then Henry VI in 1470–1. The precise role that he played during the Readeption is uncertain. He served on the Lancastrian commission of the peace in Kent but clearly watched the political and strategic situation closely. When the commissioners of array started to gather men of serviceable age in anticipation of armed confrontation, Brown saw this as an opportune moment and opted to join the duke of Clarence. Whether Brown had exploited Clarence's links in Kent through the latter's lordship of Milton and Marden is unclear. In the event, Brown accompanied the Kentish forces and was knighted on the eve of the battle of Tewkesbury.

Brown had apparently seen which way the wind was blowing during early spring of 1471. He preferred a more proactive approach to the impending crisis rather than waiting quietly on the sidelines for matters to sort themselves out. At the back of his mind appears to have been the question of how to recover his family's inheritance. He had seen how the Yorkists had treated his father and, while he does not appear to have been a committed Lancastrian in the same sense as his father, he could see the potential benefits of supporting the Lancastrian cause. Equally, however, he could also see the right moment to abandon that cause, and when Clarence chose to abandon Warwick, Brown followed suit. In doing so, he opened the way back into royal favour and once he had secured that favour, he was prepared to commit himself to the House of York. By 1479 it was reported in Paston correspondence that Sir George Brown was sleeping in the king's chamber.[42]

## DESTABILIZING EFFECTS ON LOCAL SOCIETY

Demonstrating support for one side or the other could lead to a number of unwelcome consequences for local society in general and especially for individuals. The leading gentry were aware that fresh grievances might be generated or old disputes revived within their local communities. They formed judgements around these eventualities within the context of their particular environments. Potential reprisals might include local intimidation, attacks on private property or malicious prosecutions in the law courts. That these concerns were not without foundation is shown in the suits brought into chancery during the course of the 1460s which complained about the vindictiveness of some individuals like Sir William Plumpton. Plumpton experienced difficulties during this decade because of his support for the Lancastrian cause on the battlefield right up until the Lancastrian defeat at Towton in 1461. Kirby sees him as unusual among the Yorkshire gentry for the degree of support he was prepared to give to the Lancastrian cause. Sir William's son and heir, William, had met his death at Towton in 1461 fighting for the Lancastrians. Sir William, Senior, sensibly opted for self-preservation, but the results were mixed. He entered into a recognizance for £2,000 for his good behaviour but was unable to raise the sum. As a consequence he found himself confined to the Tower of London. It was not until 1462 that he obtained a pardon but he was required to remain in London. Moreover, his dispute with Henry Pierpoint rumbled on and made him vulnerable to attack from those with a grievance against him. This is precisely what happened in 1463 when he was accused of treason. Although tried and acquitted, he made a pragmatic decision and sought the lordship and protection of Warwick, and became the earl's deputy at Knaresborough until his ill-judged support for the Readeption regime in 1470-1 cost him his office.[43]

Of course, men like Plumpton who found themselves in difficulty were not beyond engaging in intimidation. He does not appear to have been averse to the risks involved. In the wake of the battles of Wakefield and Towton, Robert Percy of Scotton in Yorkshire claimed in chancery that he was the object of Sir William Plumpton's venom. Percy was one of a handful of Neville of Middleham retainers in the Duchy of Lancaster lordship of Knaresborough, which brought him to the attention of Plumpton. Despite Plumpton's Percy and Lancastrian affiliations, he was prepared to take out his anger and frustration on Robert Percy.[44]

Some degree of retribution, victimization or intimidation was, in fact, a potential risk for anybody who had ended up on the losing side in a battle or simply shown too strong a preference for one party. This consideration had presumably been incorporated into their framing processes. Sir Thomas Malory found himself imprisoned during the late 1460s as a consequence of his association with Warwick. He was excluded from the pardon issued by Edward IV in 1470 and it seems likely that he was only released when Warwick was able to seize power in the name of Henry VI during the autumn of 1470. Various political prisoners are known to have been released at about this time. Malory presumably prospered briefly thereafter, and was buried in the fashionable Greyfriars at Newgate.[45]

Undermining effects on local society are evident in a number of instances after the Lancastrian defeats at Barnet and Tewkesbury in 1471. After the battle of Barnet, Sir James Lee of Aston in Staffordshire found himself on the receiving end of malicious litigation. Lee had probably been recruited into the earl of Warwick's forces shortly before the latter left Coventry for London in April 1471.[46] Lee came from a respectable background. His father, William Lee, had been a successful lawyer and had settled in Staffordshire where he had purchased Aston manor. He had also been closely associated with the Delves and Audley families, and in the context of 1471 and the Readeption regime of Henry VI, it was probably these particular connections that prompted his son to respond positively. It is likely that James Lee was knighted on the eve of the battle. He later claimed that he was the victim of a malicious prosecution which was accepted by the crown, which valued stability over instability, and all process against him stopped on 21 June 1472.[47]

Similarly, Sir John Guildford of Rolvenden in Kent did not appear to participate in the Wars of the Roses battles yet found himself a victim of retribution. Guildford had been Warwick's lieutenant of Dover Castle from 1465–70 and possibly his man of affairs in the shire.[48] Despite an apparent closeness to the earl, there is no evidence to suggest he took up arms at all during the political and military crises of 1470–1. His personal and emotional connections were apparently much weaker than those that tied the Richmondshire gentry to the Nevilles of Middleham. He avoided participation at Barnet and Tewkesbury and was conspicuously quiet when Thomas Neville, bastard of Fauconberg, raised rebellion in Kent in May 1471. In fact, he acted quickly to obtain a general pardon in the wake of the rebellion's collapse, which suggests his principal concern was seeking reconciliation with the regime and avoiding any unfavourable repercussions.[49]

His association with the earl of Warwick during the 1460s and with the restored regime of Henry VI during 1470–1 was enough to earn him the personal enmity of certain unspecified individuals. In the wake of Edward IV's restoration and Fauconberg's rebellion he found himself the victim of a malicious suit at the hands of one Petronilla Standish of Bedfordshire. This was apparently initiated shortly after the Barnet and Tewkesbury campaign and one of Guildford's co-defendants, Sir John Plummer, had also been linked to Warwick and had served the Readeption regime in London as keeper of the great wardrobe. There is a definite hint that somebody was taking the opportunity to settle a score now that Guildford and Plummer were politically vulnerable.[50]

Not only could the gentry elite find itself divided by the actions of a few, the introduction of newcomers into local society added further complications to the maintenance of local stability, especially when they had benefitted from forfeited estates or the misfortune of local families. Newcomers were normally absorbed into the local network of families over the course of successive generations. The marriage of Thomas Vaughan to Eleanor Brown might have been accepted in the longer term if it was not for his treatment of the rights of George Brown and his brothers. Although an accommodation was subsequently reached during the 1470s, George Brown was forced to shift his interests into neighbouring Surrey. His own restoration to favour apparently came with a personal price. Not surprisingly, Vaughan was judged by Edward IV to be the more important man of the two.[51]

Royal attitudes towards newly located supporters also reinforced negative signals to traditional gentry within a locality. This formed a significant local cue, or signal, within their framing processes. After Richard III's usurpation in 1483 Sir John Fogge found himself faced with a dilemma. Fogge had been one of Edward IV's principal servants in Kent and Richard had initially sought to court his favour. Unfortunately for Fogge, Sir Ralph Ashton, one of Richard III's leading servants, had married Elizabeth, widow of Sir Thomas Kyriell.[52] It had quickly brought Ashton and Fogge into conflict. Fogge's first wife had been Alice Kyriell, co-heiress of Sir Thomas Kyriell and niece of John and Elizabeth Kyriell. The Ashton–Fogge dispute seems to have arisen from Fogge's role as a feoffee for John Kyriell. Kyriell had settled his manors of Westenhanger, Great Mongeham and Walmer on Elizabeth for life. Fogge, however, had refused to hand over the deeds to Elizabeth and Ashton. Richard intervened on Ashton's behalf by pressuring the prior of Christ Church in Canterbury to surrender the documents that Fogge had placed in his keeping. Fogge and the prior had little choice but to comply.

Fogge clearly harboured a grievance over his treatment in this incident. Yet it is likely that by this stage Fogge was already unhappy with the influence being exerted by Ashton and others in his immediate sphere of local influence. Their presence formed a direct challenge to his traditional authority and can be regarded as an environmental cue that had much greater significance for him than most other gentry within the shire. This was probably aggravated by Ashton's personality. As one scholar has suggested, he had earned himself 'an unenviable reputation for severity'. Legend has it that Ashton, known as the Black Knight because of his armour, liked to indulge in violent and cruel behaviour to prisoners. A contemporary rhyme circulating at the time ran 'Save us from the axe of the Tower (of London), And from Sir Ralph of Assheton'. Ashton appeared to have a hard reputation and a personality that could only upset the established gentry of Kent.[53]

Another instance of the mixed political blessings of marriage at about the same moment in time in Kent is provided by William Malyverer who had married Joan, the widow of William Langley of Knolton, near Sandwich. Malyverer, from a leading Yorkshire family, went one stage further than Ashton, though, by seizing custody of William Langley's heir, John, and taking control of his lands. This brought him into conflict with another major Kentish family, the Guildfords. After William Langley died on 20 February 1483, Richard Guildford occupied Langley's lands because of his appointment as John Langley's guardian. Guildford held the lands until the following All Hallows, that is, 1 November. He was then expelled by Malyverer who continued in possession until 30 August 1485.[54] If this chronology is true, the seizure took place the day before Buckingham was executed and at a time when local conditions were clearly not favouring the Guildfords. Malyverer probably took advantage of the general confusion and disgrace of the Guildfords to secure possession of the lands. It has been suggested that he was acting in his capacity as county escheator. This could only be the case if he had taken control of the property after his appointment on 6 November 1483, but the inquisition states that Guildford held the property until All Hallows. Malyverer must have seized the property after his marriage in the hope that he could get away with it.[55]

Similarly, the dispute in the West Country between Sir John Arundel of Lanherne in Cornwall and the Ricardian Sir James Tyrell caused significant local disruption at a time of considerable political tension. These local cues were of particular relevance to Arundel. Elizabeth, Arundel's daughter by his first marriage, had married Tyrell. Arundel's second marriage, however, produced a son and five daughters, one of whom had married Giles Daubeney. This brought Daubeney into conflict with Tyrell. On the surface this seemed a relatively minor dispute, but it had potentially far-reaching consequences. Arundel's son Thomas had inherited significant estates in Devon and Cornwall from the de la Poles and Morleys. These were claimed by Elizabeth and Tyrell. The accession of Richard III and Arundel's backing of the 1483 rebellion brought these lands to Tyrell through a settlement confirmed in parliament. That could well have acted as a contribut-ing factor for Arundel's rebellion and subsequent support of Henry VII.[56]

The effect of Richard III's supporters' high-handed treatment of gentry across the south of England before and after Buckingham's rebellion was obvious. In the normal course of events parvenus were normally absorbed into local society. This was not the case following Richard III's treatment of the gentry who had supported the rebellion. The ill-will that was already gathering a head of steam before the rebellion remained bubbling under the surface thereafter. It had dis-torted the local environment and forced the gentry to adopt non-compensatory strategies based on limited evidence to cope with their altered circumstances. Indeed, Richard created a significant constituency, many attached to the previous regime, who had a vested interest in obtaining the restoration of their estates. This ill-feeling was compounded further by his policy of planting members of his northern affinity in south-east England because of his fundamental lack of trust. The scale on which this happened generated even greater acrimony, which was related by contemporary chroniclers. According to the *Crowland Chronicle*, Richard distributed the forfeited lands 'amongst his northerners whom he had planted in every part of his dominions, to the shame of all the southern people who murmured ceaselessly and longed more each day for the return of their old lords in the place of the tyranny of the present ones'.[57]

Some of Richard's senior retainers had moved into Kentish society and appeared to alienate the local gentry very quickly. Richard used eight men in Kent, all drawn from a tightly knit group of northern gentry: Sir Ralph Ashton, Robert Brackenbury, Sir Edward Stanley, Sir William Harrington, Sir John Savage, Sir Marmaduke Constable, Sir Ralph Bigod and William Malyverer. Ashton quickly became the most significant based on his recently acquired interests.[58] Richard's other northern associates did not have any Kentish interests, however. Instead, they were granted rebel lands, custody of royal lands and crown offices. At first it looked as if Sir Marmaduke Constable, a knight of the body, would become Ashton's local deputy. Between December 1483 and January 1484 he was made steward and constable of Tonbridge Castle, and given control of the honour of Tonbridge and the Stafford lordships of Penshurst, Brasted, Hadlow and Ealding.[59] However, by March 1484 it was clear that Robert Brackenbury of Selaby in Durham, an esquire of the body, had been designated Ashton's principal colleague.[60] In March 1484 he was granted the receivership of the lordships of Tonbridge, Hadlow, Penshurst, Milton and Marden, and lands forfeited by Earl Rivers, Walter Roberts and the Cheynes;[61] in May 1484 he was appointed surveyor of Tonbridge, Hadlow and Penshurst;[62] and in January 1485, as a knight of the body, he was made constable of Tonbridge Castle.[63] Brackenbury was also appointed steward of the archbishop of Canterbury's lands during 1484.[64]

After Ashton and Brackenbury had received sizeable grants of royal patronage in Kent, Richard was only able to give his other followers a modest landed stake in the county. Sir William Harrington, king's servant and royal annuitant, acquired John Darell's manor of Calehill;[65] Sir John Savage, knight of the body, was granted John Pympe's manor of Nettlestead and the marriage and custody of the lands of Thomas Culpeper, son of Richard Culpeper;[66] Sir Edward Stanley was granted Sir John Guildford's manor of Rolvenden; and William Malyverer was granted some lands forfeited by Sir John Fogge. He was also commissioned to receive the issues from some of Sir George's Brown's lands.[67]

Political bias aside, the *Crowland Chronicle* reflects what mattered at a local level. Not only had some of the leading members of the gentry been forced from their lands and offices, they saw complete strangers wielding considerable influence and power in their own communities. The gentry understood the importance of local stability. Yet actions like this directly undermined that. It would hardly be a surprise that those affected would maintain a grudge against the current regime and the principal beneficiaries of their misfortune. Moreover, this constituency was in the east of Kent where gentry influence was at its strongest and most independent.

## CONCLUSIONS

This chapter has shown that the framing process of the leading gentry could be based on more than service considerations alone. The leading men within the regions and localities were quite clearly influenced by considerations that stemmed directly from the social environments in which they conducted their daily lives and transacted their personal business. The extent to which these factors impacted upon their decision frames depended in large measure on their individual circumstances. The leading gentry in service relationships, who exercised public or seigneurial authority, were likely to have drawn upon both in the creation of their decision frames. Furthermore, the extent to which cues from the private domain influenced the formation of judgements and any subsequent decisions probably depended on the connection they felt to their locality.

On the other hand, those who had not entered into direct service relationships or shunned public service in local administration in all probability placed more weight upon cues within their immediate social environments, creating quite different decision-frames as a result. Nevertheless, disruption to their immediate environments offered the potential for sudden behavioural changes and could exert a profound influence upon the leading gentry. A strategic shift in an area or the outbreak of rebellion could alter the relative importance of particular factors that governed the operation of social networks and relationships, which might in turn prompt a change to a decision-making strategy. Leading gentry might find themselves forced to take up arms, albeit unwillingly. Where there was no pressure exerted upon the leading gentry, the core elements of the decision frame were likely to have remained much more stable. The fear for the safety of family, along with the long-term survival of family lineage and inheritance, could prompt powerful, but contradictory, responses in leading gentry. These sorts of concerns influenced those who engaged in the political and administrative realm as well as those who avoided entering the public domain. Nevertheless, some were spurred into action; others continued to hang back in the hope that action would prove unnecessary. It is unlikely that any leading gentry, other than those on the most extreme fringes of the kingdom, found themselves completely immune to these considerations. For the majority it would appear that local and regional environmental factors rather than service considerations occupied the dominant position in their decision-making process.

# 7

# The Personal Domain:
## Contradictory Responses to Conflict

## INTRODUCTION

A model of human behaviour can make a significant contribution to our understanding of the decision-making process. As we have already seen, gentry decision making was the result of judgements that were formed on the basis of cues from different environments. For some the more powerful determining factors arose from professional service within the public domain, either to the crown or to the nobility; for others, especially those who shied away from any form of public service, cues from the local environment were more relevant. Nevertheless, although there is much to recommend an approach that structures the cognitive process, thereby allowing us to identify the relevant cues and judgements that underpinned eventual choices, no model is perfect. Even advocates of Prospect Theory, which has formed the framework for analysis in this book, have acknowledged that their own more flexible approach has limitations.

In Chapter 3 we saw that there were two principal drawbacks. The first concerned the biasing mechanisms that affect people's judgements and choices. People are poor at predicting how they will react to future events, as well as recollecting how they felt about events in the past. In fact, social scientists have shown that people are particularly prone to reshaping previous experiences in a way that they find more acceptable and which allow them to justify their actions in the present. The second shortcoming, building on the distorting effects of memory and recollection, is the impact of emotion. In recent decades an increasing number of social scientists have started to recognize the link between emotion and decision making. In particular, they have identified the emotional markers that people place on events which can affect subsequent choices. However, they remain uncertain about how strong the cognitive distortion on the decision-maker's frame is and acknowledge that evidence is still being gathered.[1]

Whereas in the two preceding chapters we were able to ground many aspects of decision making in the cues found in public and private domains, the discussion in this chapter will focus on those leading gentry whose reactions were not necessarily straightforward to identify or explain. The length of time that has elapsed since the Wars of the Roses can distort the nature of the surviving evidence, while any interpretation of the distorting effects of memory or emotion upon the leading gentry can be problematic. Consequently, it is not always possible to reconcile this evidence with their basic decision-framing process. At the same time, it reminds us that no model of behaviour can effectively account or explain every action, particularly volatile and unpredictable variables.[2] Where gentry experienced ambiguous circumstances, their behaviour appeared to reflect their personal uncertainties. These men might have found themselves being asked to make a decision at short notice, or perhaps found themselves in volatile, unstable or unpredictable situations. Such instances are to be found primarily where the leading gentry had to consider whether they would provide initial or continuing support to either side. In some cases in the following discussion it will prove necessary to examine certain situations that appeared in earlier chapters from the perspective of different individuals.

## THE AMBIGUITY OF CHOICE

The ambiguous nature of some gentry choices arises in particular instances because we cannot be absolutely confident about their cognitive processes at key moments in time. This is due, in turn, to uncertainties about the extent of the information they had access to which formed the basis of their judgements and attitudes. The evidence is not strong enough to draw firm conclusions about its emotional impact on individuals. There was probably a significant amount of readily available information, perhaps more than we can truly appreciate. It is certainly known and accepted that details about events, past and present, circulated throughout the country. Communal memory preserved details about local stories and figures. Accounts of deeds of arms and of individual reputations acquired in warfare, stories of past conflicts, military campaigns and personal experiences would have circulated within local communities and no doubt remained part of their oral traditions. These would have included the experiences of men like Thomas Hostelle, a soldier who had loyally served the Lancastrian dynasty in the French Wars. In a petition to Henry VI for financial assistance he described a gruesome list of wounds he had received: at Harfleur he had served Henry V and was blinded in one eye by a crossbow bolt; he then fought at Agincourt, where he suffered a smashed hand and a crushed body.[3] It is probable that the story of John Cattys would also have circulated locally. Cattys was a gentleman of Mereworth in Kent who fought at the battle of Towton in 1461, probably in the retinue of Edward Neville, Lord Abergavenny. Cattys had been left for dead on the battlefield but had somehow managed to work his way back home, and his tribulations were later acknowledged by the grant of an annuity by the crown.[4]

These accounts would have been especially pertinent where they concerned families from those areas and where they were subsequently preserved down the generations. In one instance the Tudor chronicler John Leland related details of the dispute between William, Lord Hastings, and Lord Roos, in which the former attacked Belvoir Castle and took the lead from the roofs of his own residence at Ashby de la Zouche. Local reputations were also remembered within communities. Elsewhere Leland had clearly picked up on a story that related to Sir Richard Frogenhale of Teynham in Kent, who had a distinguished career in Lancastrian Normandy. He remarked that 'of this very auncient house was a knight that did great feates in France'.[5]

Contemporary chroniclers also incorporated reports of battles, along with the deeds and actions of some of the leading participants, into their own works, allowing a much wider audience to become familiar with current events and issues. Some stories were told and retold, like the exploits of Sir Thomas Colville in France, which were drawn upon by the leading fourteenth-century chroniclers.[6] Chroniclers compiled accounts for men who fought in battles, and in some instances heard first-hand accounts of what had transpired. Froissart recorded that he met and spoke with various English and Scottish knights who were able to provide him with details of what happened at Otterburn in 1388.[7]

It was news of current events, however, which were of more immediate importance to the leading gentry during the Wars of the Roses and most likely to influence their responses. After the second battle of St Albans in February 1461 it was reported by the Burgundian soldier and diplomat Jean Waurin that the veteran military campaigner Sir Thomas Kyriell had lamented what a terrible event had come to pass when the young Lancastrian Prince Edward passed the sentence of death on him and William, Lord Bonville. Kyriell and Bonville had remained to protect Henry VI despite knowing the Yorkists were heading for defeat. In a similar manner to Froissart, Waurin possibly came into contact with Kentishmen who had witnessed the events or heard the rumours circulated by some of Kyriell's Kentish friends. An opinion attributed to Kyriell is likely to have carried some weight among the local gentry and those who were aware of his military and chivalric reputation.[8]

During the Wars of the Roses news of battles and other noteworthy events spread much quicker than we might think. News of the outcome of Wakefield reached London 3 days after it was fought; news of Towton 5 days later; and Barnet, unsurprisingly, reached London the following day. False rumours might also be spread, feeding local paranoia like those in Norfolk after the battle of Tewkesbury when it was reported that Henry VI had been victorious.[9] Each side disseminated details in a number of ways. Series of messenger relays were able to pass news which would also have been picked up by local communities and distributed across the region. After the battles of Towton, Losecote Field and

Tewkesbury the victorious Yorkists sent out newsletters across the country. The use of the proclamation sent to sheriffs and justices of the peace was another vital tool used by both sides. The news of the Yorkist victory at Towton was declared at Paul's Cross on the day it was actually confirmed in London.[10]

The limitations identified within our model of behaviour, however, mean that it cannot identify how gentry reacted to news of events; nor can it offer significant clarity to their reactions when placed on the spot. While the model enables us to see that it was part of the judgement-forming process, it does not determine to what extent it shaped their reactions. A non-compensatory strategy can explain the process by which people make decisions based on limited information, but it does not necessarily explain how the strategy copes in sudden, volatile circumstances.[11] When commissioners of array approached the gentry the latter were placed in potentially confusing and contradictory situations, particularly when they were faced by rival commissions. Commissions of array were used extensively during the upheavals of 1469, 1470 and 1471. Edward IV sought to employ them against the earl of Warwick and duke of Clarence during the months of March, April and May 1470. Between December 1470 and March 1471, when an invasion by Edward IV was expected, Warwick and the Readeption government issued them to its supporters. The system gradually became hamstrung, though, as individuals declined to attend or come forward. It was no doubt perceived in certain quarters as a system of compulsion. One writer alleged that when the earl of Warwick could not raise the people through their goodwill 'he straitly charged them to come forth upon pain of death'.[12]

In the manoeuvring that occurred before the battles of Barnet and Tewkesbury in April and May 1471, Yorkist and Lancastrian commissioners undoubtedly employed a combination of subtle persuasion and direct pressure on local gentry.[13] The *Arrivall* remarked that messengers were despatched across the West Country, 'sent alabout in Somersetshere, Dorsetshire, and part of Wiltshere, for to arredy and arays the people by a certeyne day, suche, algats, as the sayde lords, and theyr partakers, afore that had greatly laboryd to that entent'.[14] Numerous letters were also despatched seeking support in these regions and personal appeals were no doubt made when the opportunity arose. One such letter has survived – to John Daunt of Wotton-under-Edge in Gloucestershire from Prince Edward, dated 14 April, the very day on which Queen Margaret and her son landed at Weymouth.[15]

It is extremely rare to find evidence that offers insights into the thought processes and feelings evoked in an emotionally charged situation like this. However, we are afforded a better glimpse of cognitive processes where persuasion was exerted when the Yorkshire gentry were asked to serve in France in 1421. The leading gentry were clearly placed on the spot and asked to justify their positions by the two royally appointed commissioners Anthony St Quentin and

Robert Waterton. Their individual responses were carefully summarized by the commissioners, who were concerned to be accurate in the event that they were required to explain their report. The gentry obviously felt a need to come up with a reason. Some pleaded illness and infirmity; others the financial difficulties they had already incurred or would have to incur if they served; some pointed to the fact that they were already supporting kinsmen fighting for the king; while a few referred to prior obligations that demanded their attention. In only a very few instances did they attempt to show willingness by offering to provide substitutes. Some reasons were undoubtedly more genuine than others. Thomas Constable seemed to be playing for time when he explained that he first needed to discharge his responsibilities as executor of his mother's will. Perhaps with a hint of relief, though, Sir John Bigod explained that he had been excused service by the royal council in order to discharge his account as sheriff.[16]

This document also demonstrates that a particular instance of behaviour could be justified in a number of ways. However, our model would struggle to identify the individual feelings and emotions that underpinned each justification. In fact, the relationship between emotions and the eventual act can only be inferred by medieval historians. It is often unclear what other factors were influencing individual gentry decision-frames. This phenomenon surfaces during the Wars of the Roses when East Anglian gentry were placed on the spot after the battle of Towton in 1461. Three men responded in the same way, but in all likelihood they had very different motives for doing so. The Norfolk knight Sir Miles Stapleton, part of the duke of Suffolk's connection in the early 1450s, agreed to send men to Edward IV's army being gathered for the pursuit of the retreating Lancastrians, without attending in person. Stapleton thereby avoided committing himself too closely to the Yorkist cause just in case events favoured the Lancastrians. In contrast with Stapleton's apparent juggling of circumstances was John Paston I, who also sent men to Edward IV. Paston was locked in a dispute with Stapleton, who had recently questioned Paston's family's gentle status. Paston therefore attempted to match his antagonist by sending some of his own household men to serve with the duke of Norfolk's contingent.[17] Meanwhile, a third individual, Sir William Calthorpe of Burnham Thorpe in Norfolk, perhaps found it prudent in 1461 to join the king's army marching northwards and to cultivate the favour of his brother-in-law Edmund Grey, earl of Kent, one of the new king's supporters among the peerage.[18]

Moreover, explaining gentry involvement in terms of the emotions based upon the identification of one or two dominant factors runs the risk of oversimplifing quite complex and confusing sets of circumstances. Sir William Cary of Cockington in Devon could quite conceivably have been influenced by what had happened to his family during the previous decade. His brother, Richard, had died fighting for the Lancastrians at the battle of Wakefield in December 1460.

Meanwhile, Sir William had married Anne, daughter of Sir Baldwin Fulford, who had been executed by the Yorkists in September 1461. His brother-in-law Sir Thomas Fulford was identified as one of the leading Lancastrian adherents soon after Queen Margaret's forces had landed at Weymouth in April 1471. It would not be unreasonable to suggest, therefore, that Cary was influenced by the actions of his kinsman and this, in turn, perhaps prompted him to contact his own close neighbour Sir Sinclair Pomeroy of Berry Pomeroy.[19]

Equally, Sir John Lewknor of West Grinstead might have responded to the Lancastrian cause in 1471 because of chronic indebtedness and pressure from his links within royal circles. Lewknor had served in the royal household and his brother Walter had even served in Queen Margaret's household. He would certainly have been known to other Lancastrian sympathizers including Gervase Clifton. Lewknor had maintained a low profile throughout the conflict. Difficult personal circumstances arising from the long-standing dispute over the inheritance of his wife, Joan Halsham, and some questionable financial dealings with his half-brother Thomas Hoo could have contributed quite easily towards his decision to support the restored regime of Henry VI between 1470 and 1471. His financial position had become increasingly precarious during the 1460s and he was twice outlawed for debt. The example of Lewknor highlights the difficulty in determining the point at which local, environmental cues or emotional responses exerted the greater influence upon reactions. Lewknor obviously had options in 1471, yet for reasons best known to him, he chose to join the Lancastrian cause.[20]

A model like ours based on the principles of Prospect Theory cannot easily identify the subtlety of thought that lay behind a particular decision. Feelings and emotions rarely show through in the surviving evidence. It is possible, for instance, that in 1460 the Paston family was deeply affected by the death of their friend, the veteran soldier and campaigner Sir Osbert Mountford, a member of the Calais garrison and long-standing Lancastrian servant. Towards the end of May 1460, the Yorkist supporter John Dinham had attacked Sandwich, where a Lancastrian relief force destined for Calais was stationed under Mountford's command. Mountford's force was besieged and the victorious Dinham eventually carried the hapless commander back to Calais. He was briefly placed in captivity in Rysbank Tower before being summarily executed. The impact of this event comes across in surviving Paston correspondence. In London John Paston I subsequently resisted the suggestion of his brother Clement that he should join Warwick's muster in late 1460, pleading that personal matters in Norfolk were too unstable to allow him leave. While Paston's reluctance is suggestive of an emotional response, what continues to remain unclear is the extent to which emotions like fear, frustration or anger affected his *eventual* response in 1461 within an overall decision frame.[21]

In very few cases do either the leading gentry or the nobility directly acknowledge emotions. Yet we know that such feelings could cause considerable anguish.
In one instance, though, the fear of an accusation of cowardice is admitted. On
his way to Scotland in 1482 with Richard of Gloucester's forces, William, Lord
Lovell, despatched a letter home in which he expressed fears that if he left the
army he would be regarded as a coward. The dishonour which a refusal to serve
might attract was clearly a cause of some concern to him. Lovell acknowledged
his fear; the majority of individuals did not.[22]

It is perfectly plausible that a spur of the moment decision, resulting from
youthful inexperience, but prompted by mixture of ambition and newly generated Yorkist sympathies, led to the involvement of the young Richard Corbet of
Moreton Corbet in Shropshire in 1471. Corbet had recently married the daughter
of the long-standing Yorkist Walter Devereux, Lord Ferrers. Although his father,
Sir Roger Corbet, had probably supported the Lancastrian cause until the battle
of Towton, Corbet did not allow this to stand in the way of his advancement.[23]
Contrary to the majority of the Shropshire gentry, who had opted to follow the
example of the principal regional magnate, John Talbot, earl of Shrewsbury,
and remain neutral, Richard Corbet, Roger Kynaston and Humphrey Blount
undertook to recruit men on behalf of Edward IV. Corbet's appointment as a
commissioner at such a strategically important moment suggests that there were
few leading gentry willing to come forward.[24]

In fact, it is perhaps also necessary in some cases to admit that certain gentry
felt very little emotion when making a decision to act one way or another. They
might simply have made the decision for the sake of it or because it felt as good as
any other. Medieval historians occasionally identify maverick individuals whose
behaviour they find hard to explain in a conventional way. One Midlands esquire,
Everard Digby, comes across as being very much the opportunist. Digby had
landed interests in Leicestershire, Huntingdonshire and Rutland, and seems to
have been something of a local troublemaker.[25] His bullying tactics had certainly
created some hostility among the local gentry in the region and he had found
himself embroiled in a number of disputes during the 1440s.[26]

By the late 1450s he had become part of the group of Midlands gentry, which
included William Fielding of Leicestershire, who were increasingly associated
with the militant Lancastrian regime. While he had not gained significantly from
royal patronage and was uncommitted to a particular lord, he demonstrated
himself to be an individual who could, and would, commit himself wholeheart-
edly to one side if it suited his purposes.[27] His unpredictability soon surfaced and
attracted the attention of the Yorkists. In November 1460 he allegedly plotted with
100 others at Westminster to murder York and his allies. He was indicted before
the court of king's bench but failed to appear. By this stage he was making his way
northwards where he joined the Lancastrian forces and fought at Wakefield. He

then presumably accompanied the victorious Lancastrian army southwards in early 1461.[28] His movements after the battle of Wakefield remain unclear. After the second battle of St Albans, though, he appears to have been involved with a group of undisciplined Lancastrians who sought to force an entry into the city. However, he subsequently accompanied the retreating forces northwards again before fighting at Towton.[29] He was either killed at the battle of Towton or died from wounds shortly after, for the inquisition into his property gave his date of death as the day after the battle.[30]

The behaviour of William Tailboys of Kyme in Lincolnshire shares certain similarities with Digby's maverick tendencies.[31] Apparently Tailboys did not feel constrained by the attitudes and opinions of his fellow gentry. He had become involved in a violent feud with Ralph, Lord Cromwell, and John Dymoke during the 1440s and 1450s, which is illustrative of the way in which local politics became enmeshed in national politics.[32] Tailboys came from one of the wealthiest Lincolnshire families. He subsequently served as a knight of the shire and a justice of the peace during the 1440s. Moreover, his marriage to a daughter of Lord Bonville connected him to Henry VI's chief minister, William de la Pole, duke of Suffolk. He also enjoyed a good relationship with another court favourite, Viscount Beaumont. Yet Tailboys appears to have been a genuinely violent man, willing to back up his actions by force. In Mackman's opinion his conduct 'placed him outside the normal bounds of gentry society'. Tailboys' campaign of violence and intimidation against his opponents within the shire served to alienate a significant cross section of the Lincolnshire gentry as well as causing concern to the crown.

Perhaps the most extreme example of his behaviour is the account of his attempted murder of Lord Cromwell outside the star chamber at Westminster in 1449. Although the story is probably exaggerated, there was definitely a violent encounter. This would suggest that Tailboys was not an individual who was intimidated by his surroundings or the status of his opponents. In fact, his fortunes revived during the second half of the decade, as the Lancastrian regime was more concerned with bolstering its support among local gentry elites than with making men like him pay for their crimes. The toleration displayed by the Lancastrian government seemingly did little to curb the behaviour of Tailboys. He was attainted in the wake of Towton in 1461 along with a handful of other Lincolnshire gentry. The bulk of his lands were granted to Sir Thomas Burgh, a leading supporter of Edward IV. Tailboys managed to escape to the north with the remnants of the Lancastrian forces, after which he actively participated in military activity in Northumberland. In the winter of 1461–2 he recaptured Alnwick Castle. He finally came unstuck, however, after the battle of Hexham in 1464. Although escaping the carnage, he was caught hiding in a coal pit and beheaded at Newcastle.[33]

## THE COMPLEXITY OF BATTLEFIELD DECISION MAKING

Although we cannot be sure about the actual number of gentry who participated in the battles of the Wars of the Roses, it is worthwhile considering this decision-making environment. It would be fair to suggest that the battlefield constituted a unique, volatile environment where intense emotions and sudden events render the analysis of events by our model of behaviour extremely problematic. While not offering a model of behaviour, Verbruggen's work has gone a long way towards identifying the likely reactions of soldiers on the battlefield. In the process he has also identified certain basic emotions and reactions common to groups of combatants.

Fear and anxiety were natural reactions in the tense period that preceded a battle. Once on the battlefield combatants undoubtedly experienced a rush of adrenaline as fighting commenced and were buoyed up by the feeling of camaraderie with their fellow soldiers. For men-at-arms fighting on foot, being in large formations would have given them a feeling of confidence. Many contemporary chroniclers observed this, including Thomas Gray of Heton in his *Scalachronica*.[34] Indeed, feelings of confidence could be infectious among large groups of men. At the battle of Otterburn the English and the Scots were equally motivated to fight and neither side showed signs of cowardice. The implication is that despite any inner doubts, men were able to overcome them and fight bravely. On occasion this could also result in recklessness. At the battle of Barnet the earl of Oxford's men turned the flank of Lord Hastings. Hastings' troops fled and were pursued by Oxford. When he returned to the field with his men, they were then mistaken for Yorkists and were fired upon.[35]

While many gentry fought bravely in a battle, this does not mean that they were unafraid of the consequences. However, neither a behavioural model like the one used in this book, nor the analysis by Verbruggen, can adequately account displays of gentry courage or fear on the battlefield like that described in the 'Ballard of Bosworth Field', which refers to the courage of both standard bearers: Sir William Brandon, who carried Henry Tudor's, but was cut down when Richard III launched his desperate cavalry charge; and Sir Percival Thirwall, Richard's standard bearer and a member of his household, who would not let the royal standard fall even when his legs were hewn from beneath him.[36]

The unpredictability of the battlefield also means that our model of behaviour cannot always easily identify or explain one-off, isolated factors that might have influenced the decision-making process. Medieval chronicles provide numerous examples of the fear and panic that men felt during a battle and the resulting consequences. Furthermore, experienced and inexperienced alike might fall victim to these feelings. At Otterburn, Froissart relates that Sir Matthew Redman felt that the English cause was lost and fled the battlefield. Somebody associated with

Redman might even have told him this. Unfortunately, he was spotted and hotly pursued by Sir James Lindsay. Redman's horse stumbled and he was forced to turn and fight Lindsay and he acquitted himself well. Froissart, even allowing for the fact that he might have been drawing upon the biased testimony of Lindsay, said that Redman 'tourneyed' well but finally succumbed to exhaustion and yielded.[37] Emotion undoubtedly served to make a decision frame highly volatile and unstable. Yet so many variables could influence behaviour on the battlefield. Even bad weather could amplify feelings of uncertainty and bewilderment. The battle of Towton on 29 March 1461, for instance, was fought in a snow blizzard, while the battle of Barnet was conducted in dense fog on 14 April 1471.[38]

Confidence could quite easily plummet in response to unexpected or unwelcome developments. This was dependent largely on the level of experience of the men concerned. Although his analysis concentrates on groups of men, Verbruggen also notes that more experienced soldiers fought with much greater tenacity in battle. Inexperienced men lacked confidence and were more inclined to panic.[39] This appears to have happened during the Wars of the Roses as well. At the first battle of St Albans in 1455, the Lancastrian forces were completely caught off guard by Warwick's attack in the market square. The forces of the Northumbrian Sir Robert Ogle, drawn from the Anglo-Scottish border regions, burst into the centre of the town causing mayhem. As men rushed to meet the threat, confusion reigned as they scrambled to don their armour and snatch up their weapons. On the one hand, this can be attributed to the unusual circumstances of the engagement; on the other hand, the level of experience of at least part of the Lancastrian forces was low. Many lost heart and commentators named particular individuals, including the baron of the exchequer, Thomas Thorpe. He quickly shed his armour and fled the field of battle. He had subscribed to the military ethos of the gentry but was not prepared for the full experience.[40]

Understanding a battlefield emotion like fear can also be complicated by external perceptions of a particular action and the way in which the evidence is presented. Observers sometimes explain fear as cowardice. Such descriptions are at the mercy of the political bias of the commentator. Sir Philip Wentworth, one of the king's carvers, was accused of cowardice after the first battle of St Albans in 1455. Although settled in East Anglia, he sprang from a prominent Yorkshire family and would have been trained in arms like his contemporaries, although the extent of his own military experience is not known. Wentworth had prospered in royal service and was known to be in regular attendance about the king, along with his fellow carver Sir Richard Tunstall. As the encounter at St Albans turned against the Lancastrians, Wentworth had supposedly deserted the royal banner. This, and the arrow wound received by Henry VI left standing alone beneath it, aroused angry comments in contemporary chronicles. According to Worcester, the duke of Norfolk claimed that Sir Philip Wentworth deserved to be hanged for casting down the 'Kynges standard'. This is perhaps unsurprising, for Wentworth had made enemies in East Anglia, in particular the duke of Norfolk and Sir John Fastolf. However, despite the criticism and the apparent local hostility within certain quarters, Wentworth's subsequent behaviour in support of the Lancastrian monarchy was unaffected. Hostile commentary from political opponents did not appear to affect the behaviour of some leading gentry.[41]

Interpreting sudden, unexpected acts of violence, like the settling of personal grudges, can present similar analytical difficulties. John, Lord Wenlock, reputedly had his brains dashed out by the axe of Edmund Beaufort, titular duke of Somerset, when he failed to support the latter on the battlefield of Tewkesbury. According to Hall, Somerset interpreted Wenlock's behaviour as treason, which may or may not have been true. Similarly, why Wenlock had chosen not to support Somerset at a crucial juncture in the battle is unknown and can only be guessed at.[42] These kinds of impulsive acts were not restricted to the nobility. In the wake of the Lancastrian victory at the second battle of St Albans, it was claimed by Thomas Myrdale that Queen Margaret's trusted servant Robert Whittingham had ordered the murder of his father, John Myrdale, over a debt that he claimed had already been paid.[43]

This same difficulty of interpretation can be seen when attempting to analyse the emotions that somebody felt when they witnessed unwelcome events. The complexity of analysis required is beyond the scope of our model. One particular instance can be found in the reports of the death of Prince Edward at the battle of Tewkesbury in 1471. Despite the questions raised by the lack of evidence, Davies has still suggested that Sir Richard Croft felt uncomfortable about the role he played in the death of the prince. The precise circumstances of Prince Edward's death are unclear although one tradition presented by the Tudor chronicler Hall has suggested that the prince was captured and executed by the Yorkist commanders.[44]

According to Hall, Croft had played a significant part in his capture. Described as a wise and valiant knight, he had supposedly apprehended the prince at the same time as Queen Margaret was found in her carriage fleeing the field. After the battle had ended, Croft brought his prisoner before King Edward. Croft, it was alleged, knew nothing of the king's intentions. The fact that Croft was mentioned could simply be a device designed to lend a veneer of credibility to the idea that the prince was captured and that the former felt uncomfortable about his involvement in his fate. Whether this is true or not, Hall relates that the king struck the prince across the face and then allowed Clarence, Gloucester, Hastings and Sir Thomas Grey to finish the job. Davies argues that however the prince was captured, his death must have caused some embarrassment to Croft in subsequent years. Yet there are no grounds for assuming this affected his subsequent career in any way.[45]

## THE UNCERTAINTY OF CONTINUING PARTICIPATION

In the wake of a battle the majority of ordinary combatants were presumably left to make their own way back to their homes.[46] Yet for those leading gentry who had participated as well as those who had not, the most advisable choices were not always clear-cut. While it seems sensible to acknowledge that in some cases their decision frames had altered and that they had become more risk averse, it is by no means certain how widely this had happened, nor is it always clear how or why such an abrupt shift took place.[47]

Our model of behaviour does not easily explain why some men suddenly lost the stomach for fighting or simply became weary of the sacrifices they had made. A decision like this can be made on the spur of the moment and can perhaps be observed in the behaviour of Richard Woodville, Lord Rivers, and his son, Anthony Woodville. Up until the battle of Towton they had been loyal supporters of the Lancastrian monarchy, and at Towton itself Waurin recorded that Richard Woodville had played a prominent role in the company of Henry Beaufort, duke of Somerset.[48]

The Woodvilles had already experienced mixed fortunes during 1460 and 1461, and their personal outlook must have appeared much bleaker after Towton. Unconfirmed reports of casualties circulated for a considerable period of time after the battle, and Rivers and his son Anthony were both named in contemporary correspondence as being among the slain. Yet, as a later report to Pigello Portinaro, a Milanese merchant residing at Bruges in Flanders, indicates, they had made good their escape after the battle, following Queen Margaret, Henry VI, Somerset, Roos, Exeter and others to Bamburgh Castle in Northumberland. However, when the queen's group made its way into Scotland the Woodvilles did not; they chose instead to submit to Edward IV. One report sent to the duke of Milan, dated 31 July 1461, suggested, mistakenly as it happened, that father and son had been captured by Warwick and sent to the Tower of London.[49]

They clearly did yield to Edward IV and were pardoned on 12 July and 23 July respectively. It was reported to the duke of Milan at the end of August 1461 that father and son had supposedly offered the excuse that the Lancastrian cause was irretrievably lost. This sudden change of heart is difficult to reconcile with their previous actions and is more likely an attempt to excuse their previous position while justifying their present decision and emotions. It was by no means certain in 1461 that the Lancastrian cause was indeed lost, so it is more likely that the Woodvilles simply had no stomach for further resistance and were frightened of the potential consequences of continuing resistance.[50]

What is less certain, though, is the process by which their reintegration, or that of others, was achieved. While there were a number of variables, including personal intercession by a third party and redemptive military service against former opponents, our model of behaviour does not necessarily explain how they came to be applied or how successful they were; nor can we be sure of the point at which an individual lost heart in the process and chose to act completely differently. We can be sure, however, that the degree of leniency shown towards former opponents was not necessarily accepted with equanimity by those on the victorious side. In the wake of Edward IV's victory at Towton the new king angered many of his supporters when he displayed too much mercy to former opponents. This feeling was picked up in contemporary correspondence and was clearly circulating widely. In the Paston letters it was reported after Towton that 'for they grudge and sey, how that the Kyng resyvith sych of this cuntre, &c as haff be his gret eanemyes, and opresseors of the Comynes; and sych as haff assystyd his Hynes be not rewardyt; and it is to be consederyd, or ellys it wyll hurt'. Resentments such as these bubbled underneath the surface where some men weighed the sacrifices they had made against their meagre gains and looked with antipathy upon former opponents welcomed back into the political fold.[51]

A personal intercessor, often a friend or close family member, could sometimes help mitigate the worst effects of punishment for some. Sir Thomas Dymoke was one of the leading Lincolnshire rebels of 1470. Captured and executed at the battle of Losecote Field, Dymoke's family and lands were treated much less harshly than those of another executed rebel, Sir Thomas de la Launde. His lands were granted primarily to Richard, duke of Gloucester, even though he was not formally attainted until 1475. The Dymokes were hereditary King's Champions and one of the wealthiest families in Lincolnshire. Robert Ratcliffe probably protected their local position; Dymoke's widow, Margaret, had quickly married Ratcliffe, a Yorkshire esquire and loyal Yorkist supporter. We can never know how happy Margaret was at the prospect of remarrying, yet her underlying motivation is clear to understand. They were then granted custody of Margaret's son, Robert Dymoke, which served to cushion the inheritance from potential plunderers. Ratcliffe was able to use his connections at court to protect the family during the period of its reintegration into Lincolnshire society and the Yorkist polity. In fact, it is highly likely that a deal was reached between Edward IV, Gloucester, Ratcliffe and the Dymokes.[52]

Not all examples of intercession, though, are as straightforward to interpret as that of Margaret Dymocke and Robert Ratcliffe. While we can be reasonably confidant that highly placed intercessors were able to help kinsmen and friends, and that this was performed on a personal level and was highly reliant upon a good relationship between the respective parties, we cannot be certain about how effective it remained as a process. During the early 1460s, Gervase Clifton was able to benefit from the intervention of a prominent well-wisher, his stepson, Sir John Scott, who was by this time one of Edward IV's closest supporters. Clifton had made his peace with the Yorkists after the battle of Towton and had initially benefited from his stepson's intervention. Scott had become controller of the royal household and was a major political player at the very heart of the new Yorkist polity. He was able to smooth the process for Clifton's pardon while the latter worked towards a temporary accommodation with the Yorkists in anticipation of better times ahead. In 1461 there was no guarantee that the Yorkist regime would survive in the longer term. Waiting upon events was a sensible course of action for many like Clifton.[53]

However, our model cannot explain the contradictions in behaviour that could accompany this process. Neither can it gauge at what point or to what extent Clifton might have become dissatisfied with his personal circumstances, at which point Scott's intercession proved ineffectual or what finally prompted him to act. In all likelihood this was a piecemeal process. During the course of the 1460s Clifton came up against entrenched Yorkist interests. His marriage to Maud, Lady Willoughby, widow of Sir Thomas Neville and co-heiress of Ralph, Lord Cromwell, was an unhappy one and brought him into conflict with Anthony Woodville, Lord Scales, and Humphrey Bourchier, Lord Cromwell, husband of another Cromwell heiress. Clifton was certainly plagued by debt and in November 1465 was accused of treason by Scales.[54]

Whether these events had a direct bearing on his contact with Sir Robert Whittingham in 1468 is by no means proven. He still enjoyed the support of Scott and there was no reason to think that support would be withdrawn. A commission of oyer and terminer that same year could not find any evidence against him and his name was subsequently dropped from indictments. Nevertheless, on 1 December 1468 he was excluded from a general pardon. Curiously, he was pardoned in January 1470, probably through the good offices of Scott, but by then his choice to support the Lancastrian cause had presumably been made. Our model cannot answer why he decided to support the Readeption. His activities during 1470–1 remain obscure, although there is every chance he was in London before the battle of Barnet and departed with Somerset to meet Queen Margaret in the West Country where he met his death at Tewkesbury.[55]

In the wake of the Lancastrian defeat at Tewkesbury and the deaths of Prince Edward and Henry VI, a sensible course of action might have been to make peace with Edward IV. The evidence demonstrates that there were indeed prominent Lancastrians including Sir Richard Tunstall and Sir William Grimsby who were able to transfer smoothly into Yorkist service.[56] Sir William Grimsby was particularly fortunate. Nevertheless, incorporating luck and chance into our model is also problematic. For much of the 1460s Grimsby had languished in exile at Koeur in France along with Queen Margaret and the remnants of her supporters. Towards the end of the decade Grimsby's behaviour appears contradictory. Curiously, he had returned to England in 1469 and received a general pardon. It is not possible to know whether he had suddenly lost heart and sought to make his peace with Edward IV, or whether he was more calculating in his approach. In the event, he was certainly persuaded to join the Readeption government in 1470–1. Yet when it became clear that this unstable regime was not going to survive in the longer term, Grimsby headed west where he joined the Lancastrian ranks. Perhaps he thought that he was unlikely to receive any sympathy from a newly restored Edward IV. If this was the case then he was wrong. Lucky to survive the battle, he managed to sue out a second pardon from Edward IV. Despite his erratic behaviour between 1469 and 1471, it would seem that realism now suggested to him that the Lancastrian cause was irretrievably lost. He soon entered into the service of Edward IV's chamberlain, William, Lord Hastings, and went onto enjoy a successful career as a royal customs official and servant of the exchequer.[57]

While a sensible approach after 1461, 1471 and 1483 might have been to make peace or appear conciliatory, there were obviously still individuals who were prepared to take calculated risks, even though they faced potential ruin by doing so. Our model of behaviour does not easily accommodate this contradictory behaviour. In all probability Sir Richard Croft was content to adapt his behaviour and work within a limited framework whose limits were dictated by the current political circumstances. Croft could presumably recognize the potential benefits of service at critical moments in time. This had presumably led him to bring a substantial contribution of men to Edward IV's army in May 1471. A similar cognitive process might have prompted him to accept Richard III's usurpation in 1483. Croft had become a significant member of the prince's council in Wales during the 1470s, but in 1484 had turned to the court and become treasurer of Richard's household. Despite his newly acquired Ricardian credentials, Croft was able to survive the change of regime in 1485. It has been suggested by Davies that he was playing a double game that ultimately enabled him to avoid the fallout experienced by other close followers of Richard III. If so, Croft's mixture of calculation and ambition stood him in good stead.[58]

Some leading gentry might have felt unable to escape from the consequences of their previous choices; others that they were trapped by their current circumstances and could do little apart from be swept along by events. Although there is no way of knowing for certain, we might expect their decision frames to be much more restricted than other gentry. The experiences of the Fieldings of Lutterworth in Leicestershire suggest that poor decision-making between 1460 and 1471 had led them to support the Lancastrian cause, but had lost them their prominence in local society. William Fielding's father, John, had been killed during the first phase of the conflict. It might be argued that in 1470–1 a more prudent choice would have been to stay neutral and trust to a revival under the Yorkists. Yet William opted to support the Readeption government and fight with Lancastrian forces in 1471. The family's future was clearly at the forefront of his mind. This probably caused him to produce two genealogical narratives. One identified them with the Hapsburgs; the other placed emphasis on the collection of lordships in Warwickshire, Leicestershire and Rutland, which served to underpin the family's gentility. Both documents were produced between 1469 and 1471, a period of political upheaval. Before leaving for Tewkesbury he took steps to place them in safekeeping along with other important papers. Despite the doubt and fears that he felt about his family's position in the locality, he was still prepared to risk complete ruin on the battlefield.[59]

A similar explanation would seem to account for the responses of those who rebelled against Richard III in 1483 or who opposed him in 1485 at Bosworth. The Guildfords of Rolvenden in Kent had been courted by Richard III, possibly in the hope of appealing to former Neville and anti-Woodville sentiments. Having rejected those advances, the family's interests were now threatened by the Ricardian escheator William Malyverer, who quickly seized control of their lands. Richard Guildford had managed to flee to Brittany where he joined Henry Tudor. His father, John Guildford, though, had been hidden after Buckingham's rebellion by his neighbour Walter Roberts, before being apprehended by the royal authorities. His manor of Rolvenden was confiscated and granted to one of Richard's northern retainers, Sir Edward Stanley. The Guildfords could have done nothing and waited for events to sort themselves out, like other leading gentry in the shire.[60] This would have been an entirely logical and sensible decision to make, but the Guildfords continued in their opposition to the king and risked everything on success in battle.[61]

By contrast to Fielding or the Guildfords, the Welsh esquire Rhys ap Thomas was probably caught between opposing poles in 1485 and perhaps felt that he was being swept along by events. Griffiths has suggested a self-seeking tendency within Rhys's family, but we have no way of knowing whether these qualities can be applied to these specific events. Richard III was aware of the family's importance in south Wales and had granted Rhys a life annuity of 40 marks, although there is no indication that he was ever granted local office. There is also a suggestion that the king, aware of Rhys's local connections, took the precaution of requiring him to swear an oath of fidelity and took the latter's son hostage. He also agreed to defend Milford Haven against a possible landing and to swear the oath. By this stage it is likely that Rhys had decided to support Tudor's claim. Hall includes a tradition that Henry Tudor had also sought his support. Rhys was obviously concerned about openly renouncing his oath of allegiance to Richard and paying the price for a false move. After Tudor landed Rhys shadowed his forces before finally joining them in the Midlands. One tradition has it that he dealt the final blow that killed Richard at Bosworth.[62]

Perhaps the most extreme example of an individual who probably felt completely at the mercy of events was Sir Henry Ogard. Although we have no way of knowing this for certain, his behaviour does highlight the limitations of our model in that it cannot readily explain his responses after 1471. Ogard had been a royal ward living in the Lancastrian household since the mid-1450s and was one of the Lancastrian Prince Edward's childhood companions. He was presumably with the Lancastrian forces throughout 1459–61 and was taken north with them after their retreat from Towton. Attempts were made by John Bourchier, Lord Berners, to secure his return in 1461. Ogard was subsequently taken into exile in France with Queen Margaret. If Berners' petition is to be believed, Ogard was an unwilling exile.[63] If so, we can only speculate why he remained in exile at Koeur and did not seek to return like Grimsby. Ogard had clearly remained with them throughout the 1460s and returned with them in April 1471. The evidence, although circumstantial, would suggest that he was knighted on the eve of the battle of Tewkesbury. Fortunate to survive and be able to return to Norfolk, he then found himself fighting a constant battle with the Knyvett family over the possession of his father's former lands at New Buckenham. The Knyvetts had supported the Readeption and Ogard perhaps sought to profit from their temporary eclipse. Yet Ogard was unable to judge his environment whereas the Knyvetts had been intimately involved in local politics. Ogard found himself at loggerheads with a much more influential family. Friendless, and without significant patronage, he was unable to establish a secure place in local society, but this did not prevent repeated attempts by him to do so.[64]

## CONCLUSIONS

There is little reason to doubt that the environments in which the leading gentry lived could exert a fundamental impact upon their behaviour. However, while an environment played a major, determining role in the shaping of thought and behavioural processes, it cannot account for or explain every response and reaction. A model based on Prospect Theory has considerable merit in explaining a large proportion of likely decision frames of the leading gentry. It can indicate the most likely responses that the leading gentry would make. Yet it cannot hope to explain all the exceptions. Even though it acknowledges that factors such as memory, back projection and, crucially, emotion, can each exert powerful influences, it is unable to explain why people did not always act in a predictable manner. At best it recognizes that decision frames could become unstable and volatile.

In this chapter we have seen that it is unadvisable to readily assume a direct cause and effect relationship between certain pieces of evidence. While the reasons described previously that led to the participation of Sir John Lewknor or Sir William Cary are plausible, it does not mean that they were the only ones;

nor do they necessarily explain the emotional underpinning that led to them. The range of excuses presented in an effort to avoid service hint at some of the alternative cognitive processes involved. Indeed, the mere act of offering excuses suggests an emotional response and range of reasons. But it does not identify the reasons that could result from very different emotions. It is possible to arrive at the same decision but for vastly different reasons. We can hazard guesses at how individuals might have been influenced by events, but this does not mean that they were.

Our model, while providing a structure for the interpretation of behaviour, cannot effectively answer this conundrum or all of the apparent contradictions involved in the decision-making process. We have to recognize that some people acted on the spur of the moment without a significant amount of forethought. Elsewhere, there were many individuals who were at the mercy of events, or perhaps *thought* they were. Once on a particular path some certainly found it more difficult to change course even though they might have wanted to. This could have been the scenario that Gervase Clifton found himself in as his options for manoeuvre gradually lessened. Others, however, appeared to find themselves caught up in events by accident, rather like Henry Ogard. In their own minds they might have felt they had no choice but to act in a particular way. Others might have been past caring about the end results, even though this went against the most sensible course of action. What our model cannot do effectively is explain how somebody really felt when placed in that position. Tempting as it is to believe the suggestion that Sir Richard Croft was embarrassed by his involvement in the death of Prince Edward in 1471, the fact remains that he did not allow it to affect his future career in Yorkist or Tudor service. Instead, we see somebody content to make his own decisions in a manner that suited his own purposes.

# 8

# Conclusion

This book set out to understand the decision making of the leading gentry during the Wars of the Roses. It sought to explain why they acted in a particular way rather than simply describing what they did. The leading gentry were most likely to exercise public or private authority at a local and regional level and were crucial to the stability of the realm. In spite of the substantial quantity of publications on the fifteenth century and the Wars of the Roses, the attitudes and motives of the leading gentry have received little sustained attention. In fact, they remain the subject of sweeping generalizations, with Goodman recently asserting that 'English and Welsh lords and gentlefolk repeatedly planned and participated in rebellions in the second half of the fifteenth century'. This would seem to imply a much greater willingness by the upper echelons of landholding society to engage in this kind of behaviour and is contradicted by the evidence presented in the preceding chapters of this book.[1]

Historians shall of course always remain tempted into making assumptions about their subject of study. In most instances, the leading gentry of the fifteenth century have either found themselves subsumed within narrative accounts of the Wars of the Roses and their behaviour seen as an extension of their lords'; or else they have been bound within the constricting structure of traditional gentry-based studies and examined in geographic, social and political isolation from their social superiors and inferiors elsewhere across the kingdom. Moreover, in Chapter 2 it emerged that gentry analysis has been consistently dogged by one fundamental conceptual problem: historians are not entirely sure about who the gentry were. Despite generating a substantial corpus of material about them, along with a variety of descriptive terms such as 'greater', 'upper', 'lesser', 'urban' and 'parish' gentry, they have been unable to arrive at a generally acceptable definition. As we saw, many scholars have sought to define the gentry through a combination of artificially imposed criteria based on status, wealth, landholding and office-holding. Those that meet them have been deemed to be gentry. Although it is acknowledged that this is unsatisfactory, many medievalists continue to cling desperately to this form of approach because they cannot see any other way of defining them.[2]

However, it is misleading to talk about gentry as if they were a homogenous grouping, and to think that they can be analysed in terms of a universal template.

By grouping together all those who meet the basic criteria, medieval historians run the risk of implying that all members of this social grouping tended to think and act in a similar way. In recent years some medievalists like Coss have focused on the diversity of gentry culture and argued for a broader range of defining characteristics. This looser structure does have the recommendation of capturing a much wider cross-section of individuals as well as enabling us to see the diverse cross-section of individuals who could lay claim to gentle status. Yet ultimately we are drawn back to the question of whether one single term for a social grouping is adequate or even desirable.[3] Despite advocating a less rigid definition, Coss still argues in favour of a collective identity among the gentry. However, the extent to which this was true deserves careful thought, particularly when we take into account that the upper echelons of the gentry originated from the lesser aristocracy of the early medieval period, while their contemporaries from the lower strata of the gentry shared similar characteristics to the yeomanry and lesser landowners. Regrettably, Coss does not address the potentially differing range of attitudes, opinions and behaviour among the gentry.[4]

Nonetheless, the first significant conclusion to be drawn from this discussion should perhaps be that this combination of general characteristics shared by gentry played a determining role in shaping their subsequent behaviour and responses. It is the contention here that, while the gentry shared common characteristics, different sub-groups within the social grouping possessed particular attributes to a greater or lesser degree. In order to be included within the gentry it was surely not essential to enjoy all of them in equal measure but rather to aspire to the tenets of gentle status. As a consequence, these sub-groups within the gentry thought in different ways and harboured differing attitudes. The leading gentry were perhaps closer in thought, behaviour and aspiration to the late medieval baronage. For an obvious example of the former we need look no further than somebody like Sir John Fastolf whose wealth at the time of death was in excess of many lesser nobles and whose behaviour suggested that he regarded himself their equal on both the local and national stages.[5] Why else would a member of the leading gentry feel the confidence to so forcefully criticize the peace policy of William de la Pole, duke of Suffolk, and the Truce of Tours of 1444–6?[6]

To explain gentry behaviour a framework has been proposed that enables a more complete understanding of the leading gentry's decision-making process and, by default other elements within gentry society. It has employed an interdisciplinary approach, drawing upon key elements found within the social sciences. Debates within the field of psychology over the last 50 years have highlighted the key conceptual problems in understanding human behaviour. Nevertheless, despite differences of opinion, some of these scholars have still recognized that different physical, intellectual and emotional environments go a significant way to providing the key determinants that shape decision making. The approach adopted here has been to explore the various aspects of these environments, which were defined as the public domain, private domain and the personal domain. While these environments have been treated separately for the purposes of analysis, they are quite clearly intimately connected and not mutually exclusive.

As we have seen, all gentry, leading or otherwise, created a decision frame based on their conception of the acts, outcomes and contingencies associated with a particular choice. Within their decision frame they applied certain judgements that they had formed within each environment and which they considered relevant to that situation. An environment set the boundaries that defined behaviour in a particular way. By these means they arrived at a choice that may or may not have conformed to the Pythagorean ideal. We also saw that although the leading gentry's cognitive processes were not necessarily different from those of the lesser gentry, their defining characteristics were likely to have produced alternative attitudes towards common situations that arose within specific environments. The environments, experiences and personalities of the leading gentry shaped the relevance of particular cues to the decision frame. These had the potential to produce a variety of responses depending on the environment that was exerting the greater influence at that time.

This book has quite deliberately focused its attention on the behaviour of the leading gentry. The definition provided here includes the upper levels of that broadly-based pyramid which medieval historians have been so fond of discussing, particularly those families who stood out in terms of status, lineage and wealth, while at the same time incorporating those members of the gentry who were active politically and administratively in local, regional and national affairs, but who did not necessarily meet the other established criteria. These were the men who traditionally led their communities, and whom the Lancastrian and Yorkist leaders needed to convince for support. While recognizing that the definition of leading gentry presented here is open to challenge, a broad definition based on their activities rather than on a range of externally imposed elements enables the inclusion of the widest possible number of individuals. This allows us to draw upon the approach of Coss and proponents of gentry-culture analysis without being constrained by them.

Where, though, does this leave the actual decision-making process of the leading gentry during the Wars of the Roses? How did the leading gentry decide upon the course that would ensure an acceptable outcome? Until now the behaviour of leading gentry during this period of uncertainty has often been defined by their relative proximity to, and attitudes towards, lordship, or by their propensity towards the employment of violence, either in warfare or in settling personal disputes. The analysis here has suggested that neither of these measures is sufficient on its own to understand the true complexity of the cognitive processes that they underwent in order to arrive at a particular decision. Furthermore, as this book has suggested, lordship and the use of violence were important individual variables that may or may not have influenced the decision-making process, but they were not the only ones.

The second significant conclusion to emerge from this study is that only a relatively small proportion of the leading gentry were prepared to take up arms during the Wars of the Roses, and then only under particular circumstances. Should this really be a surprise to late medieval historians? The overwhelming majority sought to avoid the obvious risks that participation would entail. What mattered to the leading gentry were considerations centred upon local stability, administration and justice. It was shown in Chapter 5 that while the leading gentry were prepared to undertake public service within the king's administration, they would only do so up to a point. A small percentage presumably did see public service as part of an accepted career path. Even among these families, however, most were probably more concerned about surviving a period of office without incurring too many debts. The crown also seemed to recognize a general reluctance to come forward. This reluctance increased dramatically during periods of instability, which again shows through in the appointments during 1459–61, 1469–71 and 1483–5. This recognition undoubtedly accounted for an official willingness to tolerate quite high levels of administrative and judicial malpractice, as well as fraud and dishonesty by many of those who were appointed. There was little concerted effort to remove persistent local offenders like Gilbert Debenham the elder in Essex.[7]

The same considerations applied to gentry clients of noble patrons. The evidence would again suggest the leading gentry were circumspect in forging these bonds. There were, of course, regions where the leading gentry felt they had little choice but to accept these social relationships. Nevertheless, this did not prevent them from making informed choices on how to act when called upon. They did not necessarily act without question. If they did not agree with the actions of their lord they did not feel obliged to follow him blindly. It was a delicate balancing game, again, based on the particular circumstances they faced. In many regions the leading gentry remained unresponsive to magnate connections altogether. Where they were perceived as antithetical to their interests they were avoided assiduously.

It is not the suggestion here that the leading gentry were immune to political issues. They were keenly aware of constitutional considerations and the implications of particular actions. In some shires, including Kent, they seemed more politicized than others. The leading gentry were also capable of giving expression to their thoughts in parliament and through the election of candidates that met their approval rather than that of a magnate. McFarlane considered that gentry opinion counted for much within the shires. He asserted that "These men would take, as they would give, advice: they appreciated the value of "good lordship"; and they were willing to be guided by those who had claims on their support; but it was foolish to attempt to drive them with too tight a rein".[8]

Nevertheless, what appeared to matter to leading gentry in the long run was protecting and preserving their traditional position within their immediate sociopolitical environment. This remained critically important to the leading gentry. It was the environment in which they lived much of their lives. In many instances their outlook and social horizons remained as narrow as that of many lesser gentry. The relationships that they enjoyed within their locality therefore required protecting and nurturing.[9] The majority were prepared to acquiesce in, if not accept, fundamental political changes at the heart of government, not least the change of monarch. For them, maintaining local stability, defending the family patrimony, preserving good neighbourly relationships and avoiding unnecessary destabilizing disputes were seen as more important considerations than engaging in civil warfare. They were prepared to act in defence of their communities, an obligation which many did take seriously, but other forms of participation were steered clear of.

From time to time the strategic importance of an area did shift in such a way that more leading gentry were drawn into acting in support of either Lancastrian or Yorkist parties. This happened in Cheshire in 1459 at Blore Heath and at Mortimer's Coss in 1461 when the local gentry turned out in higher numbers. In some instances this support was perhaps genuinely enthusiastic, such as the support by the Kentish elite in 1460–1. Yet despite the supposed numbers and the actual rewards granted in Kent, it is unclear how many actually served other than a well-known handful.[10] Such instances were comparatively rare during the conflict. Moreover, it must be recognized that many more gentry were successful in keeping a low political and military profile. The unenthusiastic nature of support is evident at Ludford Bridge in 1459 and at Losecote Field in 1470. In the latter instance the Lincolnshire gentry sought to avoid any involvement, and the rebel army simply melted away when faced by a determined royalist force.[11]

The simple fact that most localities were not in a constant state of upheaval suggests that the leading gentry did not allow political differences to stand in the way of good neighbourly relations. Moreover, even those with strong opposing political affiliations like William Fielding and Thomas Malory did not necessarily allow their political differences to stand in the way of cooperation on a variety of local matters. It was largely instances where previous choices had damaged the local standing and prosperity of a family, or had created personal disputes between families, that led to an area becoming destabilized, or prompted an individual to try to recover his traditional place within local society. The behaviour of Sir Henry Pierpoint in 1461 was probably shaped by his family's local dispute with the Plumptons. He fought for Edward IV while the Plumptons remained committed Lancastrians. The actions and activities of George Brown in Kent were determined primarily by his father's attainder in 1461 and the grasping nature of his new stepfather, the Yorkist Thomas Vaughan. It was more by luck than deliberate planning that he was able to reintegrate himself into gentry society after 1471, and even then he never truly secured a position among the Kentish elite. Not all of those who suffered severe reverses acted with hostility when trying to recover their former prosperity. Nicholas Latimer found himself attainted after the battle of Towton but accepted that he needed to negotiate for the recovery of his lands. This was not easy and probably encouraged him to try his luck with the Readeption regime in 1470–1. Like Brown, his last-minute political shift in 1471 into the camp of George, duke of Clarence, allowed him to transfer into Yorkist service without too much trouble.

The third conclusion to emerge from the preceding analysis is that those who consistently fought for either side between 1455 and 1487 were usually the most intimate servants of the houses of Lancaster and York who identified their own interests with those of their patrons. There were certainly those like Sir Richard Tunstall or Sir Robert Chamberlain who manifested a deeply held sense of loyalty to Henry VI and Edward IV respectively, and were willing to risk a life on the run or as an exile, but they were the exceptions to the rule. There were not many who were prepared to fight beyond a certain point. In the wake of the battle of Towton there were few overtly partisan Lancastrians left who were prepared to continue the fight. Even committed Lancastrians like Sir Gervase Clifton accepted that an accommodation with the *de facto* regime of Edward IV was the most appropriate course of action based on his personal circumstances in 1461. Generally speaking, the men who fought on for any length of time during this conflict were those whose loyalties can be described as partisan, those without much to lose in either the public or private domains, or who had been genuinely unfortunate in one or more choices they had previously made.[12]

Clifton, in fact, serves to remind us, though, that in all of our discussion about gentry motives and behaviour, there are always instances that we cannot readily explain. Models of behaviour can only take us so far in understanding the leading gentry during the Wars of the Roses. They provide a structure for interpreting the influences that shaped their cognitive processes. In Chapter 7 it was seen that we can often hazard a guess at the most likely factors that prompted a reaction, but we cannot be absolutely certain. Neither can we be sure at what point a decision was made. Even the most recent models of behaviour struggle to incorporate the effect of memory, back-projection and emotions. These exert a volatile influence upon decision-frames and for this reason make it virtually impossible to interpret contradictory or inconsistent behaviour in the face of more sensible options. We have little option but to accept that there were always some leading gentry who might have acted on the spur of the moment, chose a high risk option for apparently inexplicable reasons when most others were keeping a low profile, felt that they actually had no choice at all other than one particular course of action, or simply found themselves swept along by events.

In light of this evidence the most sensible conclusion to be drawn is that the leading gentry were not cowards and were not put off by the prospect of a fight when it mattered or when their interests were threatened. Yet only a relatively small proportion fought outside their immediate localities and regions and even then they rarely did so for any extended period of time. However much they cared about points of principle or showed an interest in political issues of the day, the majority did not want to become embroiled. Civil war created too many uncertainties and carried with it many risks to family and livelihoods. John Blount, Lord Mountjoy's, advice to his sons was to beware of the 'desire to be grete about princes, for it is dangeros'. These words of wisdom were undoubtedly appreciated by a much wider audience. It was always easier, and significantly safer, to avoid any involvement in politics.[13]

# Notes

*Notes to Chapter 1: Introduction: A Fascination with Choice*

1   Newell *et al.*, 2007, p. 15.
2   Hunt, 2003, p. 88.
3   Kirby, 1996, pp. 6–9, no. 28; Dockray, 2004, pp. 616–17.
4   *Paston Letters*, III, no. 894.
5   Dickinson, 1927, pp. 258–63; Watts, 1995, p. 113; Watts, 1996, pp. 22–3; Amos, 1825, p. 221.
6   Unless otherwise stated, the following discussion is drawn from the survey of historiography in Dockray, 2002, pp. 125–94.
7   Ibid., pp. 158–60; McFarlane, 1943–5, p. 161.
8   Goodman, 2006.
9   Castor, 2004.


*Notes to Chapter 2: Who were the Gentry?*

1   McFarlane, 1944, 53–79; Richmond, 1983, 57. McFarlane's views have also been endorsed in some gentry studies. Acheson, for example, has identified the need to 'minimise the dragooning influence of predeterminism and accentuate the essentially humanising element of free will': 1992, p. 3.
2   Carpenter, 1992, pp. 35–6; Coss, 2003, pp. 1–3. A recent summary of the debate on gentility is provided in Maddern, 2005, p. 34.
3   Stubbs, III, p. 22; Pugh, 1972, p. 97.
4   Thomas, 1993, p. 193.
5   Cross, 2003, p. 11.
6   Distraint of knighthood was a practice whereby those who enjoyed sufficient wealth to support the status of knighthood declined to take it up. This refusal obliged them to pay a fine to the crown. A full discussion of this subject appears in Nichols, 1863, 189–244.
7   See especially Coss, 2003, pp. 136–201, 216–38.
8   Given-Wilson, 1996, pp. 73–4; Fleming, 1984, pp. 42–52.
9   Carpenter, 1992, pp. 35–95; Acheson, 1992, pp. 29–44; Wright, 1983, pp. 1–11.
10  Coss, 2003, pp. 3–6; Castor, 2004, pp. 101–4.
11  Wright, 1983, p. 4.

12   Acheson, 1992, p. 44.

13   Mackman, 1999, pp. 13–14.

14   Carpenter, 1992, pp. 93–4.

15   Radalescu and Truelove, 2005, pp. 1–4. See also the approach adopted by Holford to analyse locality in Yorkshire which draws heavily on sociological, anthropological, and cultural methodologies to explore how different social groupings understood this concept: 2001, pp. 5–8.

16   Coss, 2003, pp. 9–11.

17   As a consequence of her network analysis, Carpenter has suggested that different social identities existed at different levels of society: 1992, pp. 335–46. For an approach that emphasizes the cultural dynamics of gentry identity, see Denton, 2006, passim.

18   Given-Wilson, 1996, pp. 80–1.

19   For a definition of affinity and its role in the recruitment process, see pp. 51–2.

20   Pollard, 1990, pp. 121.

21   Ibid.

22   In simple terms *mesne* tenure refers to any tenure which is not held in chief. Grand serjeanty, in particular, involved the provision of personal services to the lord: Simpson, 1996, p. 14.

23   Pollard, 1975, p. 52; *Arrivall*, pp. 6–7.

24   Pollard, 1990, pp. 120–6; Arnold, 1984, pp. iii, 91–7.

25   See Harvey, 1988, especially pp. 62–85, 182–225. An account of the fifteenth-century dispute between the Berkeleys and Talbots appears in Fleming and Wood, 2003, pp. 21–79.

26   Cherry, 1979, pp. 71–97; Cherry, 1986, pp. 123–44; Thomson, 1972, pp. 230–46.

27   Carpenter, 1992, p. 630.

28   Ibid., pp. 322–4, 456–7.

29   Castor, 2000, p. 234.

30   Carpenter, 1994, pp. 345–52.

31   Carpenter, 1995, pp. 195–8.

32   Before the emergence of the royal affinity in Kent the leading gentry had gravitated towards other leading political figures at court in 'semi-royal' affinities: Mercer, 1995, pp. 1, 3.

33   The element of choice among the gentry, however, is noted in the evolution of the Kentish royal affinity. Here, local conditions, including the strength of tradition and alternative structures of patronage and loyalty, are advanced as significant reasons for gentry recruitment: Mercer, 1995, p. 228.

34   Carpenter, 1992, pp. 295–320.

35   Wright, 1983, pp. 51–92; Payling, 1991, pp. 19–62; Carpenter, 1992, pp. 307–9; Mackman, 1999, p. 70.

36   Carpenter, 1995, p. 187.

37   Payling, 1991, pp. 77–8, 87–8, 98–100.

38   Wright, 1983, pp. 124–7.

39   Arnold, 1984, pp. 373–5.

40   Wright, 1983, pp. 60–2; Payling, 1991, p. 100.

41   Arnold, 1984, pp. 132–5.

42   Jack, 1961, pp. 30–1; Payling, 1989, pp. 7–9, 13.

43  Given-Wilson, 1996, pp. 73–4, 81–2; Jack, 1961, pp. 30–1, 169, 298; Payling, 1989, pp. 888–9, 891–2.
44  Fleming, 2005, p. 56
45  Mackman, 1999, p. 75
46  Ibid., p. 77
47  Mackman, pp. 71–7.
48  Wright, 1983, pp. 63, 75, 83, 119.
49  Castor, 2000, pp. 204–5.
50  Wright, 1983, pp. 83–5.
51  Carpenter, 1991, pp. 414–16; Castor, 2000, p. 269.
52  Castor, 2000, pp. 270–5.
53  Ibid., pp. 278–9.
54  Fleming, 1985, p. 434.
55  Clayton, 1980, pp. 190–224; Worthington, 1990, pp. 59–73, 94–113. The office of escheator was much less significant and generally occupied by gentry of lesser status.
56  Bennett, 1973, pp. 24–44; Clayton, 1980, pp. 162–72, 249–56; Morgan, 1987, pp. 17–9. In contrast to Bennett, however, Carpenter argues that even Cheshire enjoyed close links with Lancashire south of the Ribble and that the county was therefore less of a cohesive force among the gentry: 1994, p. 350.
57  Coss, 2003, pp. 209–15; Acheson, 1992, pp. 133–4.
58  Kleineke, 1998, p. 191.
59  Fleming, 2005, pp. 56, 58.
60  Coss, 2003, p. 252.


## Notes to Chapter 3: The Decision-Making Process

1  Carpenter, 1992, passim; Carpenter, 2004, pp. 529–31.
2  Newell et al., 2007, pp. 102–8.
3  Ibid., pp. 108–11. A useful summary article about the framing of decisions and the psychology of choice can be found in Tverskey and Kahneman, 1981, 453–8.
4  Finn, 1911, pp. 187–98.
5  TNA, C67/40 m. 33; KB9/955/2 mm. 2, 3.
6  Three Fifteenth-Century Chronicles, pp. 73, 77; Nicholas, 1834–7, pp. 307–8; Davis, 1856, p. 108; Kingsford, 1905, p. 174; 'Gregory', p. 212; Hearne, 1728, p. 766; Paston Letters, II, no. 385; Schofield, II, p. 167.
7  Warkworth, p. 14; Arrivall, pp. 7–9; Paston Letters, II, no. 664. An analysis of magnate involvement in recruitment efforts before Barnet is provided in Kleineke, 2006, pp. 66–83.
8  The area around the Tower upon which he fired was home to many London livery companies and their members.
9  TNA, KB9/75; E163/8/10; Scofield, 1923, I, pp. 90, 92–3; English Chronicle, pp. 95–6; Three Fifteenth-Century Chronicles, p. 169; Harriss, 1972, p. 227.
10  RP, V, p. 477; Shaw, I, p. 13.

11    'Gregory', pp. 220–1; *Waurin*, V, pp. 440–1, Raine, 1864, p. cix; Scofield, 1923, I, pp. 329–30.

12    *Arrivall*, pp. 31–2. Sir William Euer, the son of Ralph Euer who had died fighting for the Lancastrian cause at Towton, was fined for supporting Warwick and the Readeption regime. He subsequently entered the service of the earls of Northumberland: *CPR, 1467–77*, p. 287; Hicks, 1971, p. 89.

13    *CCR, 1468–76*, no. 703.

14    Newell *et al.*, pp. 115–23.

15    *English Chronicle*, pp. 86–91.

16    *Arrivall*, pp. 15, 22–3.

17    Newell *et al.*, pp. 25–59.

18    Discussed in detail in Holford, 2001, parts I–III.

19    Ibid., pp. 75, 109–117.

20    Newell *et al.*, pp. 141–51.

21    Holford, 2001, pp. 1–26

22    Kirby, 1996, pp. 9–10, 60–1.

23    Collins, 2000, pp. 114–40; Pollard, 2005, pp. 16–18.

24    Newell *et al.*, pp. 135–8.

25    *Arrivall*, pp. 26–7.

26    TNA, C1/27/435.

27    Newell *et al.*, pp. 34–8.

28    This is in accordance with the reasons for adopting non-compensatory strategies found in Newell *et al.*, pp. 38–42.


*Notes to Chapter 4: Gentry, Warfare and Violence in Late Medieval England*

1    General military obligations are discussed in Prestwich, 1996, pp. 57–81. Late medieval military convention and recruitment is outlined in Goodman, 1981a, pp. 119–52.

2    Ayton, 1995, pp. 81–104; Curry, 1994, pp. 39–68.

3    Keen, 2002, p. 89; Denton, 2006, p. 178.

4    The following discussion about gentry and aristocratic education is based on Orme, 1984, pp. 182–210 and Orme, 2005, pp. 63–83.

5    TNA, C1/15/143; McFarlane, 1973, p. 245; Public Record Office, 1887, 48, pp. 243, 259, 282, 293; TNA, E101/151/21.

6    A detailed account of the family is provided in MacMichael, 1960, 12–40.

7    Ayton, 1995, p. 92.

8    Anglo, 2000, pp. 7–9.

9    Barker, 1986, pp. 14–15, 23, 37, 137–61. Unlike *jousts à plaisance* (jousts of peace), these were fought with real arms until one of the contestants was disabled or killed: Blair, 1958, p. 156.

10    *Chronicles of London*, p. 158; Black, 1840, p. 37; Bodleian Library, MS Ashmole 856 fo. 102.

11    Barker, 1986, p. 131.

12   Radulescu, 2003, pp. 41-2; Fleming, 1987, pp. 85-102.

13   Anglo, 1965, 271-83; Bodleian Library, MS Ashmole 856 fo. 102; Black, 1840, p. 37.

14   TNA, PROB11/4 fos. 163r (PCC 21 Stokton). The church, along present day College Street, was burnt down during the Great Fire of London.

15   Mercer, 1995, pp. 154, 156, 181-2, 185, 198, 199; Robertson, 1886, pp. 232-7; Mann, 1932, 138-9; Mann, 1940, 366-79; Wedgwood, 1936, pp. 125-6.

16   Pollard, 1968, pp. 35-6.

17   Dillon, 1900, pp. 32-7; Nall, 2004, pp. 88-9.

18   *CPR, 1446-52*, 18; *CPR, 1452-61*, 67

19   *Froissart*, p. 92.

20   Muhlberger, 2005, pp. 38-39; *Hall*, p. 300. Hall was, of course, writing from the perspective of a Tudor audience. It is noteworthy that Somerset is still criticized for being too rash.

21   Denton, 2006, pp. 192-6; Ayton, 1995, pp. 82-3.

22   Denton, 2006, pp. 179, 186, 195-8.

23   Curry, 1994, pp. 65-7; Keen, 2002, pp. 91-5; Denton, 2006, pp. 189-91. The excuses offered by Yorkshire gentlemen in 1421 to serving in France included one from the lawyer Jankyn Malyverer, who appeared to consider that his status a man of law exempted him: Goodman, 1981a, p. 247.

24   Wedgwood, 1936, pp. 753-4; TNA, E101/50/1; Public Record Office, 1887, *XLVIII*, p. 310; Evans, 1998, pp. 74-5, 83-8; Goodman, 1981a, p. 166.

25   Denton, 2006, pp. 191-5. Denton asserts that it was primarily veterans and their heirs who took up arms between 1455 and 1471.

26   Grummitt, 2008, pp. 93-4.

27   TNA, E101/54/16; E101/55/23.

28   *Paston Letters*, III, no. 760; Grummitt, 2008, pp. 97-9.

29   TNA, E101/54/16; C76/145, m. 23; E404/72/4/76; Griffiths and Thomas, 1985, pp. 93-6; TNA, C66/594, m. 10; *Letters and Papers, Foreign and Domestic, Henry VIII*, II ii, no. 3257.

30   BL, Harleian Ms 7457 fo. 2r, gives the sixteenth-century 'old garrison' at about 160 men, which included officers, mounted men, footmen and gunners.

31   Gillingham, 1981, p. 30; Storey, 1957, 600-1, 603-4; Robson, 1989, pp. 59, 68; TNA, E101/42/40 (West March); E 101/43/26 (East March); *RP*, V, p. 477.

32   TNA, E101/42/40. This muster dates from the first two years of the reign of Henry IV, before Oldcastle became embroiled in Lollard conspiracies.

33   TNA, E101/55/9; NAI, RC8/41, pp. 237, 313. Morgan suggests that 'In several respects Ireland ought perhaps to have been the perfect arena in which to deploy the talents of the military community'. Yet Ireland was never a popular destination for leading gentry seeking military service and remained limited primarily to the immediate affinity of a lieutenant and captains persuaded to enter into indentures of service: 1987, pp. 172-3.

34   Pollard, 1968, p. 225.

35   Chart, 1935, p. 110.

36   Grummitt, 2008, pp. 107-8.

37   Jones, 2001, 283. Sir Philip Chesnall had also acquired practical military experience in the service of the Dukes of Burgundy: Grummitt, 2001, pp. 267-8, 273.

38 For Bolingbroke's activities in Prussia and evidence of his retainers there see Smith, 1894, passim. Robert Waterton, who later became Henry IV's master of the horse, also accompanied him to the Baltic: Whitehead, 2004, pp. 576–7.

39 Goodman, 1981a, pp. 195, 277 n. 216; Merriman, 1905, pp. 134–7.

40 BL, Additional Ms 30998, fos. 50v–51r; Bodleian Library, MS Ashmole 1137, fo. 113a.

41 Field, 1977, pp. 249–64; King, 1967, pp. 63–75. This tradition appeared to survive in families even when branches were established elsewhere. Thomas Docwra, prior of the order from 1502 was from a branch of the Westmorland family which had subsequently settled in Hertfordshire: Chibi, 2004, 380–1.

42 Griffiths, 1963, pp. 26, 29; Ellis, 1851, passim.

43 Nall, 2004, pp. 133–4

44 Radulescu, 2003, pp. 39–60; Nall, 2004, pp. 109–43.

45 Kaeuper, 2001, p. 133

46 A copy of this version was also made for Sir John Paston who commissioned his own 'Grete Boke' about chivalry in about 1468–9: Nall, 2004, pp. 55.

47 Bornstein, 1975, p. 472.

48 Ibid., p. 473.

49 Fleming, 1987, pp. 88–90; Nall, 2004, pp. 105–17; Radulescu, 2003, pp. 47, 56.

50 Anglo, 2000, pp. 23–5, 45–6; Waller, 2000, pp. 148–54; Novak, 2000, pp. 94–100.

51 Statutes of the Realm 1810–28, I, 97–8.

52 Goodman, 1981a, p. 144. This aspect of gentry behaviour will be considered in more depth in Chapter 7.

53 Scofield, I, 491–3; Ross, 1983, p. 129. Appeals further abroad were likewise unsuccessful. Sir John Paston, for example, chose to remain quietly on the sidelines despite a summons: Castor, 2004, pp. 201–3; Davis, 1971, I, no. 333; II, no. 763.

54 Kirby, 1996, p. 26

55 Paston Letters, II, no. 664; Arrivall, pp. 15, 22–3; Fleming and Wood, 2003, pp. 82–3.

56 Goodman, 1981a, pp. 127–9; Curry, 1994, pp. 39–68; Grummitt, 2008, pp. 44–56.

57 Storey, 1957, pp. 603–4, 607–8; Grummitt, 2008, pp. 104, 106–7; Hicks, 1998, pp. 287–8.

58 Oman, 1924, pp. 410, 414; Dobson, 1977, 15–16; Goodman, 1981a, pp. 147–8; Finn, 1911, pp. 196–8.

59 Goodman, 1981a, p. 203; TNA, C1/45/138, C1/43/156–7.

60 CPR, 1452–61, 563–4; CPR, 1452–61, 566–7.

61 Hicks, 1995, pp. 44–5.

62 Woolgar, 1999, pp. 5, 63; Mertes, 1988, p. 212.

63 Pollard, 1976, 52–69. For Harrington, p. 97.

64 CPR, 1452–61, 553.

65 Historical Manuscripts Commission, 1888, I, 3–4.

66 Dockray, 1992, p. 244.

67 TNA, E404/74/3/17.

68 Clayton, 1980, pp. 116–17.

69 Harvey, 1969, p. 203.

70 Ellis, 1998, pp. 52–61.

71 CPR, 1461–67, pp. 117, 185.

72  *Three Fifteenth-Century Chronicles*, p. 77; Griffiths, 1998, pp. 422–3, 576–7, 732–4, 739–4, 743–8.

73  Grummitt, 2008, p. 106; Charlton, 1978, p. 18.

74  Prestwich, 1996, pp. 155–6.

75  Wedgwood, 1936, p. 644; Harvey, 1969, p. 49; TNA, E404/70/2/24; Myers, 1995, pp. 152, 181–2, 223.

76  TNA, E404/71/1/59, 77.

77  Grummitt, 2008, p. 105.

78  TNA, C1/31/446; *Three Fifteenth-Century Chronicles*, p. 77; Scofield, 1923, I, p. 263.

79  The 'Forey of Fraunc' identified by some as French was probably the Englishman John Florey, a Beaufort follower: Mercer, 2007, p. 89.

80  Gregory, 213–4; Jones, 2002, pp. 131–2.

81  Labarge, 1980, pp. 186, 219, 228; Scofield, 1923, I, pp. 518–36; Ross, 1983, p. 146; Hicks, 1998, p. 176, Grummitt, 2008, pp. 49, 105.

82  Grummitt, 2008, p. 105; TNA, KB27/841 rot. 7v, rot. 53r, 71r–v, 72v; 842 rot. 72v; *CPR 1467–77*, p. 291.

83  Crossley, 1925, pp. 18–19, 21–2, 23–4; Denton, 2006, pp. 147–8, 211–13; Wedgwood, 1936, pp. 332, 683–4; Hampton, 1979, pp. 98, 198.

84  Blair, 1958, pp. 53–111.

85  Gray, 1934, p. 627. For a discussion of the distribution of wealth in Derbyshire, see Wright, 1983, p. 5.

86  Wiedemer, 1967, pp. 61–2, TNA, E403/825 m. 6; Crawford, 1992, I, p. 568.

87  TNA, C1/27/340.

88  I am grateful for Professor Jim Bolton of Queen Mary College, University of London, for supplying the details of Lord Cromwell's 'nephew' from the accounts of the Italian Bankers, the Borromei.

89  Oakeshott, 1998, p. 77.

90  TNA, CHES29/166 rot. 34r; Wiedemer, 1967, p. 51.

91  Weaver, 1903, p. 341.

92  Clark, 1914, pp. 49–51.

93  Scott, 1876, p. 251. The exact whereabouts of the account used by Scott in his article is unclear and may no longer survive.

94  Amyot, 1827, pp. 270–1.

95  For a more detailed discussion of the weaponry employed by the Calais garrison in the fifteenth century, see Grummitt, 2008, pp. 119–40.

96  TNA, E143/26/2 no. 213; Richardson, 1997, 47–51.

97  TNA, E364/72, rot. D. Indeed, men described as 'archers' comprised the majority of the garrison. However, Grummitt has demonstrated that during the fifteenth century the term no longer related directly to the function they performed on the battlefield. It was an accounting fiction which simply showed the rate of pay they were receiving: 2008, pp. 46–8.

98  TNA, E101/195/14.

99  TNA, E101/198/13, fo. 64v. The high number of bows probably represent the remains of the stockpile accumulated for the invasion of France the previous year.

100   Maddern, 1985, esp. chapter 7; Carpenter, 1992, p. 622; Wright, 1983, pp. 122–3; Payling, 1991, pp. 208–11.
101   Wright, 1983, pp. 72–4, 125.
102   Ibid., pp. 128–33; Payling, 1991, pp. 205–8.
103   Kaueper, 2001, p. 289.
104   Ibid., pp. 108–11.
105   Ibid., pp. 158–60, 289–90; Field, 1993, pp. 96–104.
106   Payling, 1991, pp. 188; Wright, 1983, p. 138–9.
107   Mackman, 1999, pp. 141–2.
108   See pp. 29–33, 60–2.
109   Wright, 1983, p. 140.
110   Payling, 1991, pp. 213–4; Mackman, 1999, pp. 141–2; Wright, 1983, p. 137; Kleineke, 1998, pp. 187–90.


*Notes to Chapter 5:  The Public Domain: Public Service, Private Lordship and Principles*

1    There is an ever-increasing body of literature on these topics and their relevance within particular contexts. For some of the more readily accessible definitions of some of these concepts, see Keen, 1984, pp. 143–78; Vale, 1981, pp. 14–32; Watts, 1996, pp. 51–80; Kaeuper, 1999, pp. 123–60.
2    Watts, 1996, pp. 31, 39–51.
3    Fleming, 1985, p. 72.
4    See p. 8. For the particular attitudes of the gentry and government towards the office of justice of the peace, see Lander, 1989, pp. 58–78, 108–55.
5    Clayton, 1980, pp. 242–3.
6    Bellamy, 1989, pp. 1–17, 30–3; TNA, KB9/232/2/88, 235/49, 244/35, KB27/733 rex rot. 29; E404/78/2/14; *Sheriffs*, 1898, p. 88; Horrox, 1989, p. 79.
7    Despite the allegedly much broader base of office-holding in Warwickshire, Carpenter sees avoidance rather than exclusion as the main reason for those families who were not involved in local administration: 1992, pp. 274–5.
8    Acheson, 1992, p. 120; Arnold, 1984, p. 260.
9    Payling, 1991, pp. 154–5.
10   Payling, 1991, pp. 111, 139–42; Wright, 1983, pp. 97, 110; Fleming, 1985, pp. 77, 79. By contrast, however, Mackman has suggested that the socio-political structure in Lancastrian Lincolnshire produced circumstances where few individuals and families were active in local administration and even these were not necessarily the wealthiest or most politically active. An elite group of royal servants was created during Edward IV's first reign, but by the 1470s the county had returned to the pattern established under the Lancastrians: 1999, pp. 104–13, 202–15, 228–33.
11   Arnold, 1984, pp. 255–6.
12   Acheson, 1992, pp. 119–20, 228–9; Wedgwood, 1936, pp. 307–8; Nicholas, 1832, p. 355; *Letters and Papers*, II ii, pp. 394, 412
13   Wedgwood, 1936, pp. 521–2; Mercer, 1995, pp. 47–8, 81, 83.

14   Acheson, 1992, p. 119.

15   Clayton, 1980, pp. 127, 145, 220-1.

16   Griffiths, 1998, pp. 426-7; Robson, 1989, p. 59. For other Heron connections to the Percys, see also Hicks, 1971, p. 90. Although Wedgwood is not always the most reliable of sources, he cites evidence of a John Heron of Crawley in Sussex: 1936, p. 447.

17   *CPR, 1452-61*, pp. 609, 613-14.

18   Carpenter, 1992, p. 273.

19   Mercer, 1995, pp. 32, 115; Jones, 1982, pp. 218, 327, 328; Marshall, 1975, pp. 117-19.

20   *Sheriffs*, p. 45; TNA, E404/71/6/15, 36; Hicks, 1984, pp. 23-4, 26-8. The unusual office of governor of the household during the Readeption has not been the subject of any analysis. It was presumably born out of the unsettled and unstable political conditions of the Readeption. What Lewis's powers were as governor are similarly unclear.

21   The Ascoughs had only recently entered the ranks of the leading gentry through the law and by integrating with established landed society: Mackman, 1999, pp. 65, 68, 103, 214, 219, 221.

22   Acheson, 1992, pp. 102-3, 132, 218-19; Marshall, 1975, pp. 136-7.

23   Acheson, 1992, pp. 230-1; Carpenter, 1992, p. 258; Denton, 2006, pp. 162-7.

24   Hicks, 1995, pp. 27-33, 43-68.

25   Extraordinary retainers in resident outside the traditional areas of influence are termed 'agents in enemy territory' by Pollard: 1976, p. 60.

26   Watts, 1995, pp. 113-14.

27   Carpenter, 1992, p. 474.

28   Kleineke, 1998, pp. 197, 199-200.

29   Acheson, 1992, pp. 24-27, 120, 234-5; Horrox, 2004a, pp. 792-5.

30   Bellamy, 1989, pp. 79-101.

31   Watts, 1995, pp. 110-11.

32   Ibid., p. 115.

33   These themes are explored extensively in Watts, 1996, pp. 13-51.

34   Grummitt, 2008, p. 31.

35   Griffiths, 1998, pp. 509-15; *Letters and Papers*, I, pp. 278-98.

36   For Gloucester's views at the peace negotiations of 1439 and those which commenced in 1445, see, for instance, Griffiths, 1998, pp. 446-54, 494-9. Yet the duke's death in suspicious circumstances in 1447 did not stifle opposition to the proposed surrender of Maine.

37   Griffiths, 1998, pp. 507-8, 514-15.

38   Jones, 1989, pp. 298-300. Watts asserts, however, that while issues such as rivalry with Somerset, honour or pressure from old soldiers shaped the duke's behaviour, York was forced to act in 1450 once the connection was made in the popular imagination between Somerset and the loss of Normandy: 1996, pp. 269-70.

39   *PPC*, VI, pp. 109-10.

40   Mackman, 1999, p. 301; *HOP*, IV, p. 203; *CPR, 1452-61*, p. 242; Holinshed, 1808, pp. 37-42

41   *Letters and Papers*, II ii, pp. 347, 435, 436, 542, 624, 631; Holinshed, 1808, p. 240.

42   Roskell, 1937, pp. 195-8.

43   Morgan, 1987, pp. 136-9.

44  *Letters and Papers*, I, pp. 251, 252, 265; II ii, pp. 435, 543; Curry, 1994, p. 61; *CPR, 1446–52*, pp. 479–80; Massey, 1980, pp. 81, 115, 204, 207, 251, 284, 286, 308; *PPC*, VI, pp. 129–30.

45  Entwistle also appears to have had some kind of association with Somerset, although the full extent of this is unknown: Bolton, 2007, p. 108 n. 18; Boardman, 2006, pp. 58–9.

46  TNA, KB145/7/1; C1/46/169.

47  Dockray, 1983, pp. 253–6; Horrox, 1989, pp. 49, 230; Pollard, 1975, pp. 37–42, 52; Bennett, 1985, p. 173.

48  *CPR, 1452–61*, p. 553; Mackman, 1999, pp. 78, 167.

49  See Payling, 1991, pp. 154–5; Wright, 1983, pp. 75, 86–7.

50  TNA, CP 40/808 rots 188, 342, 355

51  TNA, E101/410/2; 101/409/17; Myers, 1985, pp. 212–13, 227; 'Gregory', p. 207.

52  Wedgwood, 1936, pp. 647–8; Roskell, 1961, pp. 87–112.

53  Scofield, 1923, I, pp. 180, 249, 264; *Paston Letters*, II, no. 459.

54  Scofield, 1923, I, pp. 264, 334; *Three Fifteenth-Century Chronicles*, pp. 79, 178–9; *CFR, 1452–61*, pp. 260–1 (styled 'of Nettlestead, gentleman' in 1460).

55  Wedgwood, 1936, p. 883; Scofield, 1923, I, pp. 459, 544.

56  Wedgwood, 1936, pp. 67–8; Fleming and Wood, 2003, p. 91; *Paston Letters*, II, no. 615; III, no. 671; Shaw, 1906, I, p. 15. William Sandes became much more actively involved in Hampshire affairs after Edward IV's restoration: *CPR, 1461–67*, pp. 202, 230, 550; *CPR, 1467–77*, pp. 56, 351, 405, 429, 524, 629.

57  Wedgwood, 1936, p. 265; Haward, 1929, pp. 301–3, 312; *Arrivall*, p. 2; *Warkworth*, p. 13; *Paston Letters* II, no. 66, Schofield, 1923, I, pp. 568–9. Chamberlain had been a knight of the body since the 1460s: TNA, E101/412/2 fo. 36.

58  Horrox, 1989, pp. 100–2, 172.

59  Jones and Underwood, 1992, pp. 179–80; Warnicke, 1983, 176.


*Notes to Chapter 6: The Private Domain: Locality, Neighbourhood and Family*

1  Scofield, 1923, I, pp. 51–2; Mercer, 1995, pp. 82–3; Kleineke, 1998, pp. 244–5.

2  Harvey, 1969, pp. 202–7; Herbert, 1981, pp. 108–12. See p. 53.

3  A full discussion of sources is provided in Clayton, 1980, pp. 107–19. Clayton also notes that the Tudor tradition, which asserted that the leading gentry within the county were divided among themselves, does not have a factual basis. In contrast to Clayton, Gillespie thinks that Sir Thomas Fitton did bring a substantial force to Blore Heath: 1987, pp. 83–4.

4  It is unlikely that Margaret Troutbeck was the only widow to be concerned about her future after the death of her husband: Griffiths, 1998, p. 821.

5  Clayton, 1980, pp. 123–4.

6  Examples like Brereton suggest that there is still more to be gleaned about the activities of leading Cheshire gentry during the Wars of the Roses. The precise dating of this particular case involving Brereton and Clifton is uncertain although it is apparent that the case began when Henry VI was still the acknowledged king. See, for example, TNA, KB27/804 rot. 18r, 811 rot. 19v, 814 rot. 50r.

7   *Sheriffs*, p. 128; Mercer, 2007, p. 97; Clayton, 1980, pp. 146-7.

8   Holland, 1988a, pp. 849-69; Mackman, 1999, pp. 148 n. 20, 151, 162-3.

9   Moreton, 1991, p. 261.

10  Denton, 2006, pp. 69-70, 105-9. The Cliftons were one of the leading gentry families in Nottinghamshire and moved effortlessly into Yorkist service after 1461: Payling, 1991, p. 155 n.198; Horrox, 1991, pp. 111 n. 58, 267.

11  *Paston Letters*, II, no. 514; Holford, 2001, pp. 317-21.

12  Field, 1993, pp. 130-3.

13  Murray, 1935, pp. 210-6; Fleming, 1985, pp. 81-2; Griffiths, 1998, p. 815.

14  Bohna, 2003, pp. 563-82. The full extent of leading gentry involvement remains very uncertain, however. The role played by Robert Poynings as Cade's sword-bearer is quite clearly not representative of gentry involvement as a whole during the rebellion.

15  Dockray, 1983, pp. 246-65.

16  Mercer, 1995, p. 84. John Stone, a Canterbury monk who witnessed and described the events, has nothing to say on how the Yorkist earls were received within the city of Canterbury; nor does he provide any contemporary opinions about Fogge, Scott and Horne: Searle, 1902, p. 79.

17  *HOP*, III, E-O, pp. 95-7; Walker, 1990, pp. 70, 73, 76, 112, 238, 239, 269; Mercer, 1995, pp. 73-4. For John Fogge's career, see Mercer, 1995, passim; Wedgwood, 1936, pp. 339-42; Bolton, 1980, pp. 202-9. Bolton covers all possibilities for Fogge's behaviour by suggesting Yorkist sympathies of his wife, antagonism to the House of Lancaster or shrewd calculation as motives for Fogge's switch of allegiance in 1460. Simple pragmatism, very likely at the time, is not even considered.

18  Mercer, 1995, pp. 62-3; Wedgwood, 1936, pp. 750-2.

19  Mercer, 1995, pp. 61, 81. An overview of Horne's career is available in Wedgwood, 1936, pp. 470-1. See also Robertson, 1882, pp. 363-7.

20  Wedgwood, 1936, pp. 437; *HOP*, III, E-O, pp. 324-7.

21  *Town Chronicles*, p. 149; Hearne, 1728, p. 773; *English Chronicle*, p. 95; *Three Fifteenth-Century Chronicles*, p. 73; Mercer, 1995, pp. 85-8, 91-6.

22  *RP*, III, p. 398; TNA, C219/16/3; *CPR, 1452-61*, p. 673.

23  TNA, E101/54/5, 410/6, 9; *CPR, 1461-67*, p. 35.

24  Carpenter, 1992, pp. 68-9, 468-9, 476-7, 498-500, 529-32; Griffiths, 1991, pp. 365-82.

25  Norcliffe, 1881, p. 112; Wedgwood, 1936, p. 306.

26  Griffiths, 1998, pp. 805-7; *Chronicles of London*, p. 168; *Town Chronicles*, pp. 111, 159-60.

27  TNA, E404/75/1/60; Wedgwood, 1936, pp. 683-4; Kirby, 1996, pp. 27-8.

28  Lander, 1961, pp. 139-40.

29  Unless otherwise stated, the following discussion of Tresham is based on Roskell, 1959, pp. 313-23.

30  *CCR, 1461-68*, p. 56.

31  *CPR, 1461-67*, pp. 111, 369, 430, 437, 470. Tresham had been Pecche's stepson since at least 1459: *Catalogue of Ancient Deeds*, VI, C4128; TNA, C145/328/5; *CFR, 1471-85*, p. 175.

32  *RP*, V, 477, pp. 616-17; TNA, E13/155, rots. 60, 61, 64; BL, Additional Ms 39828, fo. 19.

33  There is some evidence of ransoms occasionally being demanded during the Wars of the Roses. John Barowe, a servant of Sir Thomas Neville, for example, was taken prisoner by

a servant of the earl of Northumberland at the battle of Wakefield in December 1460 and a ransom extracted for his release: TNA, C1/27/456.

34   Acheson, 1992, p. 243; TNA, PROB11/11 fos. 237–41. There is some uncertainty whether Tyrell died at the battle. If not, it occurred shortly afterwards and his eldest son, John, was forced to negotiate with the crown for the right to succeed to his father's lands: TNA, C1/56/127.

35   Pollard, 1976, pp. 52, 66; Horrox, 2004b, pp. 383–5.

36   Evans, 1998, pp. 84–6; Newell *et al.*, 2007, pp. 116–17, 120–1, 188–9.

37   *RP*, VI, pp. 29–30; *CPR, 1467–77*, pp. 535, 615–16.

38   Bean, 1984, pp. 194–5; TNA, KB9/75; E163/8/10; Schofield, 1923, I, pp. 90, 92–3; *English Chronicle*, pp. 95–6.

39   *RP*, VI, 19–20.

40   *CPR, 1452–61*, pp. 626, 629, 631; *CPR, 1461–7*, pp. 88, 90.

41   Brown was the subject of legal action shortly after the restoration of Edward IV in 1471: TNA, KB27/841 rot. 63r; 843 rot. 46v.

42   Mercer, 1995, pp. 125–6; *Paston Letters*, III, no. 842.

43   Kirby, 1996, pp. 5–9. Plumpton's career up to 1461 is dealt with at length in Wilcock, 2004, pp. 59–71.

44   TNA, C1/31/485.

45   Field, 1993, pp. 129–34.

46   *Arrivall*, pp. 9–13. In London Warwick was also joined by the duke of Exeter, marquess of Montagu and others.

47   Harwood, 1844, pp. 42–3; Bridgeman, 1913, p. 26; Wedgwood, 1917, 168–9; Carter, 1925, p. 26. Lee evidently managed to convince the authorities that false evidence had been presented against him and that he was a loyal subject of the Yorkist regime: TNA, KB9/41 (order to cease process dated 21 June 1472).

48   Mercer, 1995, pp. 90,

49   Mercer, 1999b, p. 232; Mercer, 2002, pp. 143–51.

50   Hicks, 1978, pp. 92–5; Holland, 1988b, pp. 22, 25–8, 32; TNA, KB27/842 rots. 10r, 71v; 845 rot. 118v.

51   See pp. 98–100.

52   Mercer, 1995, p. 132.

53   TNA, C1/76/3–5, 79/2; Sheppard, 1877, p. 47; *CFR, 1471–85*, no. 668; *CCR, 1476–85*, nos. 1013, 1113; Horrox, 2004c, pp. 682–3; Hampton, 1979, pp. 101–2.

54   *CIPM, Henry VII*, I, no. 362; *Harleian 433*, I, pp. 18–19.

55   Horrox, 1989, p. 286.

56   Ibid., p. 174.

57   Pronay and Cox, 1986, p. 171; Pollard, 1977, pp. 157–8.

58   *CPR, 1476–85*, pp. 368, 397, 445, 482–3; *Harleian 433*, II, p. 55.

59   *Harleian 433*, II, p. 60.

60   *CPR, 1476–85*, p. 383. Brackenbury had moved south in July 1483 after becoming constable of the Tower of London: *CPR, 1476–85*, 364.

61   Ibid., pp. 383, 385.

62   Ibid., p. 433.

63   Ibid., pp. 521, 546.

64   Du Boulay, 1966, p. 395.

65   *Harleian 433*, II, pp. 54–5.

66   Ibid., II, p. 55; *CPR, 1476–85*, p. 534.

67   *CPR, 1476–85*, pp. 515–6; *Harleian 433*, II, p. 116.

*Notes to Chapter 7: The Personal Domain: Contradictory Responses to Conflict*

1   See pp. 29–30.

2   See pp. 30–1.

3   Ellis, 1827, II, pp. 95–6.

4   *CPR, 1467–77*, p. 110. The head injuries received by some of those discovered in the Towton gravesite show a significant number received at the front and back of the skull. While injuries to the forearms as well as to the knees are present, indicative of attempts to either fend off blows or to target vulnerable parts of the body, the majority of wounds are to the head. The vast majority of blade wounds are cuts, although thrusting stab wounds are also present. Blunt force injuries also occur, predominantly to the left side of the head and face, indicating face-to-face combat with a right-handed opponent: Novak, 2000, p. 97.

5   Smith, I, 1907–10, pp. 97–8; IV, p. 87.

6   Given-Wilson, 2004, pp. 105–7.

7   *Froissart*, p. 89.

8   *Waurin*, V, pp. 329–30.

9   TNA, C1/43/284–90, 44/248.

10   Armstrong, 1983, pp. 99–100, 110, 116–17.

11   See pp. 32–3.

12   *CPR, 1467–77*, pp. 218–20, 252; Goodman, 1981a, pp. 142, 147.

13   See pp. 49, 86–7.

14   The same chronicle records that the West Country had already been thoroughly prepared by the duke of Somerset and earl of Devon, who 'bestyrd them right greatly to make an assemblye of asmoche people for to receyve theyr comynge, them to accompany, fortyfy, and assyst'. Somerset and Devon were regarded as 'old enheritors of the contrie': *Arrivall*, p. 23.

15   *Arrivall*, p. 15; *Gloucestershire Notes & Queries*, 1885, I, p. 280.

16   TNA, E101/55/13. A detailed discussion of this document is provided in Goodman, 1981b, pp. 240–52.

17   Castor, 2000, pp. 169–70, 188; Castor, 2004, pp. 142–3; *Paston Letters*, II, nos. 384, 401, 404.

18   Castor, 2000, pp. 188–9; *Paston Letters*, II, no. 384. Calthorpe had married Elizabeth, daughter of Reynold, Lord Grey of Ruthin: TNA, KB27/650 rot. 121.

19   Vivian, 1895, p. 150; *CCR, 1468–76*, no. 703; 'John Benet's chronicle', p. 233. The Pomeroys were the second wealthiest gentry family in the county: Kleineke, 1998, p. 192.

20   Mercer, 1999a, pp. 153–60.

21  Castor, 2000, pp. 166–8; Castor, 2004, pp. 66, 67, 73, 79, 84, 86, 91, 98, 142; *Town Chronicles*, p. 149.

22  Kingsford, 1919, no. 318.

23  Wedgwood, 1936, p. 222.

24  *CPR, 1468–76*, p. 284. Interestingly, Corbet's participation subsequently brought his family into conflict with the Crofts for local hegemony during the first decade of Henry VII's reign: Davies, 1995, pp. 255–6. Kynaston had been a retainer of Richard, duke of York, before 1461 and had fought with Yorkist forces at Blore Heath. After the battle he appropriated the Audley arms as his own: Griffiths, 1998, p. 820.

25  Acheson, 1992, pp. 226–7; Wedgwood, 1936, p. 273.

26  His most serious dispute, however, was probably with Edmund, Lord Grey of Ruthin, an aristocratic troublemaker in his own right, during the early 1440s: TNA, CP40/728 rots. 88, 442d, 533d; *PPC*, V, 211.

27  During the late 1420s and early 1430s Digby appears to have been drawn into the duke of Norfolk's affinity and was closely connected with the duke's servants and the prosecution of the duke's interests, including his dispute with the earl of Huntingdon. Yet Digby appeared to make connections when they suited his own purposes. During the 1440s there is also evidence that he established a relationship with Ralph, Lord Cromwell: *Itineraries*, p. 361; *Letters and Papers*, II ii, p. 760; TNA, KB27/679 rex rot. 6, 707 rot. 65, 714 rot. 124d; CP25/1/126/76/62.

28  TNA, KB9/941/87; KB27/798 rex rot. 44.

29  In an intriguing incident, Digby became associated with a knight called Sir William Kennedy who might have been part of a small Scottish contingent that accompanied Queen Margaret out of Scotland in 1460–1. In the wake of the second battle of St Albans in early 1461, Digby and Kennedy, were involved in violent disorder in Westminster. Kennedy's indictment only identified him as 'late of Westminster, knight', a common description when an individual could not be apprehended. He was not ordered to appear at the county court and was not outlawed. The evidence of this incident is consistent with contemporary chronicles that stated that the London authorities would not allow a group of Lancastrians into the city after the battle. It would seem likely that they turned their attention to Westminster instead. The chronicler known as Vitellius remarks that three of these northerners were killed at the Cripplegate, one of the principle entry points into the city from the north: TNA, KB29/92 rot 7r; KB9/297/15; *Chronicles of London*, p. 173.

30  TNA, E149/209/7; *RP*, V, pp. 477, 480.

31  Unless otherwise stated the following two paragraphs are based on Mackman, 1999, pp. 119–24.

32  Virgoe, 1973, pp. 459–82.

33  Charlesworth, 1952, p. 64.

34  Verbruggen, 1997, pp. 177–8.

35  *Arrivall*, pp. 19–20. Warkworth suggests that confusion over Edward IV and the earl of Oxford's badges led to Lancastrian forces attacking their own side during the latter stages of the battle: *Warkworth*, p. 16.

36  Bennett, 1985, pp. 115, 116, 173; Evans, 1928, pp. 125–6; Jones, 2002, p. 170.

37  *Froissart*, pp. 97–8.

38  Giles, 1845, p. 8; *Hall*, p. 255; *Arrivall*, p. 19.

39  Verbruggen, 1997, p. 179.

40  Roskell, 1963, pp. 79–105; Bayley, 1822, p. 523.

41  *CPR, 1446–52*, pp. 31, 431; TNA, E101/410/9; Wedgwood, 1936, pp. 934–5; *Paston Letters*, I, no. 243.

42  Contemporary chronicles did not record the manner of Wenlock's death. The *Arrivall* suggests that Wenlock was killed while fleeing the field of battle. Tudor chroniclers like Hall, however, subsequently incorporated the tradition of his violent death at the hands of Somerset into their accounts: *Arrivall*, p. 30; *Hall*, p. 300.

43  TNA, C1/27/478.

44  *Hall*, p. 301. The *Arrivall* simply says that 'Edward, called Prince, was taken fleinge to the towne wards, and slayne, in the fielde': *Arrivall*, p. 30. Hall's account is only a modest embellishment of the version of events presented in the *Arrivall* and could quite easily contain an element of truth.

45  Davies, 1995, pp. 245–6.

46  Returning home was not always an easy matter. On his return journey after the battle of Towton the minor gentleman Henry Spencer found himself imprisoned in Tamworth for requisitioning horses on behalf of the earl of Warwick which he had not returned: TNA, C1/27/146.

47  In the uncertain months following a battle many leading gentry sought the protection of a general pardon – such as Sir Reginald Stourton of West Bower in Somerset in 1471, who was presumably worried about repercussions in the wake of the battle of Tewkesbury, although the underlying reason remains obscure: *CPR, 1467–77*, p. 294.

48  *Waurin*, V, pp. 338–40. For detailed analyses of the Woodvilles' reputation see Hicks, 1979, pp. 60–86; Lander, 1963, pp. 119–52.

49  *CSP Milan*, I, pp. 65–6, 68, 73, 77, 78.

50  Ibid., I, p. 102.

51  *Paston Letters*, II, no. 404.

52  Mackman, 1999, pp. 174–5.

53  *CPR, 1461–67*, pp. 25, 86; Mercer, 1995, pp. 91–2.

54  TNA, C131/73/6, 74/3; C1/66/95–6.

55  TNA, KB27/804 rot. 5d; 809 rot. 79d; KB9/319; *CPR, 1467–77*, 180; TNA, C67/46 m. 38.

56  Hicks, 1984, pp. 33–5; Wedgwood, 1936, p. 883.

57  Wedgwood, 1936, pp. 400–1; Scofield, 1923, I, p. 252; *CPR, 1467–77*, p. 152; *CFR, 1461–71*, p. 283; TNA, C67/48 m. 32. Warkworth mistakenly identified him as one of those executed after the battle: *Warkworth*, p. 18.

58  Davies, 1995, p. 253.

59  Denton, 2006, pp. 162–7; Carpenter, 1992, p. 258; Acheson, 1992, pp. 230–1.

60  Sir Richard Woodville, Richard Haute and Sir John Fogge in 1485 hedged their bets should Richard III remain king. The Hautes and Fogges were kinsmen of the Woodvilles and had formed a powerful grouping within Kent. It was in the interests of Richard III to win them over and guarantee stability in the south east. On 12 January 1485 Fogge and Woodville bound themselves in the sum of 1,000 marks to bear themselves well and faithfully towards Richard III. In February Fogge was pardoned and had some of his lands restored.

Woodville was pardoned in March, as was his kinsman, Richard Haute of Ightham Mote: TNA, C244/136/130, 132; *CPR, 1476–85*, p. 511.

61  Mercer, 1995, pp. 139, 145, 147, 148.

62  Griffiths, 1993, pp. 27–43.

63  *CPR, 1461–7*, pp. 12, 135; *Calender of Documents Relating to Scotland*, IV, no. 1320; TNA, STAC2/32/12. According to an inquisition taken in November 1460 Henry Ogard was nine years of age: TNA, E207/18/3.

64  Evidence of Ogard's impact on Norfolk society shortly after Tewkesbury can be seen in TNA, KB27/844 rot. 10r, 849 rot. 28d, 35; C1/433/39–42, STAC2/32/12. See also Virgoe, 1994, pp. 23–40.

*Notes to Chapter 8:  Conclusion*

1  Goodman, 2005, p. 236.

2  Radulescu and Truelove, 2005, p. 2.

3  See pp. 9–11, 24.

4  Coss, 2003, pp. 248–54.

5  Castor, 2004, p. 103. Fastolf's income can be compared against the calculations provided in Gray, 1934, pp. 614–18, 621.

6  Fastolf's views were reflected in the *Boke of Noblesse*, composed by his secretary, William Worcester: Nichols, 1860, p. 5. Fastolf's opposition to peace was well known. His proctor, John Daubenay, had been part of a deputation at Le Mans in 1447 demanding compensation for their losses incurred through the return of their lands to the French as part of the peace negotiations: *Letters and Papers*, II ii, pp. 687–92.

7  Haward, 1929, pp. 300–14; Ross, 1983, p. 410.

8  McFarlane, 1944, p. 63. The importance of the county as a forum for the expression of communal opinion and its interaction with parliament is discussed in Coss, 2003, pp. 209–15. Watts, however, sees little evidence of autonomous gentry attitudes and asserts that 'Parliament, of course, provided an important link between centre and locality, but neither its elections nor its sessions were altogether free of the nets of lordship': Watts, 1996, p. 75. Similarly, Carpenter does not regard gentry complaints in parliament as an expression of dissatisfaction with lordship; instead it is seen as evidence that the relationship had become unstable: 1997, p. 60.

9  Moreton, 1991, pp. 255–6, 259–61.

10  The identity of participants in Fauconberg's rebellion suggests that not all leading and lesser gentry within the shire were committed enthusiastic supporters of the House of York. While some made choices based on connections to the Nevilles, others apparently made a politically informed choice to support opposition to Edward IV and the calls for good governance: Mercer, 1995, pp. 118–19; Richmond, 1970, pp. 687–92.

11  An account of the rebellion appears in Nichols, 1847, 6–16.

12  Mercer, 2007, pp. 88–93.

13  TNA, PROB11/7 fo. 212r.

# *Bibliography*

## MANUSCRIPTS

### LONDON: THE NATIONAL ARCHIVES

C1 Chancery: Early Chancery Proceedings

C67 Chancery: Pardon Rolls

C131 Chancery: Extents for Debts, Series I

C145 Chancery: Miscellaneous Inquisitions

C219 Chancery: Chancery and Lord Chancellor's Office: Petty Bag Office and Crown Office: Parliamentary Election Writs and Returns

C244 Chancery: Petty Bag Office: Files, Tower and Rolls Chapel Series, *Corpus Cum Causa*

CHES29 Palatinate of Chester: Chester County Court and Court of Great Sessions of Chester: Plea Rolls

CP25/1 Court of Common Pleas: Feet of Fines Files, Richard I–Henry VII

CP40 Court of Common Pleas: Plea Rolls

E13 Exchequer: Exchequer of Pleas: Plea Rolls

E101 Exchequer: King's Remembrancer: Various Accounts

E143 Exchequer: King's Remembrancer: Extents and Inquisitions

E149 Exchequer: King's Remembrancer: Inquisitions Post Mortem

E163 Exchequer: King's Remembrancer: Miscellanea of the Exchequer

E207 Exchequer: King's Remembrancer and Lord Treasurer's Remembrancer: KR Bille and LTR Bille Petitones Files

E364 Exchequer: Pipe Office: Foreign Accounts Rolls

E383 Exchequer: Lord Treasurer's Remembrancer: Writ Files

E403 Exchequer: Exchequer of Receipt: Issue Rolls

E404 Exchequer: Exchequer of Receipt: Warrants for Issue

KB9 Court of King's Bench: Ancient Indictments

KB27 Court of King's Bench: Plea Rolls

KB29 Court of King's Bench: Controlment Rolls

KB145 Court of King's Bench: Crown and Plea Sides: Recorda and Precepta Recordorum Files

PROB11 Prerogative Court of Canterbury: Will Registers

SC8 Special Collections: Ancient Petitions
STAC2 Court of Star Chamber: Proceedings, Henry VIII

## LONDON: BRITISH LIBRARY
Additional Manuscripts 30998, 39828

## OXFORD: BODLEIAN LIBRARY
MS Ashmole 856, 1137

## DUBLIN: NATIONAL ARCHIVES OF IRELAND
RC8 Record Commission: Calendars of Memoranda Rolls

# PRIMARY SOURCES

Amos, A. (ed.) (1825), *De Laudibus Legem Angliae, The Translation into English and the Original Latin Text with Notes*. London: Joseph Butterworth and Son.

Black, W. H. (ed.) (1840), *Illustrations of Ancient State and Chivalry from Manuscripts Preserved in the Ashmolean Museum with an Appendix*. London: Shakespeare Press.

Brie, F. W. D. (ed.) (1906–8), *The Brut, or the Chronicles of England*, 2 vols. London: Early English Text Society.

Bruce, J. (ed.) (1838), *Historie of the Arrivall of King Edward IV in England and the Finall Recouerye of his Kingdomes from Henry VI*. London: Camden Society.

*Calendar of Close Rolls, 1422–1509* (1933–1963), 11 vols. London: HMSO.

*Calendar of Documents Relating to Scotland, 1357–1509* (1888), IV. no. 1320. Edinburgh: H. M. General Register House.

*Calendar of Fine Rolls, 1399–1509* (1931–1962), 11 vols. London: HMSO.

*Calendar of Inquisitions Post Mortem, Henry VII* (1898–1956), 3 vols. London: HMSO.

*Calendar of Patent Rolls, 1399–1509* (1897–1916), 17 vols. London: HMSO.

*Calendar of State Papers and Manuscripts existing in the Archives and Collections of Milan* (1912) I, ed. A. B. Hinds. London: HMSO.

Chart, D. A. (ed.) (1935), *The Register of John Swayne, 1418–1429*. Belfast.

Clark, A. (ed.) (1914), *Lincoln Diocese Documents 1450–1544*, London: Early English Text Society.

Davies, J. S. (ed.) (1856), *An English Chronicle in the Reigns of Richard II, Henry IV, Henry V, and Henry VI*. London: Camden Society.

Davis, N. (ed) (1971–6), *Paston Letters and Papers of the Fifteenth Century*, 2 vols, Oxford: Clarendon Press.

*A Descriptive Catalogue of Ancient Deeds in the Public Record Office* (1890–1915), 6 vols. London: HMSO.

Dickinson, J. (ed.) (1927), *The Statesman's Book of John of Salisbury*. New York: Alfred A. Knopf.

Ellis, H. (ed.) (1809), *Hall's Chronicle*. London.

Ellis, H. (ed.) (1827), *Original Letters Illustrative of English History*, Second Series, 4 vols. London: Harding and Lepard.

Ellis, H. (ed.) (1851), *The Pylgrymage of Sir Richard Guylforde*. London: Camden Society.

Evans, J. (ed.) (1928), *The Unconquered Knight: A Chronicle of the Deeds of Don Pero Nino Count of Buelna by his Standard-Bearer Gutierre Diaz de Gamez*. London: George Routledge & Sons.

Finn, A. (ed.) (1911), *Records of Lydd*, trans. and transcriber Arthur Hussey and M. M. Hardy. Ashford.

Flenley, R. (ed.) (1911), *Six Town Chronicles of England*. Oxford: Clarendon Press.

Gairdner, J. (ed.) (1876), 'Gregory's chronicle: 1189–1249', in *The Historical Collections of a Citizen of London*. London: Camden Society.

Gairdner, J. (ed.) (1880), *Three Fifteenth-Century Chronicles*. London: Camden Society.

Gairdner, J. (ed.) (1910), *The Paston Letters 1422–1509*, 3 vols. Edinburgh: John Grant.

Giles, J. A. (ed.) (1845), *Chronicles of the White Rose of York*. London: James Bohn.

Goodman, A (2006), *The Wars of the Roses: The Soldiers' Experience*. Stroud: Tempus.

Halliwell, J. O. (ed.) (1839), *A Chronicle of the First Thirteen Years of the Reign of King Edward IV, by John Warkworth*. London: Camden Society.

Hardy W. and Hardy, E. L. C. P. (eds) (1864–91), *Recueil des croniques et anchiennes istories de la Grant Bretaigne par Jehan de Waurin*, 5 vols, Rolls Series. London: Longman.

Harriss, G. L. and Harriss, M. A. (eds) (1972), 'John Benet's chronicle for the years 1400 to 1462', in *Camden Miscellany Vol. XXIV: Camden Fourth Series Vol. 9*. London: Royal Historical Society, pp. 151–233.

Harvey, J. H. (ed.) (1969), *William Worcestre, Itineraries*. Oxford: Clarendon Press.

Harwood, T (1844), *A Survey of Staffordshire containing the antiquities of the county by Sampson Erdeswick, and with additions and corrections by Wyrley et al., illustrative of the history and antiquities of that county*. J. B. Nichols and son: London.

Hearne, T. (ed.) (1728), 'Annales rerum Anglicarum' by William of Worcester, in *Liber Niger Scaccarii*, 2. Oxford: E Teatro Sheldoniano, pp. 424–521.

Historical Manuscripts Commission (1888), *Historical Manuscripts Commission 12th Report: Rutland Manuscripts*, I.

Holinshed, R. (1808), *Chronicles of England, Scotland, and Ireland*, III. London.

Horrox, R. and Hammond, P. W. (eds) (1979–83), *British Library Harleian Manuscript 433: Register of Grants for the Reigns of Edward V and Richard III*, 4 vols. Gloucester: Alan Sutton for the Richard III Society.

Kingsford, C. L. (ed.) (1905), *Chronicles of London*. Oxford: Clarendon Press.

Kingsford, C. L. (ed.) (1919), *The Stonor Letters and Papers 1290–1483*. London: Camden Society.

Kirby, J. (ed.) (1996), *The Plumpton Letters and Papers*. Cambridge: Cambridge University Press.

*Letters and Papers, Foreign and Domestic of the Reign of Henry VIII, 1509–47* (1862–1932), 21 vols. London: HMSO.

*List of Sheriffs for England and Wales* (1898), PRO Lists and Indexes, 12. London: HMSO.

Macaulay, G. C. (ed.) (1910), *The Chronicles of Froissart, Froissart, Jean; translated by John Bourchier, Lord Berners*. New York: Harvard Classics.

Nicholas, N. H. (ed.) (1834–7), *Proceedings and Ordinances of the Privy Council of the Privy Council of England*, 7 vols. London: Record Commission.

Nichols, J. G. (ed.) (1847), *Chronicle of the Rebellion in Lincolnshire, 1470*. London: Camden Society, Miscellany I.

Nichols, J. G. (ed.) (1860), *The Boke of Noblesse*. London: Roxburghe Club.

Norcliffe, C. B. (ed.) (1881), *The Visitation of Yorkshire in the Years 1563 and 1564*, London: Harleian Society, XVI.

Pronay, N. and Cox, J. (eds) (1986), *The Crowland Chronicle Continuations, 1459–1486*. London: Sutton Richard III and Yorkist History Trust.

Public Record Office (1887), *Reports of the Deputy Keeper of the Public Records XLVIII*. London: Public Record Office.

Raine, J. (ed.) (1864–5), *The Priory of Hexham, Its Chroniclers, Endowments and Annals*, 2 vols. Durham: Surtees Society.

Searle, W. G. (ed.) (1902), 'Chronicle of John Stone', in *Christ Church, Canterbury*, pt I. Cambridge: Cambridge Antiquarian Society.

Sheppard, J. B. (ed.) (1877), *Christ Church Letters*, London: Camden Society.

Sheppard, J. B. (ed.) (1887–9), *Literae Cantuariensis: The Letter Books of the Monastery of Christ Church Canterbury*, 3 vols. Rolls Series. London.

Smith, L. T. (ed.) (1894), *Expeditions to Prussia and the Holy Land made by Henry, Earl of Derby (afterwards King Henry IV) in the years 1390–1 and 1392–3, Being the Accounts Kept by his Treasurer during Two Years*, London: Camden Society.

Smith, L. T. (ed.) (1907–10), *The Itinerary of John Leland in or about the Years 1535–1542*, 5 vols. London: Thomas Hearne.

Strachey, J. (ed.) (1767–77), *Rotuli Parliamentorum, 1277–1503*, 6 vols. London.

*Statutes of the Realm*, 11 vols (1810–28). London.

Stevenson, J. (ed.) (1861–4), *Letters and Papers Illustrative of the Wars of the English in France during the Reign of Henry VI*, 2 vols in 3, Rolls Series. London: Longman, Green, Longman and Roberts.

Thomas, A. H. and Thornley, I. D. (eds) (1938), *The Great Chronicle of London*. London: Alan Sutton.

Vivian, J. L. (ed.) (1895), *The Visitations of the County of Devon*. Exeter: Eland.

Weaver, P. W. (ed.) (1903), *Somerset Medieval Wills, 1501–1530*, London: Somerset Record Society, XIX.

## SECONDARY SOURCES

Acheson, E. (1992), *A Gentry Community: Leicestershire in the Fifteenth Century, c.1422–c.1485*. Cambridge: Cambridge University Press.

Amyot, T. (1827), 'An inventory of effects formerly belonging to Sir John Fastolf'. *Archaeologia*, 21, 232–80.

Anglo, S. (1965), 'Anglo-Burgundian feats of arms: Smithfield, June 1467'. *The Guildhall Miscellany*, 2, (7), 271–83.

Anglo, S. (2000), *The Martial Arts of Renaissance Europe*. New Haven and London: Yale University Press.

Armstrong, C. A. J. (1983), *England, France and Burgundy in the Fifteenth Century*. London: Hambledon Press.

Arnold, C. E. (1984), 'A Political Study of the West Riding of Yorkshire 1437–1509', unpublished PhD thesis, University of Manchester.

Ayton, A. (1995), 'Knights, esquires and military service: the evidence of the armorial cases before the Court of Chivalry', in A. Ayton and J. L. Price (eds), *The Medieval Military Revolution: State, Society and Military Change in Medieval and Early Modern Europe*. London and New York: Tauris Academic Studies, pp. 81–104.

Barker, J (1986), *The Tournament in England 1100–1400*. Woodbridge: Boydell Press.

Bayley, J. (1822), 'An account of the first battle of St Albans from a contemporary manuscript'. *Archaeologia*, 20, 519–23.

Bean, J. M. W. (1984), 'The financial position of Richard, duke of York', in J. Gillingham and J. C. Holt (eds), *War and Government in the Middle Ages*. Cambridge and Totowa, NJ: Barnes & Noble Books, pp. 182–98.

Bellamy, J. (1989) *Bastard Feudalism and the Law*. Portland: Areopagitica Press.

Bennett, M. J (1973), 'A county community: social cohesion amongst the Cheshire Gentry, 1400–1425'. *Northern History*, 8, 24–44.

Bennett, M. J. (1985), *The Battle of Bosworth*. Gloucester: Sutton Publishing.

Blair, C. (1958), *European Armour circa 1066 to circa 1700*. London: Batsford.

Boardman, A. (2006), *The First Battle of St Albans 1455*. Stroud: The History Press.

Bohna, M. (2003), 'Armed force and civic legitimacy in Jack Cade's revolt, 1450'. *English Historical Review*, 118, 563–82.

Bolton, J. L. (2007), 'How Sir Thomas Rempston paid his ransom: or, the mistakes of an Italian Bank', in L. Clark (ed.), *Conflicts, Consequences and the Crown in the Late Middle Ages*. Woodbridge and Rochester, NY: Boydell, pp. 101–18.

Bolton, S. (1980), 'Sir John Fogge of Ashford'. *The Ricardian*, 5, (59), 202–9.

Bornstein, D. (1975), 'Military manuals in fifteenth-century England'. *Mediaeval Studies*, 37, 469–77.

Bridgeman, C. G. O. (1913), 'Notes on the Manors of Aston and Walton, near Stone, in the Thirteenth and Fourteenth Centuries A.D.', in *Collections for a History of Staffordshire*, ed. by the William Salt Archaeological Society, 179–276.

Carpenter, C. (1992), *Locality and Polity: A study of Warwickshire Landed Society, 1401–1499*. Cambridge: Cambridge University Press.

Carpenter, C. (1994), 'Gentry and community in medieval England'. *Journal of British Studies*, 33, 340–80.

Carpenter, C. (1995), 'The Stonor circle in the fifteenth century', in R. E. Archer and S. Walker (eds), *Rulers and Ruled in Late Medieval England*. London and Rio Grande, OH: Hambledon Press, pp. 175–200.

Carpenter, C. (2004), 'Catesby family (*per.* c.1340–1505)'. *Oxford Dictionary of National Biography*, 10, 529–31.

Carter, W. F. (1925), 'Notes on Staffordshire Families', in *Collections for a History of Staffordshire*, ed. by the William Salt Archaeological Society, 1–153.

Castor, H. (2000), *The King, the Crown, and the Duchy of Lancaster: Public Authority and Private Power, 1399–1461*. Oxford: Oxford University Press.

Castor, H. (2004), *Blood and Roses: The Paston Family in the Fifteenth Century*. London: Faber and Faber.

Charlesworth, D. (1952), 'The battle of Hexham'. *Archaeologia Aeliana*, 4th Series, 30, 57–68.

Charlton, J. (1978), *The Tower of London: Its Buildings and Institutions*. London: HMSO.

Cherry, M. (1979), 'The Courtenay Earls of Devon: the formation and disintegration of a late medieval aristocratic affinity'. *Southern History*, 1, 71–97.

Cherry, M. (1986), 'The struggle for power in mid-fifteenth-century Devonshire', in R. A. Griffiths (ed.), *Patronage, the Crown and the Provinces*. Gloucester: Alan Sutton Publishing, pp. 123–44

Chibi, A. A. (2004) 'Docwra, Sir Thomas'. *Oxford Dictionary of National Biography*, 16, 380–1.

Clayton, D. J. (1980), 'The Involvement of the Gentry in the Political, Administrative, and Judicial Affairs of the County Palatinate of Chester, 1442–1485', unpublished PhD thesis, University of Liverpool.

Cohen, A. P. (1985), *The Symbolic Construction of the Community*. Chichester: Ellis Horwood Ltd and Tavistock Publications.

Collins, H. (2000), 'Sir John Fastolf, John Lord Talbot and the dispute over Patay:

ambition and chivalry in the fifteenth century', in D. Dunn. (ed.), *War and Society in Medieval and Early Modern Britain*. Liverpool: Liverpool University Press, pp. 114–40.

Coss, P. (2003), *The Origins of the English Gentry*. Cambridge: Cambridge University Press.

Crawford, A. (1992), *The Household Books of John Howard, Duke of Norfolk, 1462–1471, 1481–1483*. Stroud: Alan Sutton for Richard III and Yorkist History Trust.

Crossley, F. H. (1925), 'Medieval monumental effigies remaining in Cheshire'. *Transactions of the Historic Society of Lancashire and Cheshire*, 76, 1–51.

Curry, A. (1994), 'English armies in the fifteenth century', in A. Curry and M. Hughes (eds), *Arms, Armies and Fortifications in the Hundred Years War*. Woodbridge: Boydell Press, pp. 39–68.

Davies, C. S. L. (1995), 'The Crofts: creation and defence of a family enterprise under the Yorkists and Henry VII'. *Historical Research*, 68, 241–65.

Denton, J. (2006), 'The East-Midlands Gentleman, 1400–1530', unpublished PhD thesis, Keele University.

Dillon, H. A. (1900), 'On a manuscript collection of ordinances of chivalry of the fifteenth century, belonging to Lord Hastings'. *Archaeologia*, 57, 29–70.

Dobson, R. B. (1977), 'Urban decline in late medieval England'. *Transactions of the Royal Historical Society*, 5th Series, 27, 1–22.

Dockray, K. (1983), 'The Yorkshire rebellions of 1469'. *The Ricardian*, 6, (83), 246–65.

Dockray, K. (1992), 'The battle of Wakefield'. *The Ricardian*, 9, 238–58.

Dockray, K. (2002), *William Shakespeare, the Wars of the Roses and the Historians*. Stroud: Tempus Publishing.

Dockray, K. (2004), 'Plumpton, Sir William (1404–1480)'. *Oxford Dictionary of National Biography*, 44, 616–17.

Du Boulay, F. R. H. (1966), *The Lordship of Canterbury*. London: Nelson.

Ellis, S. G. (1998), *Ireland in the Age of the Tudors 1447–1603*. London: Longman.

Evans, H. T. (1998), *Wales and the Wars of the Roses*, first published by Cambridge University Press in 1915. Stroud: Sutton.

Field, P. J. C. (1977), 'Sir Robert Malory, Prior of the Hospital of St John of Jerusalem in England (1432–1439/40)'. *Journal of Ecclesiastical History*, 28, 249–64.

Field, P. J. C. (1993), *The Life and Times of Sir Thomas Malory*. Cambridge: D. S. Brewer.

Fleming, P. W. (1984), 'Charity, faith and the gentry in Kent 1422–1529', in A. J. Pollard (ed.), *Property and Politics*. Gloucester: Sutton, pp. 36–58.

Fleming, P. W. (1985), 'The Character and Concerns of the Gentry in Kent in the Fifteenth Century', unpublished PhD thesis, University of Wales, Swansea.

Fleming, P. W. (1987), 'The Hautes and their 'circle': culture and the English gentry', in D. Williams (ed.) (, *England in the Fifteenth-Century: Proceedings of the 1986 Harlaxton Symposium*. Woodbridge and Wolfeboro, NH: Boydell Press, pp. 85–102.

Fleming, P. W. (2005), 'Politics', in R. Radulescu and A. Truelove (eds), *Gentry Culture in Late Medieval England*. Manchester: Manchester University Press, pp. 50–62.

Fleming, P. W. and Wood, M. (2003), *Gloucestershire's Forgotten Battle, Nibley Green 1470*. Stroud: The History Press.

Gillespie, J. L. (1987), 'Cheshiremen at Blore Heath: a swan dive', in J. Rosenthal and C. Richmond (eds), *People Politics and Community in the Later Middle Ages*. Gloucester: Alan Sutton, pp. 77–89.

Gillingham, J. (1981), *The Wars of the Roses: Peace and Conflict in Fifteenth-Century England*. London: Weidenfeld and Nicolson.

Given-Wilson, C. (1996), *The English Nobility in the Late Middle Ages*. London and New York: Routledge.

Given-Wilson, C. (2004), *Chronicles: The Writing of History in Medieval England*. London and New York: Hambledon.

*Gloucestershire Notes & Queries*, I (1885).

Goodman, A. (2006), The Wars of the Roses: The Soldiers' Experience. Stroud: Tempus.

Goodman, A. E. (1981a), *The Wars of the Roses: Military Activity and English Society, 1452–97*. London: Routledge & Kegan Paul.

Goodman, A. E. (1981b), 'Responses to requests in Yorkshire for military service under Henry V'. *Northern History*, 17, 240–52.

Gray, H. L. (1934), 'Incomes from lands in England in 1436'. *English Historical Review*, 49, 607–39.

Griffiths, R. A. (1963), 'The rise of the Stradlings of St Donat's'. *Morgannwg*, 7, 15–47.

Griffiths, R. A. (1991), 'The hazards of civil war: the Mountford family and the Wars of the Roses', in *King and Country: England and Wales in the Fifteenth Century*. London: Hambledon, pp. 365–82.

Griffiths, R. A. (1993), *Sir Rhys ap Thomas and his Family: A Study in the Wars of the Roses and Early Tudor Politics*. Cardiff: University of Wales Press.

Griffiths, R. A. (1998), *The Reign of Henry VI*. Stroud: Sutton Publishing, reprinted edition, 1981.

Griffiths, R. A. and Thomas, R. S. (1985), *The Making of the Tudor Dynasty*. Stroud: Sutton.

Grummitt, D. (2001), 'William, Lord Hastings, the Calais garrison and the politics of Yorkist England'. *The Ricardian*, 12, 262–74.

Grummitt, D. (2008), *The Calais Garrison: War and Military Service in England, 1436–1558*. Woodbridge: Boydell Press.

Hampton, W. E. (1979), *Memorials of the Wars of the Roses*. Upminster: The Richard III Society.

Harvey, B. R. (1988), 'The Berkeleys of Berkeley 1281–1417: A Study in the Lesser Peerage of Late Medieval England', unpublished PhD thesis, University of St Andrews.

Haward, W. I. (1929), 'Gilbert Debenham: a medieval rascal in real life'. *History* 13, 300–14.

Herbert, A. (1981), 'Herefordshire, 1413–61: some aspects of society and public order', in R. A. Griffiths (ed.), *Patronage, the Crown and the Provinces*. Gloucester: Alan Sutton Publishing, pp. 103–22.

Hicks, M. A. (1971), 'The Career of Henry Percy, Fourth Earl of Northumberland (c.1448–1489), with Special Reference to his Retinue', unpublished MA thesis, University of Southampton.

Hicks, M. A. (1978), 'The case of Sir Thomas Cook, 1468'. *English Historical Review*, 93, 82–96.

Hicks, M. A. (1979), 'The changing role of the Wydevilles in Yorkist politics to 1483', in C. D. Ross (ed.), *Patronage, Pedigree and Power in Later Medieval England*. Gloucester: Alan Sutton, pp. 60–86.

Hicks, M. A. (1980), *False, Fleeting, Perjur'd Clarence*. Gloucester: Alan Sutton.

Hicks, M. A. (1984), 'Edward IV, The Duke of Somerset and Lancastrian loyalism in the north'. *Northern History*, 20, 33–5.

Hicks, M. A. (1995), *Bastard Feudalism*. London: Longman.

Hicks, M. A. (1998), *Warwick the Kingmaker*. Oxford: Blackwell.

Holford, M. (2001), 'Locality, Culture and Identity in Late Medieval Yorkshire, c.1270–c.1540', unpublished PhD thesis, University of York.

Holland, P. (1988a), 'The Lincolnshire rebellion of March 1470'. *English Historical Review*, 103, 849–69.

Holland, P. (1988b), 'Cook's case in history and myth'. *Historical Research*, 61, 21–35.

Horrox, R. (1989), *Richard III: A Study in Service*. Cambridge: Cambridge University Press.

Horrox, R. (2004a), 'Harrington family (per. c.1300–1512)'. *Oxford Dictionary of National Biography*, 25, 383–5.

Horrox, R. (2004b), 'Hastings, William, first Baron Hastings (c.1430–1483)'. *Oxford Dictionary of National Biography*, 25, 792–5.

Horrox, R. (2004c), 'Ashton, Sir Ralph'. *Oxford Dictionary of National Biography*, 2, 682–3.

Hunt, T. (2003), *The English Civil War at First Hand*. London: Phoenix.

Jack, R. I. (1961), 'The Greys of Ruthin 1325–1490: A Study in the Lesser Baronage', unpublished PhD thesis, University of London.

Jones, M. K. (1982), 'The Beaufort Family and the War in France, 1421–50', unpublished PhD thesis, Bristol University.

Jones, M. K. (1989), 'Somerset, York and the Wars of the Roses', *English Historical Review*, 104, 285–307.

Jones, M. K. (2001), '1477 – The expedition that never was: chivalric expectation in late Yorkist England'. *The Ricardian*, 12, 275–92.

Jones, M. K. (2002), *Bosworth 1485: Psychology of a Battle*. Stroud: The History Press.

Jones, M. K. and Underwood, M. G. (1992), *The King's Mother: Lady Margaret Beaufort Countess of Richmond and Derby*. Cambridge: Cambridge University Press.

Kaueper, R. W. (2001), *Chivalry and Violence in Medieval Europe*. Oxford: Oxford University Press.

Keen, M. H. (1984), *Chivalry*. New Haven and London: Yale University Press.

Keen, M. H. (2002), *Origins of the English Gentleman: Heraldry, Chivalry and Gentility in Medieval England, c.1300–c.1500*. Stroud: Tempus.

King, E. (1967), *The Knights of St John in the British Realm, being the Official History of the Most Venerable Order of the Hospital of St John of Jerusalem by the Late Colonel Sir Edwin King, Revised and Continued by Sir Harry Luke*, 3rd edn revised and continued. London: St Johnís Gate.

Kleineke, H. (1998), 'The Dinham Family in the Later Middle Ages', unpublished PhD thesis, University of London.

Kleineke, H. (2006), 'Gerhard von Wesel's newsletter from England, 17 April 1471'. *The Ricardian*, 16, 66–83.

Labarge, M. W. (1980), *Gascony, England's First Colony, 1204–1453*. London: H. Hamilton.

Lander, J. R. (1961), 'Attainder and forfeiture, 1453–1509'. *Historical Journal*, 4, 119–51.

Lander, J. R. (1963), 'Marriage and politics in the fifteenth century: the Nevilles and the Wydevilles'. *Bulletin of the Institute of Historical Research*, 36, 119–52

Lander, J. R. (1989), *English Justices of the Peace 1461–1509*. Gloucester: Alan Sutton.

Mackman, J. (1999), 'The Lincolnshire Gentry and the Wars of the Roses', unpublished PhD thesis, University of York.

MacMichael, N. H. (1960), 'The descent of the manor of Evegate in Smeeth with some account of its lands'. *Archaeologia Cantiana*, 74, 1–47.

McFarlane, K. B. (1943–5), 'Bastard feudalism'. *Bulletin of the Institute of Historical Research*, 20, 161–80.

McFarlane, K. B. (1944), 'Parliament and "bastard feudalism"'. *Transactions of the Royal Historical Society*, 4th series, 53–79.

McFarlane, K. B. (1973), *The Nobility of Later Medieval England*. Oxford: Clarendon Press.

Maddern, P. (2005), 'Gentility', in R. Radulescu and A. Truelove (eds), *Gentry Culture in Late Medieval England*. Manchester: Manchester University Press, pp. 18–34.

Mann, J. G. (1932), 'Two helmets in St Botolph's Church, Lullingstone, Kent'. *Antiquaries Journal*, 12, 138–9.

Mann, J. G. (1940), 'A tournament helm in Melbury Sampford Church'. *Antiquaries Journal*, 20, 366–79.

Marshall, A. E. (1975), 'The Role of English War Captains in England and Normandy, 1436–61', unpublished MA thesis, University of Wales, Swansea.

Massey, R. (1987), 'The Lancastrian Land Settlement in Normandy and Northern France, 1417–1450', unpublished PhD thesis, University of Liverpool.

Mercer, M. (1995), 'Kent and National Politics, 1437–1534: The Royal Affinity and a County Elite', unpublished PhD thesis, University of London.

Mercer, M. (1999a), 'Driven to rebellion? Sir John Lewknor, dynastic loyalty and debt'. *Sussex Archaeological Collections*, 107, 153–60.

Mercer, M. (1999b), 'Lancastrian loyalism in Kent during the Wars of the Roses. *Archaeologia Cantiana*, 119, 221–43.

Mercer, M. (2002), 'A forgotten Kentish rebellion, September–October 1470'. *Archaeologia Cantiana*, 122, 143–52.

Mercer, M. (2007), 'The strength of Lancastrian loyalism during the Readeption: gentry participation at the battle of Tewkesbury'. *Journal of Medieval Military History*, 5, 84–98.

Merriman, R. B. (1905), 'Edward Woodville: Knight-Errant'. *Proceedings of the American Antiquarian Society*, 16, 127–44.

Mertes, K. (1988), *The English Noble Household 1250–1600: Good Governance and Politic Rule*. Oxford: Basil Blackwell.

Moreton, C. (1991), 'A social gulf? The upper and lesser gentry of later medieval England'. *Journal of Medieval History*, 17, (3), 255–62.

Morgan, P. (1987), *War and Society in Medieval Cheshire 1277–1403*. Manchester: Chetham Society.

Muhlberger, S. (2005), *Deeds of Arms: Formal Combats in the Late Fourteenth Century*. Highland Village, TX: The Chivalry Bookshelf.

Murray, K. M. E. (1935), *The Constitutional History of the Cinque Ports*. Manchester: Manchester University Press.

Myers, A. R. (1995), *Crown, Household and Parliament in Fifteenth-Century England*. London: Hambledon.

Nall, C. (2004), 'The Production and Reception of Military Texts in the Aftermath of the Hundred Years War', unpublished PhD thesis, University of York.

Newell, B. R., Lagnado, D. A. and Shanks, D. R. (2007), *Straight Choices: The Psychology of Decision Making*. Hove and New York: Psychology Press.

Nicholas, N. H. (1832), *History of the Battle of Agincourt*, 2nd edn. London.

Nichols, F. M. (1863), 'On feudal and obligatory knighthood'. *Archaeologia*, 39, 189–244.

Novak. S. (2000), 'Battle-related trauma', in V. Fiorato, A. Boylston and C. Knüsel (eds), *Blood Red Roses: The Archaeology of a Mass Grave from the Battle of Towton AD 1461*. Oxford: Oxbow Books, pp. 90–102.

Oakeshott, E. (1994), *The Sword in the Age of Chivalry*. Woodbridge: Boydell Press.

Oman, C. (1924), *The Art of War in the Middle Ages, Volume Two: 1278–1485AD*, reprinted edn 1991. London: Greenhill Books.

Orme, N. (1984), *From Childhood to Chivalry: The Education of the English Kings and Aristocracy 1066–1530*. London: Routledge Kegan & Paul.

Orme, N. (2005), 'Education and recreation', in R. Radulescu and A. Truelove (eds), *Gentry Culture in Late Medieval England*. Manchester: Manchester University Press, pp. 63–83.

Payling, S. J. (1989), 'The Ampthill dispute: a study in aristocratic lawlessness and the breakdown of Lancastrian government'. *English Historical Review*, 104, 881–907.

Payling, S. J. (1991), *Political Society in Lancastrian England: The Greater Gentry of Nottinghamshire*. Oxford: Clarendon Press.

Pollard, A. J. (1968), 'The Family of Talbot, Lords Talbot and Earls of Shrewsbury in the Fifteenth Century', unpublished PhD thesis, Bristol University.

Pollard, A. J. (1975), 'The Richmondshire community of gentry during the Wars of the Roses', in C. D. Ross (ed.), *Patronage, Pedigree and Power in Later Medieval England*. Gloucester: Alan Sutton, pp. 37–59.

Pollard, A. J. (1976), 'The Northern retainers of Richard Nevill, Earl of Salisbury'. *Northern History*, 11, 52–69.

Pollard, A. J. (1977), 'The tyranny of Richard III'. *Journal of Medieval History*, 3, 147–65.

Pollard, A. J. (1990), *North-Eastern England during the War of the Roses: Lay Society, War and Politics, 1450–1500*. Oxford: Oxford University Press.

Pollard, A. J. (2005), *John Talbot and the War in France 1427–1453*, reprint of 1983 Royal Historical Society edition. Barnsley: Pen and Sword.

Prestwich, M. (1996), *Armies and Warfare in the Middle Ages: the English Experience*. London and New Haven: Yale University Press.

Pugh, T. B. (1972), 'The magnates, knights and gentry', in S. B. Chrimes, C. D. Ross and R. A. Griffiths (eds), *Fifteenth Century England 1399–1509: Studies in Politics and Society*. Manchester: Manchester University Press, pp. 86–128.

Radulescu, R. (2003), *The Gentry Context for Malory's Morte D'Arthur*. Cambridge: D. S. Brewer.

Radalescu, R. and Truelove. A. (2005), *Gentry Culture in Late Medieval England*. Manchester: Manchester University Press.

Ramsay, J. (1892), *Lancaster and York: A Century of English History 1399–1485*, 2 vols. Oxford: Clarendon Press.

Richardson, T. (1997), 'The Bridport muster roll of 1457'. *Royal Armouries Yearbook*, 2, 46–52.

Richmond, C. (1970), 'Fauconberg's Kentish rising of May 1471'. *English Historical Review*, 85, 674–92.

Richmond, C. (1983), 'After McFarlane', *History*. 68, 46–60.

Robertson, S. (1882), 'Chapel at Horne's Place, Appledore'. *Archaeologia Cantiana*, 14, 363–7.

Robson, R. (1989), *The Rise and Fall of the English Highland Clans: Tudor Responses to a Medieval Problem*. Edinburgh: John Donald.

Roskell, J. S. (1937), *The Knights of the Shire of the County Palatine of Lancaster, 1377–1460*. Manchester: Chetham Society.

Roskell, J. S. (1959), 'Sir Thomas Tresham, Knight, speaker for the Commons under Henry VI'. *Northamptonshire Past and Present*, 2, (6), 313–23.

Roskell, J. S. (1961), 'Sir William Oldhamm, speaker in the parliament of 1450–1'. *Nottingham Medieval Studies*, 5, 87–112.

Roskell, J. S. (1963), 'Thomas Thorpe, speaker in the Reading parliament of 1453'. *Nottingham Medieval Studies*, 7, 79–105.

Roskell, J. S., Clark, L. and Rawcliffe, C. (1993), *The History of Parliament: The House of Commons, 1386–1421*, 4 vols. Stroud: Alan Sutton.

Ross, C. D. (1983), *Edward IV*. London: Methuen.

Scofield, C. L. (1923), *The Life and Reign of Edward the Fourth, King of England and of France and Lord of Ireland*, 2 vols, London: Longman.

Scott, J. R. (1876), 'Receipts and expenditure of Sir John Scott in the reign of Edward IV'. *Archaeologia Cantiana*, 10, 250–8.

Shaw, W. A. (1906), *The Knights of England*, 2 vols. London: The Lord Chamberlain, St James' Palace.

Simpson, A. W. B. (1996), *A History of the Land Law*, 2nd edn, reprinted. Oxford: Oxford University Press.

Storey, R. L. (1957), 'The wardens of the Marches of England towards Scotland, 1377–1489'. *English Historical Review*, 72, 593–615.

Stubbs, W. (1903), *The Constitutional History of England*, 5th edn, 3 vols. Oxford.

Thomas, H. M. (1993), *Vassals, Heiresses, Crusaders and Thugs: The Gentry of Angevin Yorkshire, 1154–1216*. Philadelphia: University of Pennsylvania Press.

Thomson, J. A. F. (1972), 'The Courtenay family in the Yorkist period'. *Bulletin of the Institute of Historical Research*, 45, 230–46.

Tversky, A. and Kahneman, D. (1981), 'The framing of decisions and the psychology of choice'. *Science*, 211, 453–8.

Vale, M. (1981), *War & Chivalry: Warfare and Aristocratic Culture in England, France, and Burgundy at the end of the Middle Ages*. Georgia: The University of Georgia Press, Athens.

Verbruggen, J. F. (1997), *The Art of Warfare in Western Europe during the Middle Ages*, 2nd edn, revised and enlarged. Woodbridge: Boydell Press.

Virgoe, R. (1973), 'William Tailboys and Lord Cromwell: crime and politics in Lancastrian England'. *Bulletin of the John Rylands Library*, 46, 459–82.

Virgoe, R. (1994), 'Inheritance and litigation in the fifteenth century: the Buckenham disputes'. *Legal History*, 15, 22–40.

Walker, S. (1990), *The Lancastrian Affinity 1361–1399*. Oxford: Oxford University Press.

Waller, J. (2000), 'Combat techniques', in V. Fiorato, A. Boylston, and C. Knusel (eds), *Blood Red Roses: The Archaeology of a Mass Grave from the Battle of Towton AD 1461*. Oxford: Oxbow Books.

Warnicke, R. M. (1983), 'Lord Morley's statements about Richard III'. *Albion*, 6, 173–8.

Watts, J. L. (1995), 'Ideas, principles and politics', in A. J. Pollard (ed.), *The Wars of the Roses*. Basingstoke and New York: Macmillan and St Martin's Press, pp. 110–33.

Watts, J. L. (1996), *Henry VI and the Politics of Kingship*. Cambridge: Cambridge University Press.

Wedgwood, J. C. (1917), 'Staffordshire parliamentary history from the earliest times to the present day', in William Salt Archaeological Society (ed.), *Collections for a History of Staffordshire*, 1–464.

Wedgwood, J. C. (1936), *History of Parliament: Biographies of the Members of the Commons House 1439–1509*. London: HMSO.

Whitehead, J. R. (2004), 'Waterton, Robert (d. 1425)'. *Oxford Dictionary of National Biography*, 57, 576–7.

Wiedemer, J, E. (1967), 'Arms and Armour in England, 1450–1471, Their Cost and Distribution', unpublished PhD thesis, University of Pennsylvania.

Wilcock, R. (2004), 'Local disorder in the Honour of Knaresborough, c. 1438–1461 and the national context'. *Northern History*, 41, 39–80.

Woolgar, C. (1999), *The Great Household in Late Medieval England*. New Haven and London: Yale University Press.

Worthington, P. (1990), 'Royal Government in the Counties Palatinate of Lancashire and Cheshire 1460–1509', unpublished PhD thesis, University of Wales, Swansea.

Wright, S. M. (1983), *The Derbyshire Gentry in the Fifteenth Century*. Chesterfield: Derbyshire Record Society.

# Index

Members of the nobility are indexed under family name rather than under title. Members of the royal family are indexed under their Christian names. References to groups of gentry can be found under the relevant county. To avoid confusion between gentry or noble families principal seats have been included where necessary.

Aberystwyth Castle 47
Agincourt, battle of (1415) 57
Aleyn, William 51
Alnwick Castle, Northumberland 55, 114
Ampthill manor, Bedfordshire 19
Ap Thomas, Rhys 122
arbitration 17–18, 30, 60–2, 63, 64, 93, 94
Archer
    family of 14
    Richard 72
Armourers' Company, London 57
arms and armour 57–60
*Arrivall* 110
Arundel, Sir John 103–4
Ashby de la Zouche, Leicestershire 109
Ascough, John 70, 141n. 21
Ashton, Sir Ralph 102–3, 104
Astley, Sir John 39, 46
Aucher, Henry 70
Audley
    family of 101, 146n. 24
    James, Lord 87

Babington
    family of 45
    William 68
Bamburgh Castle, Northumberland 118
Barley
    family of 41
    Robert 57
Barnet, battle of (1471) 53, 56, 80, 94, 97, 101, 102, 109, 110, 115, 116, 120, 135n. 7
Barry, Sir John 43–4
Baskerville, family of 45
Basset, family of 21

bastard feudalism
    *see* lordship
battlefield injuries 106, 145n. 4
Beauchamp, earls of Warwick
    family of 14
    Richard, earl of Warwick 14
Beaufort
    affinity 70, 93, 95
    Edmund, duke of Somerset 42, 44, 51, 75, 76, 80, 94, 95, 141n. 38, 142n. 45, 145n. 14, 147n. 42
    Edmund, styled duke of Somerset 40, 44, 117, 120, 137n. 20
    Henry, duke of Somerset 50, 52, 118, 139n. 79
    Margaret, countess of Richmond and Derby 82
Beaumont
    family of 41
    William, Viscount 47, 114
Bedford, John of Lancaster, duke of 43, 54, 76
Bedfordshire 19, 102
Bedingfield, Sir Edmund 2
behaviour
    *see* decision making
Bellers, John 70
Bellingham, Sir Henry 28
Belvoir Castle, Leicestershire 109
Berkeley of Berkeley Castle, Gloucestershire
    family of 13, 134n. 25
    Thomas, Lord 13, 47
    William, Lord 81
    William 82
Berkeley of Beverstone, Gloucestershire
    family of 82
    Sir Maurice13, 81

Berkshire 15, 16, 94
Bermingham, Richard 54
Berwick-upon-Tweed, Northumberland
   garrison of 50, 55
   town of 40, 42
Bigod
   Sir John 111
   Sir Ralph 82, 104
Bissipates, Sir George 56
Blore Heath, battle of (1459) 77, 86, 129,
   142n. 3, 145n. 24
Blount
   family of 41
   Humphrey 113
   John, Lord Mountjoy 131
   Walter 21
Bold
   family of 43
   Sir Robert 43
Bonville, William, lord 13, 109, 114
Booth, Sir William 69
Bordeaux, Gascony 75
Bosworth, battle of (1485) 59, 78, 82, 115, 122
Bosworth Field, ballard of 78
Boucicaut, Jean le Meingre, marshal 37
Boteler, William 54
Bourchier
   Henry, earl of Essex 38
   Humphrey, Lord Cromwell 120
   John, Lord Berners 87, 123
Boyle, Philip, of Aragon 39
Brackenbury, Sir Robert 104, 144n. 60
Brandon, William, of Knowle, Warwickshire 48
Brandon, Sir William 56, 115
Brereton, Sir Ralph 87, 142n. 6
Brézé, Pierre de, seneschal of Normandy 55,
   90
Bricqbec, lordship of 77
Brokestowe, John 62
Brown, Richard 51
Brown
   Eleanor 102
   Sir George 70, 98–100, 102, 105, 130,
     144n. 41
   Sir Thomas 27, 98–9
Browning, William 38
Brunever, John 77
*Brut* 45, 46, 48
Buck, Sir George 3
Buckinghamshire 15, 16, 19, 96
Bueil, de, Louis 47

Burgh, Sir Thomas 88, 114
Burgundy
   Anthony, bastard of 38, 58
   Charles the Bold, duke of 44, 60
   dukes of 44, 137n. 37
   gunners from 55
Bury, Lancashire 51
Butler, James, earl of Ormond and Wiltshire
   54

Cade, Jack, rebellion of 90, 142n. 14
Caen 76
Calais
   garrison 38, 41–2, 44, 49, 50, 55, 56, 59,
     60, 112, 139n. 95
   marches of 37
   siege of (1436) 74
   town of 86
Calthorpe, Sir William 111, 145n. 18
Calveley, Sir Hugh 54
Canterbury, Kent 91, 92, 102
Canterbury
   archbishop of 104
   Christ Church, prior of 102
Carlisle, Cumberland 42
Carte, Thomas 3
Cary, Sir William 111–2
Catesby, Sir William 25–6
Cattys, John 108
Chalers
   Sir John 79
Chalons
   family of 47
   Sir Robert 47
Chamberlain, Sir Robert 81, 130, 142n. 57
chancery 32, 100, 101
Chandée, Philibert de 55
Charles I, king of England 1
Charles VII, king of France 75
Chaworth
   family of 18
   Chaworth, Sir Thomas 18
Cherbourg 77
Cheshire 22, 54, 57, 66, 69, 76, 86, 87, 88, 129,
   135n. 56, 142n. 6
Chester
   earldom of 15, 22
   palatinate of 22, 87
Cheyne
   family of Eastchurch, Kent 104
   Sir John 69

Cheyne, Sir John, of Falstone-Cheyne, Wiltshire 38, 82
chivalric literature 45–7, 62, 63, 72, 138n. 46
 *see also* military manuals
chivalric values 64–5
choices
 *see* decision making
Christine de Pisan, *Livre du Corps de Policie* 46, 47, 48
Cinque Ports 51, 90, 91
Clarence, George, duke of 53, 54, 55, 81, 88, 94, 99, 100, 110, 117, 130
Clerke, John 77
Clifford
 family of 12, 18
 Sir Thomas 37
 John, Lord 94
Clifford, Robert 38
Clifton of Clifton, Nottinghamshire, family of 89, 142n. 10
Clifton, Sir Gervase, of Brabourne, Kent 69, 76, 87, 90, 91, 112, 119–20, 124, 130, 142n. 6
Cockayne, John 62
Cokesey, Sir Hugh 43
Colt, Thomas 53
Colville, Sir Thomas 109
commissions of array 2, 9, 32, 49, 69, 110
Conisbrough Castle, Lincolnshire 53, 78
Constable of Flamborough
 family of 17
 Sir Marmadue 104
 William 59
Constable of Halsham
 family of 17
 Thomas 111
Constantinople 56
Conwey, Hugh 42
Conyers
 family of 91
 Sir John 77, 78
 John 78
 Sir William 78
Coppini, Francesco, bishop of Terni and papal legate 56
Copuldyke, family of 17
Corbet
 Sir Richard 113, 146n. 24
 Sir Roger 113
Cornwall 103
county administration 8, 22, 66–70, 73, 82–3
county court 10, 22, 66, 87, 146n. 29

court of chivalry 37,
Courtenay
 family of 45
 affinity of 13, 64, 73
 Sir Piers 37
 Thomas, earl of Devon 13, 145n. 14
Coventry, Warwickshire 50, 51, 59, 101
Croft, Sir Richard 117, 121, 124, 146n. 24
Cromwell, Ralph, Lord 15, 18, 58, 114, 120, 146n. 27
Crowland Chronicle 104, 105
Culpeper
 Richard 90, 105
 Thomas 105
Cumberland 90
Cumberworth
 family of 17
 Sir Thomas 59

Danyell, family of 45
Darell
 family of 45, 91
 Sir John 105
Dartford, rising at (1452) 27
Daubeney
 Sir Giles the elder 58
 Giles, Lord 58, 59, 103
 William 58
Daunt, John 110
Dawes, John 60
De'Bardi, family of, armourers 58
Debenham
 family of 81
 Gilbert, the elder 128
 Sir Gilbert, the younger 81
decision making
 back projection 31, 107, 123, 130
 battlefield emotions 115–7
 cognitive distortion 29, 31, 107
 compensatory and non-compensatory strategies 33, 86, 87, 104, 110
 decision frames 29, 30, 32, 33, 68, 70, 72, 79, 85, 86, 89, 90, 92, 94, 95, 96, 97, 105, 106, 111, 112, 116, 118, 121, 123, 127, 130
 emotions 25, 30, 31, 74, 81, 94, 96, 101, 107, 108, 110, 111, 112, 113, 115–7
 environments 5, 8, 11, 16, 21, 24, 29, 30, 31, 37, 64, 66, 68, 85, 86, 88, 89, 100, 103, 104, 105, 106, 107, 112, 115, 123, 126–7, 129

decision making (*continued*)
 judgements 29, 30, 32, 33, 40, 66, 68, 70,
  72, 74, 79, 85, 89, 92, 94, 95, 96, 98, 100,
  105, 107, 108, 110, 127
 principles 74–7
 prospect theory 29, 107, 112, 123
 preference ordering 28–9
 rational theories 26, 28–9, 30
 risk aversion 26, 27, 97
 'sure thing' principle 26, 28
Delves
 family of 101
 Sir John 28, 87
Denbigh Castle 97
Derbyshire 9, 15, 17, 18, 19, 20, 21, 27, 41, 46,
 60, 64, 68, 73
Devereux, Sir Walter, Lord Ferrers 86, 97, 98,
 113
Devon 13, 23, 47, 64, 103, 145n. 14
Digby
 family of 41
 Everard 79, 113, 114, 145n. 27, 146n. 29
Digges, John 58
Dinham
 family of 64, 73
 Sir John 64
 John, later Lord 73, 112
distraint of knighthood 87, 133n. 6
Docwra, family of 45
Dokeray, James 54
Donne
 family of 43
 John 95
Dorset 39, 40, 110, 145n. 14
Douglas, Sir Archibald 40
Dover 86
Dover Castle, lieutenant of 90, 92, 101
Drury, John 90
Dunstanborough Castle, Northumberland 80
Durfort, Gaillard de, Lord of Duras and
 Blanquefort 55
Dymoke
 family of 119
 John 114
 Margaret, wife of 119
 Robert, son of John and Margaret 119
 Sir Thomas 119

East Anglia 27, 61, 67, 81, 96, 111, 116, 117
Edgecote, battle of (1469) 78
Edmond, Thomas 39

Edward I, king of England 8, 35, 49, 73
Edward II, king of England 49
Edward III, king of England 49
Edward IV, king of England 1, 12, 16, 27, 28,
 38, 44, 49, 50, 51, 53, 55, 56, 58, 59, 69, 71,
 73, 77, 78, 80, 81, 82, 87, 88, 93, 94, 95, 96,
 98, 99, 101, 101, 110, 111, 113, 114, 118,
 119, 120, 121, 124, 130, 140n. 10, 142n. 56,
 144n. 41, 146n. 35, 148n. 10
Edward V, king of England 81
Edward of Lancaster, prince of Wales 49, 69,
 80, 109, 110, 117, 120, 123, 124, 147n. 44
Entwistle, Sir Bertin 76, 77, 141n. 44
escheators 9, 22, 66, 70, 91, 93, 96, 103, 122,
 135n. 55
Essex 69, 70
Euer
 Ralph 94, 136n. 12
 Sir William 94, 136n. 12
Evereux 76
Everingham, Sir Thomas 44, 68

Fairfax
 family of 45
 Sir William 67
Fastolf, Sir John 9, 31, 47, 59, 75, 117, 126,
 148n. 5, 148n. 6
Fauconberg, Thomas Neville, bastard of 56,
 101, 102, 148n. 10
feats of arms
 *see* tournaments
Ferrers of Chartley
 affinity of 14, 21
 family of 15
 William, lord 18
Fielding
 family of 41, 121, 122
 John, father of William 89, 121
 William 70–1, 89, 97, 113, 121, 129
 John, son of Sir William 89
Findern, Sir Thomas 28, 55
Fitton
 Sir Lawrence 58
 Sir Thomas 53, 142n. 3
FitzEustace, Sir Roland, Lord Portlester 54
FitzGerald, family of, earls of Kildare 54
FitzHarry, Sir Thomas 86
FitzHerbert
 family of 56, 63
 Sir Nicholas 56
 Ralph 56

FitzHugh
    family of 45
    Thomas 46
Fogge
    Sir John 91–2, 102, 105, 143n. 16,
      143n. 17, 147n. 60
    Sir Thomas 91
Foljambe
    family of 61
    Thomas 62
Formigny, battle of (1450) 41
Fortescue, Sir John 66, 72
    *De Laudibus Legum Angliae* 2
Foster, Agnes
Fougères, attack on (1449) 74–5
France 31, 36, 37, 40, 41, 42, 44, 47, 48, 49, 52,
    70, 74, 75, 76, 79, 91, 92, 109, 110, 120, 123,
    137n. 23, 139n. 99
Frogenhale, Sir Richard 70, 91, 109
Froissart, Jean 39, 40, 109, 115, 116
Fulford
    Sir Baldwin 51, 112
    Sir Thomas 28, 112
Fullhurst, Sir Robert 69

Gascoigne, Sir William 2
Gascony 54, 55, 75
Gate, Sir Geoffrey 56
gentry
    definitions of 7–11, 125–6, 127
    disputes 17–18, 19, 21, 56, 72, 89, 92–4,
      100, 102–3, 109, 111, 112, 113, 127–8,
      129–30, 146n.26, 146n. 27
    education 36–9
    households 52
    loyalty 13, 27, 28, 53, 56, 65–6, 70, 71, 72,
      77–83, 134n. 33
    military experience 40–5
    networks 11, 14, 15–17, 20, 29–30, 33,
      102, 105, 134n. 17
    violence 35, 60–64, 65, 81, 94, 114, 127–8
Gloucester, Humphrey, duke of 47, 75, 91,
    141n. 36
Gloucester, Thomas, duke of 47
Gloucestershire 13, 17, 110
Glyndwr, Owain 43
Graville, Seigneur de 55
Gray, Thomas, *Scalachronica* 115
'Gregory's Chronicle' 55
Green
    family of 92

Sir Thomas, senior 92
Sir Thomas younger 92
Greene, Godfrey 1
Gresley
    family of 41
    John 18, 21, 61
Greville, family of 17
Grey, Sir Thomas 117
Grey of Codnor
    Henry, 1st Lord 18, 61–2
    Henry, 2nd Lord 43, 53, 63
    John, Lord 44
Grey of Groby
    Edward, Lord 14
Grey of Ruthin
    Reynold, Lord 19, 145n. 18, 146n. 26
    Edmund, Lord and earl of Kent 19, 52,
      95, 111

Greyfriars (Newgate), London 101
Griffith, William 54
Grimsby, Sir William 120–1, 123
Guildford
    family of 91, 122
    Sir John 70, 101–2, 105, 122
    Sir Richard 45, 103, 122

Hall, Edward 2, 40, 117, 122, 125, 137n. 20,
    146n. 44
Halsham, Joan 112
Hammes Castle 55
Hammes, Sir Symond 28
Hampden, Sir Edmund 79
Hampden, John 80
Hanford, Sir John 57, 76
Hansard, Thomas 38
Harcourt
    family of 44
    John 79
    Sir Robert 58, 79
Harfleur 108
Harlech Castle 80, 97
Harrington
    family of 43
    Sir Richard 76
    Sir Thomas 53, 97
    Sir William 104, 105
Hastings of Kirby Muxloe, Leicestershire
    family of 41, 69, 96
    Sir Leonard 73
    Ralph 96

Hastings of Kirby Muxloe, Leicestershire
    (*continued*)
    William, Lord 42, 47, 73, 81, 91, 93, 109,
        115, 117, 121
Hastings, Sir Hugh, of Fenwick
    Northumberland 90
Hatfield manor, Hertfordshire 53
Haute
    family of 47
    Richard Haute 147n. 60
    William 92
Hauley, family of 17
Hedgeley Moor, battle of (1464) 28
Henry IV, king of England 78, 93, 137n. 32,
    138n. 38
    as earl of Derby 17, 44
Henry V, king of England 74, 75, 78, 92,
    108
Henry VI, king of England 15, 16, 20, 25,
    27, 32, 40, 41, 47, 51, 56, 68, 69, 70, 74,
    76, 77, 78, 79, 80, 93, 96, 97, 98, 99, 101,
    102, 108, 109, 112, 114, 116, 118, 120, 130,
    142n. 6
Henry VII, king of England 45, 59, 82, 104,
    146n. 24
    as Henry Tudor, earl of Richmond 42, 55,
        115, 122
Herbert
    Sir Richard 98
    Sir William, lord Herbert, earl of
        Pembroke 86, 97–8
Herefordshire 86
Heron of Ford
    family of 43, 141n. 6
    Sir John 28, 69
Heron of Chipchase, family of 43
Hertfordshire 69, 70
Heworth, skirmish at (1453) 19
Hexham, battle of (1464) 28, 52, 80, 114
Heydon, family of 47
High Peak, Derbyshire 15, 19, 20, 21
Hillyard, Robert 91
Holinshed, Raphael 76
Holland (Netherlands) 81, 89
Holland
    Henry, duke of Exeter 19, 51, 99, 118,
        143n. 45
    John, duke of Exeter 39
Hoo, Sir Thomas 91, 112
Hopkynson, John 39
Horton manor, Kent 17

Horne
    family of 91
    Robert 51, 90, 91, 92, 143n. 16
Hostelle, Thomas 108
Hotoft
    family of 41
Howard, Sir John, duke of Norfolk 52, 58, 95
Hungerford
    family of 16
    Robert, lord 55
Hunsdon, manor of, Hertfordshire 79, 80
Huntingdonshire 113
Hutton, William 3

Ingloys, family of 44
Inns of Court 36
Ireland 31, 42, 43, 44, 49, 54, 74, 137n. 33
    lordship of Wexford 43
    lordship of West Meath 43
    Meath, liberty of 43

Jargeau, battle of (1429) 36
Joan of Arc 36
John of Salisbury, *Policraticus* 2
jousts
    *see* tournaments
justices of the peace 8, 9, 29, 49, 61, 66, 68, 70,
    91, 110, 114, 140n. 4

Kendal, family of 44
Kent
    county of 69, 70, 86, 90, 99, 101, 102
    gentry of 68, 90, 91, 92, 99, 103, 104, 105,
        109, 128, 129, 130, 134n. 32
Kesteven, Lincolnshire 67
king's bench, court of 2, 56, 113
Kirketon, lordship of, Lincolnshire 76
Knaresborough
    deputy-steward of 2, 100
    honour of 101
Knightley, family of 17
*Knyghthode and Batayle* 47
Knyvett
    family of 123
    Sir Thomas 1
Kynaston, Roger 113
Kyriell
    Alice, daughter of Sir Thomas 102
    Elizabeth, wife of John 102
    Kyriell, John 102
    Kyriell, Sir Thomas 40–1, 68, 90, 91, 102, 109

Lancashire, gentry of 43, 87, 135n. 56
Lancaster
    affinity of 20, 22, 28, 68, 73, 78
    duchy of 12, 15, 20, 21, 22, 28, 73
    dukes of 15, 31, 68, 78, 93, 101, 130
    House of 31, 78, 93, 130, 143n. 17
Langley, William 103
Latimer, Sir Nicholas 95, 130
Launde, de la, Sir Thomas 88
Lee
    Sir James 101, 143n. 47
    William 101
Leek, family of 41
Leicester 50
Leicestershire 9, 17, 20, 23, 27, 41, 68, 69, 70, 73
Leland, John 109
Lewis
    Sir Henry 70, 95, 141n. 20
    Sir Philip 17
Lewknor, Sir John 112, 123
Lincolnshire 9, 17, 20, 88, 129, 140n. 10
Lindsey, Lincolnshire 17
Liberi, Fiore Dei 48
Lincolnshire rebellion (1470) 88
Lindsay
    Sir James 116
    Sir William 40
Lisle, Margaret 13
localities, strategic importance of 85–8,
    105–6, 129
London
    city of 88, 91, 92, 101, 102, 103, 109, 110,
        112, 120
    livery companies 135n. 8
    Tower of 80, 98, 100, 118
Longford
    family of 41
    Edward 79
Losecote Field, battle of (1470) 88, 109, 119, 129
Lovelace, Richard 42
Lovell
    family of 19
    William, Lord 113
Ludford Bridge, battle of (1459) 77, 80, 129
Luttrell, Sir Hugh 52,
Lydd, Kent 51

Mainwairing
    Sir John 87
    Randle 57
Malorte, Sir Cardot 55

Malory
    family of 17
    Sir John 45
    Sir Robert 45
    Sir Thomas 62, 89, 101, 129
Malyverer
    Jankyn 136n. 23
    William 103, 104, 105, 122
Mancini, Dominic 82
Manston, Richard 77
Margaret of Anjou, queen of England 13,
    20, 21, 27, 29, 53, 54, 55, 79, 80, 81, 82, 87,
    93, 95, 96, 110, 112, 117, 118, 120, 123,
    146n. 29
Masse, Pierre de 39
Mercenaries 53–5
Mescua, Sir John de, of Navarre 54–5
Meverell, family of 21
Middleham, lordship of 52 77
Middleton, family of 45
Middlesex 69, 70
Milan 57, 59
Milan, duke of
    see Sforza, Franceso
military manuals 45–8
    see also chivalric literature, Christine de
        Pisan, Vegetius
Milton and Marden (Kent), lordship of 99, 104
Missaglia, family of, armourers 58
Molyneux, family of 43
Montgomery, family of 20–1
More, Sir Thomas 2
Morley, family of 103
Mortimer's Cross, battle of (1461) 53, 54, 55,
    86, 97, 129
Moton, Sir Robert 67
Mountford
    family of 14, 93
    Sir Baldwin 93
    Sir Edmund 93, 94
    Sir Osbert 75, 112
    Sir Simon 69, 93, 94
    Sir William 14, 15, 93
Mowbray
    affinity 146n. 27
    family of 81
    John, duke of Norfolk 38, 76, 111, 116, 117
    Anne 38
Myrdale
    John 117
    Thomas 117

Nancy, battle of (1477) 44, 60
Naworth Castle 80
Neel, Richard 97
Neville, family of 44
Neville of Middleham
  family of 12, 50, 70, 72, 77, 78
  affinity of 19, 70, 101, 148n. 10
  Edward, lord Abergavenny 108
  George, bishop of Exeter, archbishop of
    York
  Neville, John, lord 32
  Neville, John, Lord Montagu, earl of
    Northumberland, marquis Montagu 42,
    53
  Neville, John, son of Richard, earl of
    Salisbury 87
  Neville, Richard, earl of Salisbury 12, 97
  Neville, Richard, earl of Warwick 3, 14, 77,
    88, 93, 100, 101, 102, 110, 116
  Neville, Sir Thomas 32, 87, 120, 143n. 33
Neville of Raby, earls of Westmorland 52, 94
Newark, Nottinghamshire 49
Newcastle-upon-Tyne, Northumberland 42,
  114
Newport, John 32
nobles
  affinities 16, 51, 71–2, 73, 78, 128
  definition 8
    see also gentry, definitions
  estates 19, 23, 73
  households 52
  lordship 4, 10, 11–16, 18, 20–1, 23, 24, 32,
    52, 61–2, 64, 71–3, 77, 127–9
    see also gentry, disputes; gentry, violence
Norfolk 2, 49, 109, 112, 123
Normandy 41, 54, 55, 74, 75, 76, 77, 79, 90,
  109, 141n. 38
Northampton, battle of (1460) 27, 51, 58, 79,
  87, 92
Northamptonshire 17, 69, 95–6
Norwich, Norfolk 51
Nottingham, Nottinghamshire 50, 62
Nottinghamshire 15, 17, 18, 20, 27, 41, 45, 61,
  67–8, 88, 89, 94, 143n. 10

Ogard
  Sir Andrew 54
  Sir Henry 122–3, 124
Ogle, Sir Robert 43, 52, 116
Oldcastle, Sir John 43, 137n. 32
Oldhall, Sir William 38, 79–80

Olney, Robert 19
Order of the Garter 55, 75, 78
Otterburn, battle of (1388) 39, 109, 115
Oxfordshire 15, 16, 17, 58, 79

parliament
  complaints to 73, 148n. 8
  house of commons 79, 95, 96
  legislation 39, 98, 104
  members of parliament 31, 128
  petitions to 93, 96, 99
Papplewick Moor, affray at (1457) 94
Paris 39
Passhley, Sir John 36, 37
Paston
  correspondence 30, 100, 112, 119
  family of 4, 42, 89, 112
  Clement 30, 112
  Edmund 42
  John I 39, 89, 111
  Sir John 42, 46, 58, 138n. 46
  Margaret, wife of John I 89
Patay, battle of (1429) 31
Pecche
  Sir John 38
  Sir William 26–7, 57, 58, 96, 143n. 31
Pemberton, family of 45
Pembroke Castle 97
Percy
  affinity 12, 18, 28, 43, 50, 69, 101, 136n. 12
  family of 44
  Henry, Lord Poynings 72
  Henry, 1st earl of Northumberland 40
  Henry, 2nd earl of Northumberland 94
  Henry, 3rd earl of Northumberland 94,
    143n. 33
  Henry, 4th earl of Northumberland 1–2,
    12, 28
  Sir Ralph 39
Percy, Henry 59
Percy, Robert, of Scotton 101
Pickering, Sir James 53, 78
Pierpoint, Sir Henry 18, 57, 61–2, 94, 100,
  129,
Pilkington, Sir John 1
Plummer, Charles 3
Plummer, Sir John 102
Plumpton
  correspondence 1–2, 30
  family of 94, 129–30
  Edward 30

Sir Robert 30
Sir William 1–2, 49, 61, 100, 101, 144n. 43
Pole, de la
family of, earls of Suffolk 103
Sir Alexander 36
William, earl and duke of Suffolk 36, 77, 111, 114, 126
Pomeroy
family of 145n. 19
Sir Sinclair 112
Portinaro, Pigello, merchant of Milan 118
Poyntz, Robert 82
Preston, John 62
Pury, John 79
Pympe, John 105
Pythagoras 1, 127

Ramsay, Alexander 40
Ratcliffe, Robert 119
Reading, Berks 50
Reddisham, John 32
Redesdale, liberty of 43
Redford, Sir Henry 75–6, 77
Redman, Sir Matthew 115–6
retinues
indentures of service 11–12, 41, 42, 49–50–1, 52–3, 71, 137n. 33
Rhodes, English gentry at 44–5
Richard III, king of England 67, 78, 82, 102, 103, 104, 115, 121, 122, 147n. 60
as duke of Gloucester 1, 44, 67, 77, 78, 81, 82, 113, 117, 119,
Richmond, honour of 12
Richmondshire 77, 91, 101
Rither, Sir William 67
Roberts, Walter 104, 122
Robin of Holderness, rebellion of (1469) 90–1
Robin of Redesdale, rebellion of (1469) 49, 78, 81, 91
Rokewode, William 51
Romney, Kent 51, 91
Romney, John 58
Rondelle, Martin 58
Roos, Sir Robert 47
Roos, Thomas, Lord 109, 118
Rouen 75, 76
Roxburgh Castle 43
Royal household 58, 59, 67, 69, 70, 76, 78, 79, 81, 82, 93, 95, 112, 115, 120, 121, 123, 141n. 20

Rutland 67, 93, 113, 122
Rysbank tower 112

St Albans, first battle of (1455) 2, 51, 52, 53, 54, 75, 76, 78, 80, 94, 95, 116
St Albans, second battle of (1461) 27, 28, 51, 55, 92, 109, 114, 117, 146n. 29
St Amand, family of 19
St John of Jerusalem, knights of 44–5
St Quentin, Anthony 110
Sandes, William 81
Sandwich, Kent 86, 90
Savage, Sir John 57, 104, 105
Say, William, Lord Say and Sele 81
Scales, Thomas, Lord 99
schools of arms 37
see also tournaments
schools of defence 37
see also gentry, military training
Scotland 31, 40, 44, 49, 55, 80, 82, 113, 118, 146n. 29
Scott
family of 91
Sir John 59, 91, 92, 119–20, 143n. 16
William 91
Scott, Sir Robert 54
Scott, Sir Walter 3
Scudamore
family of 41
Sir John 41, 53, 97–8
Sir Henry 53
Sir Maurice 53
Sir William 41, 53
Secreta Secretorum 46
Seyntlo
Giles 42
Sir Nicholas 47
Sforza, Francesco, duke of Milan 118
Sheffield, lordship of 18
sheriffs 8, 9, 19, 22, 27, 61, 66, 67, 68, 69, 70, 73, 81, 87, 88, 91, 93, 94, 110, 111,
Shrewsbury, battle of (1404) 63
Shropshire 113
Skipwith
family of 17
Sir William 53, 78
Smithfield, tournaments at 38, 39
Somerset 110
Somervyle, Hugh 39
Stafford, family of, dukes of Buckingham
affinity of 21

Stafford, family of, dukes of Buckingham
(*continued*)
    Henry, duke of Buckingham 30, 94, 103,
      104, 122
    Humphrey, duke of Buckingham 14, 21,
      61, 76, 93
Staffordshire 21
Standish, Petronilla 102, 174
Stanhope of Rampton
    family of 17
    John 68
    Sir Richard 17
Stanley of Lathom
    family of 42, 69
    Sir Edward 104, 105, 122
    Sir William 87
Stapleton, Sir Miles 111
star chamber 114
Stathum, family of 41
Statute of Additions (1413) 8
Statute of Winchester (1285) 48–9, 60
Staveley, Sir Richard 17
Stoke, battle of (1487) 2
Stonor
    family of 15–16, 17
    correspondence 30
Stourton, William, Lord 82
Stradling
    Edward 45
    Sir Henry 45
Strange, family of 44
Strelley
    family of 63
    Sir Robert 18, 68
Stubbs, William, bishop of Chester, bishop of
Oxford 7, 11, 74
Surienne, François de, of Aragon 74–5
Surrey 45, 69, 92, 102
Sussex 36, 37, 69, 92
Sutton of Dudley, family of 15
Swayne, John, bishop of Armagh 44
Symson, John 39

Tailboys, Sir William 28, 64, 114
Talbot
    family of 12, 13, 18, 25 45, 134n. 25
    Sir Christopher 39
    John, Lord Furnival, 1st earl of
      Shrewsbury 31, 39, 43, 44, 52
    John, 2nd earl of Shrewsbury 18, 113
    Sir Thomas 43

Talhoffer, Hans 48
Teutonic Knights 44
Tewkesbury, battle of (1471) 26, 28, 40, 49,
    53, 55, 71, 80, 81, 87, 94, 96, 98, 99, 101,
    102, 109, 110, 117, 120, 122, 123, 129,
    147n. 47, 148n. 64
Thirwall, Sir Percival 115
Thorpe, Sir Thomas 116
Tirwhit, family of 17
tournaments
    jousts 37, 38, 39, 47, 136n. 9
    tourneys 37, 47
Tours, truce of (1444–6) 126
Towton, battle of (1461) 12, 25, 27, 28, 45,
    48, 49, 50, 51, 54, 77, 80, 92, 93, 94, 95, 98,
    100, 101, 108, 109, 110, 111, 113, 114, 116,
    118, 119, 120, 123, 130, 135n. 12, 145n. 4,
    146n. 46
Tresham, Sir Thomas 79, 95, 96, 143n. 31
Trollope, Andrew 42
Troutbeck
    Sir William 87
    Margaret, wife of 142n. 4
Troyes, Treaty of (1420) 75
Trussell
    family of 17, 41
    Sir William 69
Tudor, Jasper, earl of Pembroke 97
Turner, Sharon 3
Tunstall
    Brian 46
    Sir Richard 28, 80, 116, 120, 130
    Thomas 46
Turnbull, John 44
Turre, della, Antonio 56
Tutbury, honour of, Derbyshire 15, 20, 21
Tybeaudis, William 51
Tynedale, liberty of 43
Tyrell
    Sir James 103
    Sir William 97, 144n. 34

universities 36

Vaughan, Thomas 99, 102, 130
Vavasour, Sir Henry 67
Vegetius, *De Re Militari* 46, 47, 48
Venables, family of 43
Vere, de, earls of Oxford
    John, earl of Oxford 2, 27, 49, 58, 81, 97,
      115, 146n. 35

Sir Robert 75
Sir Thomas 56, 81
Vergil, Polydore 2, 3
Vernon
    family of 18, 21, 41, 63
    Henry 32, 53
    Richard 18, 21, 62

Wakefield, battle of (1460) 27, 28, 32, 43, 92,
    95, 101, 110, 111, 114, 143n. 33
Wales 41, 42, 47, 49, 80, 97, 121, 122
Walpole, Horace 3
Warkworth, John 27, 146n. 36, 147n. 58
wardens of East and West March 12, 42, 43,
    50, 131n. 31
Warwickshire 14, 16–17, 20, 21, 61, 62,
    69–70, 72, 89, 93, 94, 122, 140n. 7
Waterton
    family of 52
    Robert 111, 137n. 38
Waurin, Jean 109, 118
Wawton, Sir Thomas 19
Weaponry see arms and amour
Welles
    family of 20
    Richard, Lord 88
    Sir Robert, 88
Wenlock, Sir John, later Lord 99, 117,
    147n. 42
Wentworth
    Henry 56
    Oliver 80
    Sir Philip 28, 80, 116–7
Westmorland 90
Weston, family of 45
Weymouth, Dorset 110
Whittingham, Sir Robert 54, 80, 117, 120
Whittington College, London 38

Willoughby of Eresby, Lords, family of 20
    Maud (née Stanhope), Lady 120
Willoughby of Willoughby-on-the-Wold,
    family of 88
Willoughby of Wollaton
    family of 41, 46, 61
    Sir Hugh 67
    Ralph 67
Wiltshire 16
Woodville
    family of 38, 81, 92, 147n. 48
    Anthony, Lord Scales, 2nd Earl Rivers 38,
        118, 120
    Sir Edward 44, 82
    Richard 36
    Sir Richard, 3rd Earl Rivers 147n. 60
    Richard, 1st Earl Rivers 39, 118
Worcester, William 59, 86, 116, 148n. 6
    Itineraries 86
Worcestershire 17

York 90
York
    duchy of 12
    House of 31, 73, 100, 148n. 10
    Richard, duke of 3, 12, 27, 38, 41, 43,
        44, 53, 54, 73, 75, 76, 77, 78, 79, 80,
        81, 86, 95, 97, 98, 113, 130, 141n. 38,
        146n. 24
    Richard, duke of, son of Edward IV 38
Yorkshire 1, 7, 12, 18, 28, 30, 44, 53, 68, 78,
    82, 88, 90, 94, 100, 110, 134n. 15, 137n. 23
    East Riding of 17, 90
    West Riding of 12, 18, 19, 67, 68

Zouche
    family of 44, 46
    William, Lord 18